MW00622903

PRAISE FOR
TRANSFORMING COMMUNICATION

Evangelical missions theory has too often conceived what is termed *cross-cultural* communication as an obstacle race in which missionaries strive to surmount the hurdles of understanding alien cultures in order to reach the finishing line of winning converts. Vee J. D-Davidson's book challenges this assumption by employing instead the concept of *intercultural* communication, a two-way process in which communicators and recipients of the message enter into a mutual relationship and together bring their cultural understandings under the authority of the gospel. This well-written book will guide both students and practitioners of Christian mission from Global North and Global South backgrounds into wise pathways of missional discipleship.

> BRIAN STANLEY, professor of World Christianity,
> University of Edinburgh

Transforming Communication is a tour-de-force that should become a standard text in the field of cross-cultural communication. I recommend this book if you believe Christianity is inherently cross-cultural, bringing people from different cultures together to learn from each other in Christ and so become intercultural believers. I recommend this book if you are willing to reflect on your own cultural shaping and engage your cultural perspective at an intellectual, spiritual, and practical level. I recommend this book if you want to grow spiritually and be stimulated in prayer and for a desire for a closer relationship with God in Christ. If you want to learn from the experiences of Christian scholars and practitioners across the ages and the world's continents—experiences the author draws on throughout—then *Transforming Communication* is the book that will equip you to undertake the challenging task of sharing the gospel of God's love in the myriad human cultures he has created around the world.

> CANON DR. CHRIS SUGDEN, PhD programme leader,
> Oxford Centre for Religion and Public Life

Vee J. D-Davidson's new book, *Transforming Communication*, not only shows us her firm belief in how Christians can communicate Christ incarnationally in a multicultural context but also how she, as a missionary to China for many years, has exemplified what it means to identify ourselves with the local context where Christ has called us to serve. This book is an excellent example of how we interplay our text into our context, mediated by our lives as agents of communication with others. I highly recommend this book to those who want to learn about and pay the price of being an incarnational missionary to the nations.

DR. JOEL AGPALO TEJEDO, director for the Asia
Pacific Research Center (APRC), director for the Institute
for Church Action on Poverty Studies (ICAPS)

TRANSFORMING
COMMUNICATION

TRANSFORMING COMMUNICATION

PROGRESSING FROM CROSS-CULTURAL TO
INTERCULTURAL COMMUNICATION OF CHRIST

VEE J. D-DAVIDSON

ZONDERVAN
ACADEMIC

ZONDERVAN ACADEMIC

Transforming Communication
Copyright © 2022 by Vee J. D-Davidson

Requests for information should be addressed to:
Zondervan, *3900 Sparks Dr. SE, Grand Rapids, Michigan 49546*

Zondervan titles may be purchased in bulk for educational, business, fundraising, or sales promotional use. For information, please email SpecialMarkets@Zondervan.com.

ISBN 978-0-310-12441-7 (audio)

Library of Congress Cataloging-in-Publication Data

Names: D-Davidson, Vee J., author.
Title: Transforming communication : progressing from cross-cultural to intercultural communication of Christ / Vee J. D-Davidson.
Description: Grand Rapids : Zondervan, 2022. | Includes bibliographical references and index.
Identifiers: LCCN 2022009771 (print) | LCCN 2022009772 (ebook) | ISBN 9780310124382 (hardcover) | ISBN 9780310124399 (ebook)
Subjects: LCSH: Intercultural communication--Religious aspects--Christianity. | Communication--Religious aspects--Christianity. | Evangelistic work. | Missions.
Classification: LCC BV2082.I57 D33 2022 (print) | LCC BV2082.I57 (ebook) | DDC 261--dc23/ eng/20220330
LC record available at https://lccn.loc.gov/2022009771
LC ebook record available at https://lccn.loc.gov/2022009772

Cover design: Lucas Art & Design
Cover photo: © *Caner CIFTCI/ Alamy Stock Photo; Angelina Bambina / Shutterstock*
Interior design: Kait Lamphere

Printed in the United States of America

22 23 24 25 26 27 28 29 30 31 32 /TRM/ 15 14 13 12 11 10 9 8 7 6 5 4 3 2 1

To Mia M. Young,

my very dear sister and also sister in Christ.

*If it hadn't been for your loving and faithful support during
these past almost three decades of overseas ministry, this
book would never have come about quite as it has.*

*Thank you so much for ministering with me from afar through handling
the missionary logistics of prayer letters, fielding communications from
supporting churches and prayer partners, airport pickups and drop offs, and
the loving refreshment through your unwaveringly generous hospitality.*

*It has been wonderful to enjoy simplicity on our many adventures
together and reveling together in the presence of our Savior, Jesus.
Thank you for modeling perseverance through all kinds of trials.*

*May your delight in Jesus be increasingly contagious
and bear rich fruit in all seasons.*

Contents

Figures and Tables

Acknowledgments

Many people have been part of putting this book together, not least long-term colaborer Julie (Jewels), who has ministered with me in multiple Asian settings and continues to share both the trials and delights of different facets of intercultural ministries. Thank you, Jewels, for your self-denial and sacrificial perseverance as we lived out and prayed through so many ministry storms together and also sang and rejoiced in the victories. Because you stand gloriously firm in God's love and calling, there will be even more to rejoice over in the times to come.

Thanks too to my cherished mentor Rev. Dr. Hugh Osgood for encouraging me to complete the doctoral studies whilst on the mission field, which opened up so many more opportunities for teaching in mono- and multiple-culture settings. I am indebted to many former students who kindly allowed me to use excerpts from their course assignments, including: Génesis J. Géron, Oh Oun mi (Sarah), Jefté C. Salazar, Ely Sebiano, Eunice Angeles, Jeon Myong soo (Luke), Imelda P. Sedano, Buenavieln B. Valasco, Rholda Cayabas, Rachel Chng, Claudia Janneth Mendoza, Jessica Ortiz, Josiah Nari, Misael Cornelio, Aya Uchimara, Erita Sipahutar, Lyreen Alunes-Cheung, Rut Vretonko, Julie E. and a great many other students, colleagues, and friends who preferred to stay anonymous for various reasons. Thanks to Regnum International for kindly allowing me to use overlapping parts of my "Empowering Transformation" missions textbook with varying degrees of editing. Heartfelt thanks to intercultural mentors, Doreen Dormun (Young Baptist church, NSW, Australia) enjoying life to the fullest now, (Dr.) Ruth Peever (of Canada, and formerly China and the Philippines), and also special friends KY and Dong (Malaysians in Hong Kong) who have been longtime caring intercultural encouragers along with Yau whose continual kindness and wise insights make the intercultural friendship such a God-planned delight. Dear Caroline and Paul Gibson, your spiritual and practical input has been so much appreciated, and Paul, I'm indebted to you for also using your skills to turn my freehand diagrams into electronic format.

Profound thanks, once again, to a long-time dear friend and sister in Christ Moyra Trimby for very kindly persevering through initial proof-reading and offering invaluable advice and comments. With the timeless parts of decade-old teaching notes incorporated into the book, I may have missed acknowledging some sources. I very much hope this is not the case, but if it is, profuse apologies as the fault is entirely mine.

Finally, I'm privileged to have had this writing project taken on so enthusiastically by Dr. Stan Gundry of Zondervan so as to provide a concise and updated version of David Hesselgrave's cross-cultural communication classic and am appreciative of all the teamwork involved in bringing the project to fruition.

Preface

Due to God's opportunities and glorious grace-filled adventures, my life has unfolded in ways I would never have expected. My exposure to other cultures began in my early twenties when I set off on a three-month overland trip to Kathmandu via Europe and the Middle East. En route, I had an encounter with God in Jerusalem that brought me to Christ, and after eventually arriving in Nepal, I continued backpacking through Asia and Australasia. Once my travel money was spent, I learned to live very simply and trust God for all my needs before arriving back in the UK eighteen months later via North America and Canada. I then spent two years in Pakistan with Operation Mobilization before seminary in the UK and being prayed out to China in 1994 where I have lived and ministered in six different areas over twenty-seven years.

In 2008 I had begun taking annual trips away from China to teach "Perspectives in Missions" for master's-level students from all over Asia at Asia Pacific Theological Seminary (APTS) in the Philippines. I completed my PhD in 2009. This was followed by teaching "Cross-Cultural Communications" at APTS and then these two courses and "Spirituality and Spiritual Growth" at Ecclesia Theological Seminary in Hong Kong, as well as various other ministries at Asian Bible schools and seminaries. I compiled the appropriate parts from my PhD into a missions textbook, yet I found it rather unwieldy to use the same text for every "Cross-Cultural Communications" course despite the overlap of material. With each course, I had to rework the text and add the communications-related perspectives. The intercultural nature of the different teaching and learning environments has always brought the joy-filled challenge of how to be appropriately creative, as have all the years of teaching in Chinese in China. I have often used the church-planting and teaching ministry in China to provide illustrations for both missions and cross-cultural communications principles. Teaching notes inevitably get revised year by year and modified to best fit each different group of students, but some principles—especially those that are Spirit-inspired—are timeless and supracultural. Every course brought new perspectives from students' background cultures. While the majority of my students have been Asian, I was delighted to discover how many other cultural perspectives have contributed to the makeup of this textbook—from Africa and Eastern Europe to the Pacific Rim and North and South America. I hope the text will be an interesting, challenging, and inspiring read, regardless of your motives for reading. As I continue walking with Jesus in the adventure of lifelong-learning, I become increasingly aware of my own limitations. May you be drawn beyond any limitations, be touched by God's timeless presence, and inspired for greater fruitfulness in communicating about our Lord and Savior.

CHAPTER 1

Foundations for Communicating Christ

As It Happened: After eight months of language study in China, my left shoulder started hurting. A nurse colleague diagnosed a "frozen shoulder" and advised some exercises to improve movement of the joint, but the exercises caused me even more pain. A Chinese friend, whose mother had taken a great liking to me, passed me a gift from her mother "to help." It was a heavy green bottle containing rocks, plants, and a liquid that smelled like strong alcohol. I put the bottle on the windowsill and enjoyed seeing the morning sun shine through the bottle's green glass onto the plants and rocks inside. I had been too embarrassed to ask my friend whether I should drink this kind offering from her mother or just rub the liquid into my shoulder, and in fact, I would not have wanted to drink the alcohol. Eventually, as my nurse colleague had assured me, the shoulder healed itself, and my friend's mother was very happy too.

INTRODUCTION

How often are we confused by another person's suggestion simply because we are too embarrassed to ask them to clarify? Any time we communicate with another person, we're bringing our own personality quirks, cultural backgrounds, and social expectations into the conversation. When we're communicating with someone from a different cultural background, the potential for confusion and awkwardness can increase to the point that it seems easier to just back off.

With all the tools and information readily available via multiple forms of media, we might wonder why cross-cultural communication is such a challenge. After all, with so much international travel and people migrating from one country to another with relative ease, the world seems to be getting smaller. People from different nations can be seen congregating in the world's bigger cities (and even many smaller ones), so that engaging with people from other nations is far less of a geographical challenge than it used to be.

So why do we—people living in this "global village"—still face difficulties communicating the gospel with those of other nations? Now that the Global South sends out more cross-cultural missionaries than the Global North (Ma 2016, 94),[1] how might we adapt our communication to more fruitfully reach people of other communities throughout the world as well as engage effectively with colaborers from other nations? Chapter 3 notes two different approaches to culture, one which sees culture "as a given and the other as a construct" (Handford, Van Maele, Matous, and Maemura 2019, 163). For our purposes here, we will consider culture and cultural distinctives (i.e., definable and observable differences) as a prevailing reality as we examine terminology and ask the question: What is the difference between cross-cultural interaction, intercultural interaction, and life in a multicultural society?

This chapter begins by examining and describing the different terms, then addresses the nature of people as communicators, and concludes with a deeper look at the term *evangelism*. A timeline is then given to show the historical emergence of liberal, evangelical, and fundamentalist theology and how these theologies affect the communicated content of the gospel message. Finally, the essentials of the gospel message are laid out from an evangelical perspective.

INTERACTIVE TERMINOLOGY AND COMMUNICATION

Let's look at the terms mentioned so far and see the implications for interaction and building relationships to communicate the gospel of Christ and Christian beliefs according to God's Word, the Holy Bible.

---

1. See Jenkins (2002; 2006) for Global North and Global South distinctives, and Wonsuk Ma (2016: 94) on the Asian missionary perspective: "Before the turn of the [twenty-first] century, missionaries from the non-Western churches outnumbered those from the traditional Western churches." See too Claudia Wärisch-Oblau on the African Pentecostal/Charismatic perspective (2009, 254–62) and Brandner (2009, 218) on the internationalization of communication of Christ, which "is originating in all parts of the world and moving in all directions."

Multicultural Societies

A multicultural society or setting, whether a large city or a smaller town, has groups of people from two or more national or cultural backgrounds so that there are people from multiple cultures within the same setting.[2] Multiple cultures are represented, but the members of each group tend to congregate and communicate largely with those of their own background. The setting has different groups of people, but they do not tend to socially interact with members from any of the other groups. They may have their own language, which is widely used in the home and with those of the same culture community, but some of the group—often the older members—may not speak or understand any language other than their own.

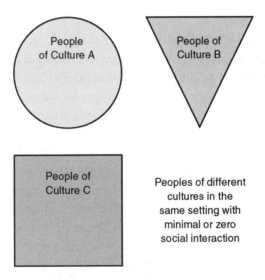

Figure 1.1: A Multicultural Society

Example: German nationals communicate using German but have probably also learned English in school. Germany has additional community groups such as Turkish migrant workers, Polish nationals, and Japanese workers involved with operations at the Nissan car

---

2. I differentiate the terms *multicultural* and *multiple-culture*, with the former indicating the presence of people from multiple but non-mutually-engaging cultures in contrast to the latter, which is a setting with people from multiple cultures engaging with each other with varying degrees of willingness in interaction.

manufacturing plant, to name a few. None of these non-German group members are likely to be inclined to socialize with members of the other groups. Turkish migrant workers, whose lifestyle-influencing religious background is Muslim, are unlikely to have much in common with Catholic-background Polish nationals. The Japanese car-plant workers may not be interested in using their limited relaxation time to socialize with their German counterparts, even though the Japanese employees will likely need to be reasonably conversant in the German language. What we see, then, is a multicultural setting with people from multiple cultural backgrounds who generally prefer to limit their social engagements to people of their own background.

Cross-Cultural Interaction

The terms *cross-cultural* and *intercultural* are often used interchangeably in communications and culture-related literature.[3] This can be less helpful in relation to cross-cultural cultural-competence studies since, according to each term's adjectival component parts, they are clearly not pure synonyms. The prefixes *cross-* and *inter-* have quite different meanings. In cross-cultural interaction, people from one cultural background seek relationships and communication with people whose culture is different from theirs. They tend to consider the other culture entirely in comparison to their own, using their own culture as the benchmark from which to discern appropriate interaction. Appropriate, inappropriate, and questionable actions and behavior are largely discerned in light of the communicating outreacher's conscious and subconscious cultural preferences. Their choices and actions are motivated by a desire to cross the divide between cultures, and the approach is comparison based. At least in the early stages, there is minimal or no attempt by people from the other culture to cross the divide toward the outreacher's culture. As far as the ones being reached out to are concerned, the outreachers are unusual and are being engaged with largely in terms of the immediate perceived benefit that might come from getting to know them.

---

3. See, for instance, Chu (2019, 3), whose work is on intergenerational differences amongst Chinese pastors in Australia. Chu advises in footnote 1 that he uses the terms *cross-cultural* and *intercultural* interchangeably.

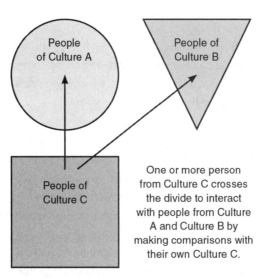

Figure 1.2: Cross-Cultural Interactions

Example: Consider a French Protestant missionary wanting to share the gospel with German-speaking people in the German setting from the previous example. In order to build a bridge over the divide between his culture and that of the German-speakers and to facilitate fruitful cross-cultural interaction, the missionary has had to learn a new language, German. If they are German nationals, then the divide between French culture and German culture will not be as great or complex as the divide between his French culture and that of a German-speaking Japanese car-plant worker. For the former, both have a common European geographical base, albeit with differing cultural specifics and different languages. For communicating with the Japanese German-speaker, however, our French missionary has both language and the specifics of Asian perspectives to consider. Our French missionary may also find himself called to share the gospel with the Turkish migrants. Again, he will need to find ways of crossing the divide between his culture and that of the Turkish migrants in order to bring about fruitful cross-cultural outreach. In addition, he will need to consider what is appropriate in relation to Muslim perceptions as well. As he reaches out cross-culturally, he will be using his cultural background as the benchmark from which to decide how to reach out to the Germans in his neighborhood, how to engage with Japanese workers, and how to interact with the Turkish migrants who might be living in a

largely single-culture location. As the French missionary builds bridges
to cross the cultural divides and become friends with different members
of each cultural group, it is unlikely that any of them will have known or
engaged with those of the other cultural groups.

Note the implications for cross-cultural communication: there needs
to be, at the very least, some kind of common ground from which to begin
communication with another person or group of people. In monocultural
workplaces or social settings, relationships usually are formed on the basis
of similarities (Bennett 2013: 4). Friendships are grown from commonality
or, at the very least, differences that are seen as attractive, and from there,
the combination of commonality and differences in perceptions and interests become the guiding paths on which the journey to deepening relationships is either heightened or called off. Language and/or common values,
such as religious adherence, may be the basis for the common ground, but
without establishing any common ground between the outreacher and the
outreachees, any reciprocity by the outreachees to "different others" would
have no useful purpose or motivating relevance for them.

Intercultural Interaction

Intercultural interaction involves two or more people from different cultural backgrounds who have managed to form relationships that
have crossed the cultural divides to some degree. These relationships are
marked by sensitivity to the differences between cultures (Bennett 2013,
11), are devoid of oppression or disrespect (15),[4] and instead manifest
empathy (20, 47).[5] Unlike cross-cultural relationships, which are based on
comparison of one's background with the other's, intercultural relationships have progressed beyond assurances of security due to one's own

---

4. Note that Bennett's highly secular approach to the subject of intercultural competence
(more of which in chapter 8) prefers to leave aside what he terms *ideological issues*, suggesting that
"purely ideological analyses yield a lot of heat and not much new light" (15). See too Bennett's earlier
edition of the text published in 1998. For our purposes in communicating Christ we cannot help but
base our approach and analysis on the ideology and wholehearted application of Christian love, for
which sensitivity, mutual respect, and compassion are essential life principles, outlook values, and
attitudes in any form of communication by Christians.

5. See also Bennett (1979), which provides the basis for his attention to empathy.

culture[6] and are marked by increasing mutual respect for those of other cultures. A mutual affirmation of dignity comes through lived-out respect for each other and recognizing that cultural differences need not be barriers to growing relationships. Intercultural communication can be most effective in relationships of mutual respect and affirmation of dignity amongst people of different cultures without any party losing the immediacy of their own cultural background. Rather than differences undermining communication, the differences become a means for celebrating diversity.[7] Higher degrees of intercultural relationship, or interculturality, between members of different cultures are marked by an increasing willingness to lay aside prejudices. Relationships of increasing interculturality between a Christian and non-Christians of other cultures are marked by the Christian not only laying aside prejudices but also caringly submitting to the others for God's purposes to be fulfilled.

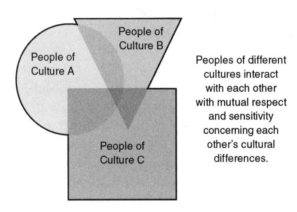

Figure 1.3: Intercultural Interactions

---

6. See also the distinction by Omori (2017, 309) in the context of research: "Cross-cultural communication and intercultural communication are differentiated based on the focus of the research: whereas intercultural communication focuses on the interaction with different cultures, cross-cultural communication focuses more on the comparisons of different cultures." Using one's own culture as the basis for comparison in the early days of building cross-cultural relationships must not provoke a sense of ethnocentric superiority. Relying on generalizations of other cultures can lead to naive stereotyping.

7. Note some earlier definitions of intercultural communication: "acts of communication undertaken by individuals identified with groups exhibiting intergroup variation in shared social and cultural patterns" (Damen 1987, 23), or a "symbolic process in which people from different cultures create shared meanings" (Lustig and Koester 2003, 49–51). Unlike these and other definitions, Bennett cited above hones in on the interpersonal dynamics for facilitating what results in intercultural communication.

Example: A church with members from multiple different cultures who engage lovingly with each other regardless of personal backgrounds is a fine example of an intercultural body. A church in a multicultural city may well have smaller congregations composed of people from a similar background (e.g., a Korean congregation, a Filipino congregation, an English-speaking congregation, and a Japanese congregation), but an intercultural church in a multicultural city will see members of the smaller congregations happily interacting with members of the other smaller congregations (as much as they are able) when the entire church congregates. A merely multicultural church will see the members of the smaller congregations limiting their interactions to those of their own congregation. For instance, the Koreans may sit in one area, the Filipinos may sit elsewhere, the English-speakers may carry on their usual weekly interactions with each other, and so on. An intercultural church, on the other hand, will see members of the different smaller congregations intermingling as an intercultural body.

Intercultural communication is difference based (Bennett 2013, 5) and so needs to be more intentional than casual interaction with those similar to ourselves. But our motivation for intentional interaction is best served by sensitivity to differences and to God's leading and calling, whether outreach is amongst individuals, small groups such as families, or wider communities. Hopefully we can see how intercultural relationships are much more attractive than cross-cultural relationships for sharing the message of the gospel. The journey to interculturality begins with having the courage to take on the risks of cross-cultural interaction. What do the risks include? Being judged by others and found wanting, being misunderstood and rejected, being (rightly or wrongly) perceived as projecting superiority or a threat and so provoking resentment or hatred, or being perceived as being inferior and considered contemptible and worthless.

Cross-cultural example from Pakistan: My missionary activity in the 1980s involved being part of a multiple-culture women's team with Operation Mobilization in Pakistan, working cross-culturally with the church and reaching out cross-culturally to Muslim women. Our team included young female Christians from Malaysia, Singapore, Korea, and Pakistan, as well as my British self. I had a naive awareness of our different outlooks on the mundane day-to-day aspects of life, and my interactions with my equally young-in-Christ teammates were very much cross-cultural rather than intercultural. We took turns cooking for the team week by week, and my British preference for bland food was very soon judged as unacceptable because my teammates all preferred spicy food. Even though this reaction was shocking to me, when it was my turn to cook, I had to put my own cultural preference and personal tastes aside and take a cross-cultural approach by cooking food that they liked to eat. I didn't grow up eating curry, and I didn't enjoy it. I had to regard eating meals with Pakistani families and at church gatherings as part of sacrifice and self-denial in ministry. For two years, I spent most of the daily team meals in Pakistan eating rice with tomato sauce, which I bought by carefully saving the small weekly allowance allotted to each team member.

Cross-cultural and intercultural examples from China: In 1994, I found myself placed with an American organization in China and threw myself into language study. I enjoyed using and developing the language I was learning in real-life settings, such as travelling and buying bus, train, and boat tickets; ordering food from noodle vendors; and negotiating for permission to stay in the least expensive hostels that were only supposed to admit Chinese travellers. In the early days, my interactions with my American teammates followed a cross-cultural approach when I compared and discovered the Americans' alternative use of the English language and outlook on life. In fact, at one point an American team leader advised me to be as cross-cultural in my interactions with the Americans as I needed to be with Chinese people. Two and half years later, I was teamed up in a remote setting with another non-American, Dr. Co, who is a Filipina of Chinese descent. We became long-term colaborers ministering together in six different parts of China over nearly three decades. What began as a cross-cultural relationship moved almost imperceptibly into an intercultural relationship as my respect for her giftings and abilities, and her appreciation of mine, bound us together in God's purposes despite our differing cultural backgrounds. We could both see the fruitful ways God used our strengths and weaknesses complimentarily, and

> this was communicated through our lifestyle to the Chinese villagers as we lived and worked together in a remote village in China. By grace, we began a village house-church network and trained Christian disciples who became emerging leaders and eventually took on full leadership when we sensed our part of the work was done (as in D-Davidson 2012, 226–31). Growing the relationship into interculturality was just as important for us as missionaries from different backgrounds as moving from cross-cultural to intercultural relationships with those we were reaching out to together.

Missionaries largely used to be from the Global North, and they compared other cultures to Western concepts of appropriate and inappropriate behavior and action. The growth of missionaries from the Global South, as well as the multiple-culture approach to outreach that is conducive to purposeful outreach in our global-village world, has made it all the more important for traditional monocultural outreach organizations and groups to recognize the contribution that can come by welcoming and respecting input from Christians of differing background cultures. This is particularly important for Western organizations that have long been accustomed to taking Western orientations as the benchmark for their members, despite the fact that some of their members might now have a non-Western background.

> **Cross-cultural example of a Filipina working with Germans:**[8] "I'm now working with an orphanage that was established in the Philippines by a German organization, so many of my colleagues and the administrative team are Germans. I just have to remember they are being German because they are so straight when they speak compared to Filipinos. It would be much harder if I hadn't already worked in Germany before this. I'm getting used to adjusting to them, and it means my German is improving too."

---

8. Throughout this book I will be presenting examples and illustrations in quotation marks that are largely from my former students, as well as from missionary colleagues and other friends, from a variety of Global North and Global South nations. Some of the examples are from assignments in which my students interviewed people from other cultures, and the wording and phrasing has been modified where necessary for accuracy in English and coherency of context. Permission was given for use of interview material.

Monocultural Global South organizations, which are engaging increasingly in ministry with those from other nations and backgrounds, do well to be aware of the need for mutual cultural awareness too. It can enrich our hearts and lives to learn about the backgrounds and perceptions of other Christians with whom God has brought us to minister together for him. Growing in understanding of the different backgrounds and learning how God has worked in each person's life and background community can encourage and challenge us to a life of greater love. The world will see that we are living as disciples of Jesus as we respect and love each other in celebration of God's glorious creative diversity (John 13:35). A consistent and long-term lifestyle demonstration can be more persuasive in communicating the truth of the gospel of Christ than mere words.

Devotional comment: Moving from cross-cultural relationships to intercultural relationships involves a process. As obstacles are overcome and time is spent, how the process unfolds will vary from individual to individual and group to group. No single program or plan can be applied uniformly as every society and community has distinct structures and expectations—much of which are created and defended according to the desires and distinctives of the specific members. We can, however, bring out universal, transferable principles that can be modified according to the dynamics of different settings. For instance, sharing the gospel of Christian love with others in a culturally appropriate way can only truly come about with passion as we grow more deeply in love with the Lord Jesus. Being sensitive to the leading of the Holy Spirit will help us make appropriate choices as we engage with those of other perceptions and outlooks. A key part of moving from cross-cultural interaction to intercultural relationships comes as we grow more willing to lay aside our ambitions and walk in God's leading, courageously facing the challenges laid out for us to take up in building and growing relationships.

PEOPLE AS COMMUNICATORS

Defining *communications* is the starting point for considering people as communicators. The *Oxford English Dictionary* defines *communications* as "the means of sending or receiving information."[9] How do we, as people, communicate? Unlike animals and other created entities, we communicate in a variety of ways, using literal and symbolic meanings. We use symbols, such as the grouping of component parts of the alphabet, to indicate literal and/or figurative ideas in the form of words. These are interacted with as either written or spoken symbols. We also use creative means, such as pictures and objects, both to aid comprehension in communication and as a means of enjoyment. Enjoyment or despair of life is communicated by how we interact with the world and with others. The use of symbols, such as through language and behavior, varies from culture to culture in communicating common concerns, such as respect, gratitude, apology, and so on. These differing cultural forms, whether verbal or behavioral, are understood by the members of a community to have particular meanings when the forms and symbols are used in expected ways. Misunderstanding of communication comes when we use the forms and symbols either in an incorrect way or in a way that brings confusion.

> **Important principle:** As people communicating the gospel, we want to send information about Christ and have it both understood and received as relevant by those to whom we communicate. In fact, we want to communicate more than factual information; we also want to communicate the reality of the love and the power of the gospel of Christ so that others are attracted to a life reborn by the forgiveness of sin on the cross. Furthermore, we are following the command of Jesus to "go and make disciples of all nations" (Matthew 28:19–20) because we want to obey his command out of love for him and express that love to others.

THE DIFFERENCE BETWEEN MISSIONS AND EVANGELISM

When communicating about Christ to people of all nations, it is important that we consider the rationale underlying our communications, as well as

---

9. *Concise Oxford English Dictionary*, 11th ed., CD-ROM (Oxford: Oxford University Press, 2004). Licensed to Focus Multimedia Ltd. This source will also be used for the other *OED* definitions in this book.

our platform for being relevant and credible.[10] This is why it can be helpful to distinguish between missions and evangelism.

- Bosch (1991, 420) notes that the concept of evangelism has been interpreted over the years in multiple different ways but prefers to "summarize evangelism as that dimension and activity of the church's mission which, by word and deed and in the light of particular conditions and a particular context, offers every person and community, everywhere, a valid opportunity to be challenged to a radical orientation of their lives . . . which involves such things as deliverance from slavery to the world and its powers; embracing Christ as Savior and Lord; becoming a living member of his community, the church; being enlisted into his service of reconciliation, peace, and justice on earth; and being committed to God's purpose of placing all things under the rule of Christ."
- The Greek New Testament term we associate with evangelism, εὐαγγέλιον, means "the good news," and rather than referring to the one bringing the message, it refers to the actual message. So we can certainly say it refers to *what* we communicate and not *how* we communicate it. For instance, we may build relationships cross-culturally through many ways, such as the dental clinic Dr. Co set up in the remote village or our American colleagues' efforts to teach English in Chinese colleges, but these activities are not the gospel message. Rather, they are the missions platform for bringing the message and through which the love of God could be lived out and bring transformation.
- Kirk (2000, 57) urges that "missions is not synonymous with evangelism. If evangelism [sharing the good news] is made to bear the full weight of the entire missions calling of the Church, its sharp characteristic will disappear. . . . [However] there can be no authentic evangelism apart from a living testimony to the transforming power of the Gospel in action."

We should never forget that we are God's vessels for communicating the gospel message, and God is the source of the power that brings transformation—the power that is Spirit-derived, unquenchable, immeasurable, unconditional love. Hesselgrave (1991, 85) suggests we are

---

10. This section is a modification of D-Davidson (2018, 2–3).

communicating to persuade, as of the verbal form πειθω in Acts 26:28 and 2 Corinthians 5:11, so that *persuasion* encapsulates the aim of people communicating Christ.

THEOLOGY IN RELATION TO PERCEPTIONS OF THE GOSPEL OF CHRIST

Following the death and resurrection of Jesus, the early church had a passion for sharing the gospel of Christ that began with the outpouring of the Spirit at Pentecost and saw initial cross-cultural evangelism to Jews and gentile converts who had gathered in Jerusalem from as far away as Rome, Libya, Mesopotamia,[11] and Cappadocia[12] (Acts 2:5–11). Indeed, before Jesus' ascension and the day of Pentecost, Jesus had advised his disciples that the Holy Spirit would empower them to be his witnesses in Jerusalem, Judea, Samaria, and to the ends of the earth (Acts 1:8). In Matthew's gospel account we read of the command given by Jesus that, in light of the complete authority given to him, his followers should "go and make disciples of all nations, baptizing them in the name of the Father and of the Son and of the Holy Spirit, and teaching them to obey everything I have commanded you. And surely I am with you always, to the very end of the age" (Matthew 28:19–20). The disciples could have little understood the implications of Jesus' words, but the empowering at Pentecost and the persecution of the early church started bringing about through them that of which Jesus had spoken.

The continual unfolding of Jesus' instructions and direction before his ascension also shows us the history of missions and expansion of communication of the gospel. Prior to Jesus' incarnation the Alexandrian Empire had made Greek a common language. The succeeding Roman Empire then brought an infrastructure of roads that enhanced the possibilities of extended travel and rapid communication of the gospel message. The message of Christ was communicated with urgency as his return was expected to be imminent. The Didache, or the Teaching of the Twelve Apostles, was a collection of teachings put together after the first century[13] to provide instruction for Christian community and church life, and was the universal manual for evangelists and travelling teachers. The centuries unfolded with no return of Christ, and by the fourth century attention turned to

---

11. Present-day Iraq.
12. Present-day Turkey.
13. Sommer (2007, 333) "probably compiled sometime between A.D. 90 and 110, in Syria."

questions of doctrinal delicacy: How was Christ both fully human and fully divine? How could the divine associate with the profane? What might be understood of the ontology of the Godhead? The answers put forward to these crucial questions became part of the meat of teaching of the different schools of theological thought and influenced the beliefs and doctrines propagated by different parts of the universal or *catholic*[14] church. By the sixteenth century this catholic church had become the Catholic Church, a towering institution with the priesthood wielding control of the church and sacraments in a way that undermined the gospel.

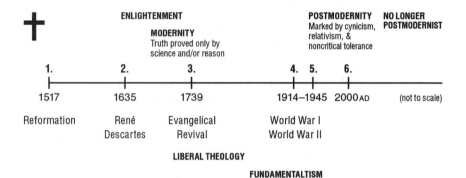

Figure 1.4: Timeline Showing the Emergence of Liberal, Evangelical, and Fundamentalist Theology

1. In AD 1517, Martin Luther memorably pinned his objections to the door of the Wittenberg Cathedral, heralding the beginnings of the Reformation of the Catholic Church and the eventual establishment of the Protestant church body, for whom salvation was, once again, as professed by Luther, to be understood as by grace, through faith, and according to Scripture.

2. In AD 1635, French philosopher and mathematician René Descartes links the ability to think with unquestionable proof of existence in the phrase that is translated "I think, therefore I am." He is often referred to as the "father of modern philosophy" for moving away from the standard approach to philosophy that had relied on the senses to discover knowledge. For Descartes anything that could be doubted had the potential to be untrue. He urged

---

14. The term *catholic* can be seen to come from the Greek component parts of καθολικος, κατά (per, in respect of) and ὁλός (all).

that truth could only be discovered by scientific (or law-revealing) method or by unquestionable reason. This ushered in the Age of Enlightenment and the period known as *modernity* in which truth was validated only through science and reason. An eventual consequence was the beginning of liberal theology since the divinity of Jesus and proof of his miraculous power could not be reproduced by scientific method. The Enlightenment era and modernity had little place for faith, so for Liberal Theologians and the Protestant church following its influence, certain "unprovable" parts of the Bible were dismissed as unauthoritative.

3. Despite the Enlightenment era's faith-quenching nature, the Holy Spirit was still moving, and AD 1739 saw the Wesleyan revival in the United Kingdom,[15] which became known as the Evangelical Revival. This move of faith brought multitudes into personal relationship with God through Jesus and a new appreciation by faith of God's Word so that "evangelical Christians" considered the entire canon of Scripture to be authoritative. In further opposition to the liberal theology, the late nineteenth century saw the arising in the United States of the fundamentalist movement, which influenced Protestant church denominations into the early twentieth century. To undermine liberal theology's limitations on the authority of the Bible, the fundamentalist response was to declare that the entire canon of Scripture could be and should be taken literally in its entirety.

4. The years AD 1914–1945 saw the death and destruction caused by two world wars. Modernity's melioristic metanarrative of the potential for human betterment through the increase of knowledge and discovery of truth was seen to be unfounded.

5. In the wake of those wars came the start of postmodernity. Sampson, Samuel, and Sugden (1994, 7) give us a helpful definition for postmodernity in relation to modernity: "Modernity is the intellectual and cultural heritage of the Enlightenment project—namely the rejection of traditional and religious sources of authority in favor of reason and knowledge as the road to human emancipation. From this point of view, postmodernity refers to the

---

15. Concurrent with the Great Awakening in the North American colonies and the series of revivals in the 1730s and '40s.

progressive loss of confidence in, if not failure of, the enlightenment project since 1945."

Why do Sampson, Samuel, and Sugden suggest postmodernity began in 1945? Carter (2006, 54) writes:

> The optimistic, humanistic liberalism of the nineteenth century had been savaged by the tragic events of the first half of the twentieth century: two world wars, the Depression, the Holocaust, the development and use of the atomic bomb, racism, eugenics, increased barbarism in war, the rise of Communist totalitarianism in the Soviet Union. These horrific events had shaken the twin doctrines of the Enlightenment: the doctrine of progress through science, technology, education, and democracy and the doctrine of the perfectibility of humanity.

So by 1945 the optimism of modernity was undermined worldwide and the age of postmodernism began. Following Erickson (1998, 19), Stetzer (2003, 120) specifically offers that "postmodernism is based on the denial of personal objectivity, the uncertainty of knowledge, the death of any all-inclusive explanation, the denial of the inherent goodness of knowledge, the rejection of progress, the supremacy of community-based knowledge, and the disbelief in objective enquiry."

In summary we can say that postmodernism and postmodernists are marked by (D-Davidson 2018, 4–5):

- o *Cynicism,* because expectations of global improvement were undermined;
- o *Relativism,* which promotes there being no ultimate standards for truth and the belief that what's true for one person isn't necessarily true for everyone else; truth is constructed by society; and
- o *Noncritical tolerance,* which uncritically urges that everyone can believe whatever they like but may not insist that everyone else should believe it too.

6. Whereas postmodernism brought with it a deconstruction of what had previously been considered to be true and real along with something of a reinvention of what was considered to be creative across the arts and in literature, the second millennium

seems to be heralding a desire for reconstruction of a new sort. It appears to be a post-postmodern era with no consistent terms or premises emerging to name or define it. Themes have begun to emerge but are not widely established in the academic realm, not least the "digimodernism" ubiquity of technology-driven social media influences and the effect upon their users (Kirby 2009). Here we see something of the lifestyle changes and the shared global concerns that the internet and social media have brought about through the instant revealing of news throughout the world along with the opportunity for critical replay and detailed analysis of unfolding events. The post-postmodern era brings something of a reclaiming of the objectivity that was lost to postmodernism and welcomes engagement with how communities might respond to accommodate issues of gender dysphoria and gender fluidity, varying perspectives on human rights, and questioning the expectations of political figures when economics or personality appear to undermine the value of integrity. The twenty-first century is also notably marked by a millennialist narcissism, as those growing up in the new millennium have led the way in preoccupation with self, as seen in selfieism[16] on social media, concurrent with the GoFundMe[17] mentality that asks others to assist with one's financial burdens—some requests of which have been a catalyst for generosity whilst others bring merely mass derision for an "entitlement" mentality. Global concerns for internationally agreed policy on combatting global warming and attention to environmental issues abound, along with the need for cooperation in managing humanitarian needs related to large-scale disasters and fatal pandemics such as due to SARS (severe acute respiratory syndrome), Ebola, and coronavirus diseases. Our aim in communicating Christ is to bring a message that is perceived as relevant in spite of, or particularly in the face of, the seemingly insurmountable difficulties and concerns that are present at both individual and community level.

---

16. *Selfieism* is the activity of taking multiple "selfie" photos (i.e., photos of oneself) in both unusual and mundane situations and posting them onto a social media platform so that others may register their like or dislike.

17. This internet platform is used to request financial donations for described needs from paying hospital bills to a desire to take a holiday somewhere. It appeals to a sense of philanthropy although the platform takes a cut of the money raised.

IMPLICATIONS OF UNDERLYING LIBERAL
AND FUNDAMENTALIST THEOLOGIES

As we have seen, liberal and fundamentalist theologies differ on their perceptions of the authority of the Bible and hence its relevance for life. These perceptions or beliefs about the Bible can't help but influence the message communicated about Christ. The liberal message that is unable to fully present the faith-requiring truths of the gospel can result in communicating a message that merely presents Jesus as a good man, a good teacher, or an excellent model of love and compassion, all of which he is, thereby introducing only the human side of the Savior. The salvation associated with communicating this representation of Jesus cannot get much beyond presenting his benefit for the development of individuals and communities in purely physical and emotional terms and on a temporal basis only. Another factor of liberal theology is its tendency to suggest that the gospel will change with different cultures and settings. As an evangelical, I prefer to suggest that although emphases related to application of the biblical truths may differ, certain essentials of the gospel message should never change, in that same way that Clark (2003, 120) advises that "the Bible itself is not acultural but it is transcultural."

In contrast to liberal perceptions of the Bible, the fundamentalist desire to take the entire Word of God literally misses the critical scholar's perspective that not all Scripture can be read and understood through a literal approach. Poetic genres of the Bible are full of figurative language, and Jesus frequently taught using parables with a clear indication that not all would understand his teaching—only those with "ears to hear" (Mark 4:9). Perhaps the greatest problem that can come from taking a purely literal approach to Scripture is exactly what Jesus accused the Pharisees of: they sought to follow the law according to every tiniest detail but lacked the love that was fundamental to obeying the commandments. When asked by one of the teachers of the law which was the most important commandment, "'The most important one,' answered Jesus, 'is this: "Hear, O Israel: The Lord our God, the Lord is one. Love the Lord your God with all your heart and with all your soul and with all your mind and with all your strength." The second is this: "Love your neighbor as yourself." There is no commandment greater than these'" (Mark 12:29–31). The Pharisees would have been well aware of these laws but were not living them out. As a result, the Pharisees came across as legalistic, demanding, and unloving. Fundamentalist churches whose members communicate an entirely literalist understanding of Scripture can easily fall into this same trap so that the message of the gospel becomes little more than a new life marked by an unhelpful legalism.

Communicating the gospel from a liberal perspective can result in a humanistic understanding of Christ that limits spiritual growth as there would seem to be no need for faith. In contrast, communicating about Christ from a fundamentalist perspective can introduce new believers into the bondage of sets of manmade lifestyle and churchmanship rules that restricts believers from living in the freedom that the gospel promises. Instead, we do well to communicate Christ from the evangelical perspective.

ESSENTIALS OF THE GOSPEL FROM THE EVANGELICAL PERSPECTIVE

Whilst emphases on application of biblical truths may well vary from culture to culture and setting to setting, there are truths in the gospel message which should never change. How we present them in terms of communication style from formal teaching to interactive conversation may vary according to the culture and setting, but the truth content is nonvariable and nonnegotiable. These truths relate to:[18]

- **Who** Jesus is
- **What** Jesus did
- **Why** Jesus did it

If we omit even one of these three aspects, we will not have presented the full gospel message. For instance:

- **If we omit the truth that Jesus is the Son of God**, fully divine and fully human, then he may be understood merely as a very good human teacher who modeled the concept of love in light of the law with self-sacrificing excellence. In this case Jesus would not be qualified to atone for sin.
- **If we omit what Jesus did**, that he died on the cross and rose again to destroy the power of sin and the curse of death so that our sins could

---

18. These principles are taken from Vee J. D-Davidson, *Empowering Transformation: Transferable Principles for Intercultural Planting of Spiritually-Healthy Churches* (Oxford: Regnum International, 2018), 94–96. ISBN 9781912343713. Used by permission as are all further excerpts throughout the book.

be atoned for, then salvation in Jesus' name has little practical application with respect to a change of life and lifestyle with regard to sin.

- **If we omit why Jesus did what he did**—namely, so that we can be
born again of the Spirit and come into a personal relationship with
God with good works prepared for us each to do according to God's
glorious eternal purposes—then although our lifestyle may reflect
our dislike of sin, the path we choose, albeit a good one, may not be
the one that God had planned for us for his glory. In fact, rather than
seeking the Holy Spirit to intuit to us God's specific will, we may
well end up doing all manner of good works through our strength
and not in step with the Holy Spirit.

In the process of developing a friendship and relationship that has built
the trust necessary to share gospel truths, we may well only communicate
aspects of the gospel message at certain times. The order we present each
truth is likely to vary depending on the context of the person or people we
are communicating with. We will not necessarily present all three truths
in a single encounter or in the order listed. But by the time we sense the
Holy Spirit's leading to offer an evangelistic invitation, all three aspects
need to have been communicated clearly during the outreach process. We
also need to be careful that there has been correct understanding of the
different concepts shared. If the offer is not taken up, it may not be the
gospel that is being refused but rather a poorly communicated and misunderstood message.

Let us consider the three essentials again since the message we communicate is crucial:

- If we do not fully communicate that Jesus is the Son of God, he may
be understood to be merely a good teacher and a profoundly impres-
sive model of love in action. But in that case, lacking the perfection,
holiness, and sinless purity of a member of the Godhead, he would
be ineligible to pay the price for sin that separates people from God.
- If his death and resurrection are omitted, so is the truth of the price
he paid for the sin that separates us from God, along with the truth
of forgiveness, removal of guilt, and the unchangeable hope that is
brought by knowing that he has thoroughly defeated sin and death.
- If the reason he died for us is omitted, then potential followers of
Jesus will be unaware of the fullness and richness of purpose in following him—let alone the mighty potential of the depth of God's

love working in and through those who come to him through Jesus, or the fruitfulness that not only transforms society but also leads to the eternity that is both now and yet to come.

Important principle: We must communicate fully the essentials of the gospel with sensitivity to the Holy Spirit concerning how much our listeners are ready to receive each time we meet with them. As we pray to be in step with God's timing, he will lead us in communicating who Jesus is, what he did, and why he did what he did.

CONCLUSION

We seek to communicate the gospel of Christ because we have been persuaded of the wonder of his sacrificial love that brings forgiveness of sin and restoration of relationship with God. In communicating this gospel to others we do well to continue developing our relationship with God and increasingly become sensitive to the leading of the Holy Spirit. As evangelicals we need to be aware of the theology that underlies liberal and fundamentalist approaches to the gospel message so that we don't confuse or mislead our listeners. As we reach out to people of other nations and cultural backgrounds, our relationships invariably begin as cross-cultural relationships. Our goal is to build relationships that progress from cross-cultural relationships to life-transforming intercultural relationships. Such relationships will involve increasing sensitivity to the cultural differences, empathy for the life and situation of the other and others, and will inevitably be marked by the mutual respect that results from cherishing the dignity of the other by the love of Christ. Through such relationships, communication of Christ is both transforming and transformed.

In the next chapter, we will look at the technicalities of communication and their means for heightening effective communication of Christ.

QUESTIONS FOR REFLECTION
AND DISCUSSION

1. In the "As It Happened" scenario at the start of the chapter, did my Chinese friend and I have a cross-cultural relationship or an intercultural relationship? What evidence do you have for your choice?

2. In the "As It Happened" scenario at the start of the chapter, apart from my desire to escape from drinking the alcohol in the bottle gifted to me, how else might misunderstanding cause us embarrassment? How might we deal with these issues?

3. Consider colleagues, friends, or relatives from a different cultural background than you. How long have you known each one? Which relationships are multicultural, which are cross-cultural, and which are intercultural? Wherever you sense a lack of care for one of them, pray for insight into how you might deepen your relationship.

4. Consider the three essentials of the gospel message referred to in the chapter. Which of the three might you start from if you were sharing the gospel with an ex-drug addict who is overcome by guilt at having abused his body? Which would you start with if you were sharing the gospel with a young student who is passionate about the injustice of racism in society?

CHAPTER 2

Communication Theory and Models of Communication

As It Happened: An American couple had moved into a new house in a rural community. It had been constructed according to their design via an interpreter and featured a fully functioning Western-style kitchen. The wife was making friends with young girls in the community and invited two of them back to the house to make cookies and learn some English. She told them they could come once a week for an English lesson. A few days later the two girls came to the foreigners' house with some of their friends.

> **Husband:** "Your English-class students are here with some friends."
> **Wife:** "But I told them it's just once a week. I really can't see them now. Can you tell them I'm busy?"
> **Husband:** "They're your students. You tell them!"

INTRODUCTION

Have you ever been surprised to discover you've been misunderstood and had to face the difficulty and embarrassment of trying to make things right? Sometimes the misunderstood issue doesn't cause a big problem, but in other cases the consequences of miscommunication can be devastating for relationships.

This chapter begins with attention to different aspects of life and human interaction that are vehicles for communication, and then it provides a brief background to communication theory in relation to the development of models of communication. These models include classic linear, interactive, and transactional models. The chapter culminates with a model for Christian communicators of Christ.

VEHICLES FOR COMMUNICATION

We now turn to different aspects of life and human interaction that are vehicles for communication in order to begin to understand why our communication with others can be so easily misunderstood, particularly when we are communicating with people of other cultures.

Language

We saw in chapter 1 that people use symbols to communicate with each other and that these symbols can be expressed through language and behavior. Popenoe (2000, 56) defines a symbol as "anything that a group of people have agreed upon as a way of meaningfully representing something other than itself." As we apply this definition to language, it is clear that different nations can express similar concepts in their own language, but they can also use words to express concepts and ideas that don't translate well into other nations' languages. Those concepts and ideas and the associated language symbols were agreed upon by people in that nation only.[1] If the language isn't understood, then neither can the symbols' meanings be understood.

> **Example from South Korea:** "We have the word *Kibun*, which has no exact English meaning, but it's like pride or self-esteem and that we are careful not to hurt others' feelings."

Terms in any language can have more than one meaning depending on how the words are used. Context is essential for understanding.

> **Example in English:** Notice how many ways the word *saw* is used in this sentence: "The father saw the son saw the log whilst the mother saw that[2] their daughter saw[3] the doctor." Note that the third and fourth uses are more complex than the first two uses.

---

1. Note too that graphics or visual presentations of ideas can also be a technical form of language. As for verbal language, if the graphic icons aren't understood, neither can the graphic presentation's meaning be understood correctly.

2. Meaning "made sure that."

3. Meaning "had a consultation with."

Example from Spain: The word *mañana* can mean both "morning" and "tomorrow," but in English it is often used in a satirical manner to describe procrastinators who may or may not complete a task until some unspecified time in the future. In that sense, *mañana* might never come.

Learning the heart language, or "mother tongue," of the people we are reaching out to opens us up not only to how words are used in their culture but also to the often hidden dynamics of the worldview underlying their cultural behavior.

Example from Japan: "It is very important that the missionary intending to go to Japan should at least be able to speak and understand conversational Japanese, especially in the provinces where purely *Nihongo* is being used. It is very difficult to communicate through sign language, and sometimes those signs and waving-the-arms communication can be misunderstood in our culture as meaning something else!"

Example from China: In my early days of language learning, I attended formal classes as well as having a private tutor. My tutor advised me to set aside the books from the formal classroom lessons and instead had us work through some books from a series used by Chinese children to learn Mandarin. I enjoyed learning to read and write the words and phrasings of short classic poems and stories, and as my tutor pointed out, we were learning about Chinese culture and beliefs the same way that Chinese children did. The colorful pictures and cute puzzles provided a fun, nonintimidating way to learn the language and learn about Chinese history and culture as well.

Nonverbal Communication

North American anthropologist Edward Hall served in the United States army in Europe and the Philippines during World War II. Later he became director of the Foreign Service Institute, which provided training for overseas and diplomatic service. His observations and experience of other cultures inspired the 1959 classic *The Silent Language*, a groundbreaking work proposing that behavior acts as a language without using spoken words and that nonverbal communication through body language permeates culture.[4] Every culture has ways of being and behaving that are learned from childhood so that the meaning of what is being communicated is clearly understood by people of that culture. Just as we saw in the example from Japan above, being cross-cultural communicators requires that we become aware of what expressions of body language mean in the culture or cultures of the people to whom we are reaching out.

There are a number of vehicles for nonverbal communication through specific emphases of body language and cultural behavioral preferences and expectations, which we will look at in turn, beginning with the term *kinesics*, the technical term for body language. Additional vehicles include haptics, proxemics, human/physical characteristics, commonly used articles and artefacts, paralanguage, and contexting.

Kinesics

The term *kinesics*, coined by the anthropologist Ray Birdwhistell in 1952, has become the umbrella term for a variety of specialized fields related to communicative interaction. Hall (1976, 65) writes that "Birdwhistell has defined kinesics as the way one moves and handles one's body." This is something of a simplification of Birdwhistell's attention to both conscious and subconscious movements of different parts of the body in relation to communication.[5] Birdwhistell's succinct explanation of the *hows* and *whys* of movement looked to provide something of a universal application to understanding, but when we consider kinesics in cultural terms, the important concept of social learning is what causes cross-cultural communicators' initial difficulty.[6] An acceptable gesture, posture, or facial expression in one culture may be offensive in another. Until we have learned how local people perceive gestures and other body movements, we may easily misread body language or try to engage with people in a way that is perceived as inappropriate and perhaps even rude.

---

4. See also Knapp, Hall, and Horgan (2013); Argyle (2013), which is an updated edition of Argyle's 1975 classic *Bodily Communication* on nonverbal communication; and Sternberg and Kostić (2020).

5. For a fun video showing nonverbal behavior expressed by a child in an undesired musical performance, see Stephen Hill singing "Five Little Fingers" on the Gaither DVD *Christmas: A Time for Joy.*

6. Yet Birdwhistell (1952) was clearly not unaware of cultural factors as his bibliography includes Labarre (1947) writing on "The Cultural Basis of Emotions and Gestures."

Example from Thailand: "We never point our feet at people. Sometimes foreigners come to preach at the church, and they need to know that when they sit on the floor with us, it's offensive to have their legs point straight forward at the congregation."

Example from Guatemala: "When women meet, it looks like they kiss, but actually they are only moving their heads and air kissing, not actually touching—not like French people, who actually do kiss cheeks."

Example from India: "We shake the head to the right to agree, not bob it up and down!"

Haptics

Haptic is an adjective related to the sense of touch. Swindells et al. (2006, 1) describe *haptic behaviors* as "touch-based interactions that represent some kind of meaning to the user." Haptic communication involves the use of touch in specific mutually understood ways to convey a variety of information, including emotional acknowledgement of another or pragmatic responses to planned events or unexpected contingencies. For instance, shaking hands is a typical haptic behavior of Westerners as a sign of greeting and acknowledgement of another's presence. The rules of appropriate and inappropriate haptic behavior vary from culture to culture.

Example from New Zealand: "In New Zealand, our indigenous Maori people press their noses together when they greet."

Example from Myanmar: "For the people of Myanmar, their head is sacred, so a missionary from another nation should avoid touching it."

Example from Nepal: "Men and women are not allowed to shake or hold hands together. . . . You must never use the left hand in handling, receiving things, pointing or shaking because the left hand is considered dirty."

Example of pragmatic-response haptic behavior: With the coronavirus epidemic that began in December 2019, people worldwide were discouraged from touching each other's hands in greeting to prevent any spread of the virus. Instead, they were urged to bump each other's elbow or tap feet together. In the beginning people found it amusing or even embarrassing as it was so different from their usual manner of greeting. To others it almost seemed silly, but it was an important way of preventing cross contamination. People decided whether they would use the arm or foot to greet by observing each other carefully before initiating the greeting. These new body language communications soon became learnt responses, even if they still seemed a little silly. Based on the example from Thailand above, we would expect that tapping feet together would not have been a greeting choice for Thai people.

Proxemics

Edward Hall also provided the key insights associated with proxemics or the use of space surrounding groups and individuals in his 1966 book *The Hidden Dimension*.[7] He also provides a typology for perceptions of space. He recognized that different cultures have distinct perceptions concerning what makes for comfortable, uncomfortable, acceptable, and inappropriate use of space and that this is discerned in relation to the senses as one becomes enculturated.

Ferraro and Briody (2017, 85) present four types of distance related to middle-class North Americans by citing observations from the proxemics typology of Hall (1966):

Intimate distance: ranging from body contact to 18 inches,[8] a distance used for love-making, comforting, and protecting, at which olfactory and thermal sensations are at their highest.

Personal distance: from 18 inches to 4 feet, depending on the closeness of the relationship. At this distancing mode, people have an invisible "space bubble" separating themselves from others.

Social distance: from 4 to 12 feet, a distance used by acquaintances and strangers in business meetings and classrooms.

---

7. Note that other writers, including Sommer (1959), Kuethe (1962), and Little (1965), provided earlier publications concerning space and distance in a North American context, whereas Hall also attends to cross-cultural effects. See too his proxemic behavior notation system (Hall 1963).
8. 18 inches = 45.72 cm; 12 inches or 30.48 cm = 1 Foot.

Public distance: from 12–25 feet, at which the recognition of others is not mandatory and the subtle shades of meaning of voice, gesture and facial expression are lost.

If we compare the middle-class American distance preference to that of people from other cultures, there can be a vast difference.

Example from the Philippines: "When we meet, we easily group together with body parts like arms and shoulders touching. Riding jeepneys,[9] some foreigners don't like it, I think, because you are very scrunched up tight to the people on each side of you, and the driver doesn't start off until the vehicle's two long benches are properly crammed full."

Example from Italy: "Oh, we like to be very close when we talk, just like dancing, and eating. Well, everyone is as near as they can be and want to get the most out of talking with everyone, especially with friends or big family meal gatherings."

People of European nations can find Hall's middle-class American social distance preference to be as much as twice the distance of their own, and Asians, in relation to Americans, even more so. From the Philippines example, we can see that the American intimate distance is similar to the personal distance (or personal space[10]) for Filipinos. Whilst travelling in jeepneys, Filipinos don't appear to need the "space bubble" of separation that the Americans need to feel comfortable.

When we engage with people who are comfortable at a greater distance than we are, we might communicate a desire to intrude into their space and impose upon them, in which case they are liable to back away. Conversely, when we try to engage with people who are used to a lesser distance and who move in close to us, we likely will feel uncomfortable and will want to increase the distance. Without realizing, we might be communicating dislike or that we don't want to be with them. Of course, this will not help us build deep trusting intercultural relationships that our cross-cultural communications aspire to!

---

9. A jeepney is a privately owned vehicle with bench-like sitting platforms inside running the length of each side.

10. A term first referred to by David Katz (1937).

The hidden (worldview) rules associated with use of space are inculcated in members of each culture from a young age, and different aspects are lived out either consciously or subconsciously.

Example of conscious space and distancing rules: Teachers have children sitting at desks or tables in their classrooms with the furniture deliberately laid out as expected or required by the educational system.

Example of subconscious rules: Children go into the classroom and sit down at tables, usually in a designated place, without even thinking about the space between tables or classroom layout.

Proxemics and distancing expectations might change temporarily in the face of contingencies as a matter of pragmatics. The coronavirus mentioned earlier saw social-distancing laws enacted worldwide to try to limit the spread of the illness. Not only were ways of greeting changed, from nation to nation, but limits were also placed on the number of people who could meet together. Similarly, varying lengths of time and degrees of isolation were required of those who were infected by the virus, as well as for those who had symptoms of the virus or even had come into contact with a virus-carrier. We can note too though that isolation practices have been introduced since the days of the 1918 Spanish flu (also known as the 1918 influenza epidemic, which ran from March 1918 to March 1920). The Spanish flu infected nearly one-third of people globally and killed between 2.5–5 percent of the world's population across four successive waves. Despite the devastation of communities across the globe, Spinney (2017, 2) writes, "The Spanish flu is remembered personally not collectively. Not as a historical disaster but as millions of discrete, private tragedies." Despite that two-year long epidemic, cultural proxemics were not noticeably altered in the long term, but the memories associated with the private tragedies lingered for decades. The proxemics practices were a relatively short-term change in response to contingencies rather than being a facet of cultural orientation.

Human/Physical Characteristics

Psychology advises us that people are wary of those who look different. From culture to culture, some physical characteristics cause disgust, avoidance, or persecution while other physical characteristics command a positive response such as respect or appreciation. Characteristics that are markedly different can also be a source of fascination.

Example from China: "Western foreigners are called 'big nose' because, physically, their nose goes all the way to their forehead whereas that's not characteristic of Chinese people. It seems like a derogatory term—I suppose it is—but little children call it out because it's true and it's what they see."

Example from the Philippines: "Having the Mestizo [Spanish] look is considered really beautiful. Having a wide nose is not."

Example from Germany: "Being tall commands respect, especially in the workplace."

Example from North America: "Oh, all the girls want to have blonde hair—it's attractive to guys."

Example from Nepal: "Skin color affects your social level in my country."

When we're trying to make friends and build relationships cross-culturally, it is helpful to ask what we communicate through our appearance in relation to the physical characteristics that are considered attractive or fascinating in that culture. I can't help having the "big nose" of a Western foreigner, but I can mitigate any tension if I take the insult lightly and say, "This is how God made me, and we're all beautiful to him and wonderfully made." Of course, we do well to avoid appearing in a way considered offensive, if we can avoid it. That can have a lot to do with the clothing we wear and the items with which we choose to live.

Commonly Used Articles and Artefacts

Just as styles of housing and clothing differ from culture to culture, so too do cultures express their distinct priorities through the choice and use of particular artefacts and manmade objects. Some preferences are a result of pragmatics in relation to conditions of the environment. For instance, Inuits wear thick windproof sealskin coverings to keep warm in subzero temperatures. In contrast, Australians are accustomed to wearing a suit of short trousers and jacket whilst working in an office in their hot climate. For most office workers in Europe, wearing short trousers during working hours would be considered to be unprofessional and inappropriate. To communicate in a way that can be well received, we must be aware of what makes for appropriate clothing, colors, and use (or misuse) of other commonly used articles.

Example from Myanmar: "Men dress wearing the *lungy*, a small skirt the Burmese people acquired from India. If the missionary is willing to wear our clothing, this will create an important connection between the missionary and the local people, especially in the countryside where the people are more reserved."

Example from Fiji: "I think the tourists are better than the missionaries because the tourists in Fiji prefer to live with the people and mingle with them. We have missionaries that are there, but they have their own little castle and community where they all stay and have comfort. When they have vacations, they prefer to go to vacation hotels than to live with the islanders."

Example from Nepal: "Always remove footwear when entering a home."

Example from Bhutan: "Ladies cannot wear yellow *Rachu* (a piece of scarf worn by women, hung over a woman's shoulder) because only the Queen wears yellow *Rachu*, and only she can let the *Rachu* rest on both of her arms."

Example from Kenya: "The common meal in Kenya is maize flour, corn meal, rice, mashed potatoes, and chapatti. You'd better like it because you can expect that to be what you eat, unless you go to a big city."

Paralanguage

Para- as a prefix to the term *language* suggests that there is meaning beyond the words being communicated, usually due to the emphasis on the words spoken. For instance, note the difference with the emphasized word in italics between *"He* is my friend" compared to "He is my *friend."* The first identifies one man amongst other people, while the second emphasizes something more personal and special about the relationship.

Tonal languages can sound unusual to those who use tone levels for emphasis and vice versa, since both use the tone as a form of paralanguage but in a different manifestation. Meaning can also be affected by gestures and facial expressions. For instance, Kostić et al. note, "Micro-expressions [i.e., brief facial expressions] that last less than a quarter of a second and that appear suddenly are the biggest problem for the observer" (2020, 269), whilst Ekman (2009, 17) advises that micro-expressions may be a sign of speaking untruth, which invariably can be difficult to discern.

Paralanguage can also be seen through differing cultural ways of communicating in relation to contexting. Degrees of contexting vary on a spectrum from high-context communication to low-context communication. Edward Hall introduced the concept of contexting in *Beyond Culture*. He describes how "A high-context (HC) communication or message is one in which most of the information is either in the physical context or internalized in the person, while very little is in the" words spoken or written (1976, 79). So the actual words used by a high-context communicator do not make a major contribution to what the person is trying to communicate. Instead, communication is indirect, and the context and cultural understanding about the context provide the meaning. Further, "HC transactions feature programmed information that is in the receiver and in the setting, with only minimal information in the transmitted message. [Low-context] transactions are the reverse. Most of the information must be in the transmitted message in order to make up for what is missing in the context" (88). So low-context communication uses words, spoken or written, in a way that brings the exact meaning the communicator wants to communicate. Unlike high-context communications, there is no need to consider the surrounding context or cultural practices for further meaning because the meaning is intended to be conveyed directly through the words.

High-context example from Japan: "We communicate indirectly. The best way to communicate when we don't want to do something is to say, 'I will think about it,' which actually means no."

High-context example from Myanmar: "In my culture we don't usually tell the truth. We just go around the truth."

High-context example from China: "It is really hard to say no in my culture. Usually people will say okay at first, but you will never actually know if they mean yes or no."

Low-context example from Samoa: "People usually communicate directly, and what they say is what they mean."

Low-context example from Czech Republic: "Czech people always speak their mind."

Low-context example from Dominican Republic: "Our people are straightforward. They speak their mind and their feelings even if they offend people."

High-context example from Guatemala: "Don't ask for something directly like saying, 'Do you have a camera?' but 'Is there a camera we can use to take pictures?' Or when eating and you want to put more sugar in your coffee, we don't say to someone, 'Please pass the sugar to me,' but the equivalent of, 'Is there sugar?' Then we're not imposing on someone or making it look like we are demanding or expecting they should act as if we are higher than they are."

Author's example of unexpected low-context communication: On returning from a trip to the UK, I presented some small gifts of boxes of English tea as Christmas presents for the Foreign Affairs Bureau officials who processed our work visas each year. One official asked, "Is this a bribe?" Dr. Co immediately replied, "Of course not. It's far too small to be a bribe!"

From this example we can see that even in high-level context cultures, low-level contexting approaches to communication will also be found, particularly in institutional settings, such as engaging with officials in formal settings, registering as a hospital patient, or buying and using airplane tickets.

Contexting aids understanding of the shared assumptions concerning how communications are to be understood in a particular culture. As seen, low-context cultures value directness and assume a common understanding of specific terms and those terms' relations to specific ways of interacting regardless of the context. High-context cultures assume a common understanding beyond the actual words used in terms of expectations related to behavior and commonly accepted interactions among people. We should attend not just to the words but also *how* they are used. For instance, when a low-context communicator from a low-level context culture says yes, the affirmative response and resulting behavior reflects that, but when a high-context communicator from a high-context culture says yes, it may be couched in indirect and even ambiguous wording, and there is far less guarantee that the resulting behavior will reflect it. Moreau et al. (2014, 129–31) point out that different people communicate with differing degrees of contexting despite being of the same culture. As we have seen in some of the examples, a high-context yes might actually mean no.

What might give us a clue about the contexting in communication we are likely to encounter in a given culture? Social psychology studies suggest that "people from East Asian cultures (e.g. China, Korea, and Japan) tend to pay greater attention to contextual information than their counterparts in Western cultures" (Masuda et al. 2008, 1260). Meyer (2014, 38) suggests, "The USA is the lowest-context culture in the world followed by [some] European cultures, with the UK on the higher end of low-contexting. . . . Italy, Spain, France . . . fall to the right of centre. . . . Many African and Asian countries" fall on the high-contexting end of the spectrum. She suggests that Japan is the highest-context culture.[11] She offers that "high-context cultures tend to have a long-shared history" and are usually relationship oriented (40), which would account for Asian nations such as China, Japan, and Korea. Communities whose members are very tightly knit around their deeply held values, such as the religiosity of Muslim communities, are also likely to be higher-context communicators. In multiple-culture negotiations and workplaces, Meyer also suggests that following a low-context approach to communication and advising all members of the setting that this is the case is liable to be the best way to reduce misunderstandings in communications (55). Whilst Meyer makes this suggestion in the context of multiple-culture business settings, we can apply this same principle to avoid intergroup miscommunication if we minister as multiple-culture teams.

---

11. Note that Meyer writes into the context of international business communications and does not supply data or a data source for her findings but refers to Hofstede (1991).

Markers for High and Low Context Communication

Low contexting: Communication through speech or the written word means exactly what is said or written. No ambiguity is intended, and meaning is explicitly in the words used: "What I say or wrote is exactly what I meant."

High contexting: Communication may include spoken or written words, but the intended meaning lies beyond the actual words. In fact, the true meaning lies in how the words are interpreted according to the context and in relation to the wider nonverbal cultural understandings and expectations. The meaning might be something quite different than the words used, even the exact opposite: "I said or wrote that, but the words don't express what I actually mean."

Virtual Meetings and Negotiations

With the growth of international business negotiations held online and even more so in the wake of the COVID-19 pandemic, which limited travel opportunities and face-to-face negotiations, communication via the internet and electronic media also merits consideration. A meta-analysis by Baltes et al. (2002, 156) suggests, "computer-mediated communication leads to decreases in group effectiveness, increases in time required to complete tasks, and decreases in member satisfaction compared to face-to-face groups."

Movius (2020), albeit from a Western perspective, offers that keeping online meetings to a minimum length of time is likely to be most effective. Movius further gives some useful pointers for group meetings, including that (1) roles are assigned and understood before the meeting begins, since four or more members without assigned roles in an online meeting can easily distract attention from key issues; (2) concurrent discussions between members using other electronic or communication media are best kept short with care to keep their content private; and (3) communication is heightened by being able to see the faces of others in the meeting (i.e., video link is preferable to email, texting, or audio-only phone calls).

Particularly for people from individualistic cultures, seeing their own face or head and shoulders on screen can provoke a psychological response of comparison with others on the screen, which can distract from the issues at hand. Dressing appropriately and being thoughtful about what others can see around you is also key for presenting an appropriate image that will not detract from the meeting or negotiations being carried out. Maintaining eye contact (if and when appropriate) requires looking at the camera rather than at the person or people on the screen, and trying to multitask by concurrently attending to other tasks is not recommended since others watching may be offended by what they perceive to be disinterest when meeting-members appear distracted.

A BRIEF BACKGROUND OF COMMUNICATION SCIENCE AND COMMUNICATION MODELS

Having learned about vehicles for communication, we now consider aspects of communication theory from a historical perspective and how these aspects are developed and represented through a range of communication models.

Nearly 400 years before Christ, we find the phrase "Necessity is the mother of invention" in the writings of the Greek philosopher Plato. As need arises, people seek ways of dealing with the need and resolving root causes of the need. Rhetorical and logical prowess were an important part of Greek culture, as we can see in Paul's address to the Athenians (Acts 17:16–34), in which "he 'made a speech' (διελέγετο) in the synagogue with both Jews and God-fearing Greeks" (v. 17).

Many models of communication can be categorized as either linear, interactive, or transactional models. Aristotle was a student of Plato, and the Aristotelian model is one example of a linear or unidirectional model of communication, in which the speaker addresses the audience in a one-way fashion. The following paragraphs survey some of the primary linear models of communication.

Linear Models of Communication
Aristotle

Aristotle believed that to be able to persuade someone else of your opinion, that person needed to be able to trust you. His "model of communication" from his 300 BC writing *Rhetoric* involved five components: the speaker, the speech, the occasion, the audience, and the effect. Aristotle brought out three important aspects to aid communication: (1) *ethos*, or the credibility of the speaker, so that they would be considered trustworthy; (2) *pathos*, or having the audience see the message as connecting with them by being relevant to their life situation; (3) and *logos*, or the logical flow that gives a speech coherency. Aristotle's model was certainly influential and important, but we must be aware that, as we will see in a later chapter, not all cultures communicate according to a logical flow of ideas.

Lasswell's Model

In 1948 Harold D. Lasswell developed a model to analyze mass media propaganda presentations and mass communication for businesses, but his model has also been useful for less complex communication events. He wrote, "A convenient way to describe an act of communication is to answer the following questions:

- Who
- Says What
- In Which Channel
- To Whom
- With What Effect?" (Lasswell 1964, 37)

Lasswell's analysis attends to these five components:

1. The speaker or source of communication—analyzing *who* this source is in terms of control (i.e. what biases might be in play; how might they best or better control the communication for optimum outcome)
2. The content of what is communicated—analyzing whether or not and to what extent *what* is communicated is appropriate to the populace, market, and business aims
3. The channel or method being used—to assess the viability or potential effectiveness of the *medium* or *media*
4. Those to whom the communication is propagated—to analyze who the members of the *audience* are and how to best influence them
5. The results desired of the communication—to analyze the potential *effect* of the event

Some say that the effect component provides feedback,[12] in which case this would not be a linear model. However, most prefer to see this as a linear model since the effect is intended to be considered ahead of the

---

12. For instance, Reddi (2009, 42) suggests that the "effect" component can also pertain to feedback in public relations.

communication event in order to analyze or predict whether the desired effect is likely to be achieved.

A key difference between Lasswell's model and the Aristotelian model is the attention Lasswell's model gives to the medium or media used for communication. In Lasswell's day, radio and television were available in addition to printed materials.

Useful principle: Lasswell gives us a timeless sentence by which to check our communication plans.

Shannon and Weaver's Cybernetic Model of Communication

Claude Shannon and Warren Weaver (1949) adapted the term *cybernetics*[13] to describe the form of communication occurring through the electronic signaling of telecommunications and computerized systems. This kind of communication had been used during World War II to send coded messages that could only be decoded by those with the necessary information to decode the message. Anyone else would be aware that a message has been encoded by a sender, but they would not be privy to the meaning of its content.

Shannon and Weaver's cybernetic (code) model of communication and its components can be seen represented as in figure 2.1.

The components of the model proposed in Shannon and Weaver (1949) include:

- **Sender:** Here the sender is generally recognized as an individual, as this model is not helpful for analyzing group or mass communication. The sender may be communicating as a primary source (i.e., the originator of the message), as a secondary source by using information that originated from elsewhere, or as a tertiary source by conveying information that they got from a secondary source.
  - **Example:** Jesus (primary source) told the Centurion's messenger (secondary source) to tell the Centurion his son would be healed. If the Centurion then told his wife the messenger's good news, the Centurion would be a tertiary source.

---

13. Wiener (1948), a mathematician, introduced the concept of cybernetics when looking into communication in relation to men and machines.

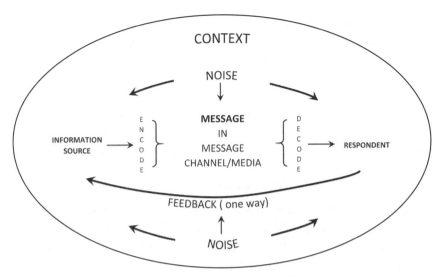

Figure 2.1: Shannon-Weaver Cybernetic
(CODE) Model of Communication

Useful principle: Communicating information from primary sources is preferable to using secondary sources as this reduces the possibility of inaccuracy. A secondary source may have misrepresented or misunderstood the primary source.

- **Respondent:** Also called a *receiver* or *receptor* (these terms are used interchangeably). This individual is somewhat passively the object of the sender's attention for whom the message is intended.
- **Encoding:** The sender puts together the message using what they consider an appropriate way by either verbal means (spoken or written words), nonverbal means (behaviors such as gestures), or a combination of these.
- **Channel:** The pathway, medium, or combination of media through which the message is sent so that one or more of the receiver's senses might be stimulated.
- **Decoding:** The receiver engages with the message content and discerns meaning from the receiver's perspective.
- **Feedback:** The receiver sends back a response to the sender. This can provide an indication of whether and to what extent the message has been understood correctly.

- **Noise:** Anything in the environment or message channel that might hinder effective communication by distorting the message content and causing the receiver to misunderstand the sender's intended meaning.

Shannon and Weaver's key contribution recognizes the factor of noise in causing miscommunication. While this is not so clear from their original model, noise can affect any element of the model. Notably, the concept of feedback is included, but the feedback is only one-way, from receiver to sender.

Useful principle: As we engage cross-culturally, we soon find that for communication to be effective, feedback between both the sender and receiver is essential. We cannot assume our communication has been understood in the way we intended.

Kubota details four spheres of noise as follows:

1. Physical noise such as noise from construction outside of the classroom or room temperature.
2. Psychological noise such as prejudice, biased attitude towards the other person.
3. Biological noise such as disease, fatigue or hunger of a sender and/ or a receiver.
4. Semantic noise such as slang or [technical] terms (Kubota 2019, 55).

Physical noise is related to external factors, while psychological noise manifests as internal noise. We can add to these physical, mental, and/or emotional discomfort; any of the distractions caused by the sender's inattention to what makes for appropriate kinesics, haptics, proxemics, physical characteristics, and use of articles and artefacts in the receiver's culture; the respondent's awareness (or not) of paralanguage; and the communicator's attention to the degree of contexting in the respondent's culture.

Author's Example from China: By UK standards, I am short in height, but in the remote village in China, I was slightly above average height for women. When my sister (who is taller than average for British women) visited, her height caused much fascination among the villagers. They were distracted from listening to anything she had to say via my interpretation because she was so interesting and unusual to look at. Her height was a source of noise.

Berlo's S-M-C-R Model

The sender-message-channel-receiver (SMCR) model of communication pays attention to the details of four component steps to facilitate the process of communication (Berlo 1960).

- Of the sender: aspects include their communication skills; attitudes (in relation to self, the receiver, and the environment); knowledge (especially in relation to the message subject matter); particularities of the sender's background social system, communication setting, and background culture.
- Of the message: factors considered include its content (in terms of the overall body of the message); elements (including verbal and non-verbal aspects); treatment (i.e., how the content is put together and/ or conveyed without causing distraction or confusion); structure (i.e., how the parts relate to each other); and code (i.e., the way the message is put across such as through body language, music, speaking, or a combination of these).

Useful principle: Intentional attention to coherency, simplicity (as far as this is possible), and attractiveness of the message influences its degree of receivability and accuracy of decoding.

- Of the channel: covers the five senses of seeing, hearing, touching, smelling, and tasting, which of these senses are engaged with, and how, so that communication can be mediated through engaging one or more of these possible channels.
- Of the receiver: the same considerations as for the sender so that potential for miscommunication may be avoided.

Note that the more similar the communication skill level of the receiver is to the skill level of the sender, the greater the likelihood for effective communication.

This model is limited in that it does not acknowledge the need for feedback to increase understanding of the message. In addition, it pays no attention to the place of the cognizant skills of thinking and analyzing in order for the receiver to come to an accurate interpretation of the message.

Interactive Models of Communication

Interactive communication models go beyond linear communication by recognizing that effective communication is a *dynamic* two-way process.

Osgood and Schramm's Model

In criticizing linear models, Schramm (1954) argues, "It is misleading to think of the communication process as starting somewhere and ending somewhere. It is really endless. We are really switchboard centers handling and rerouting the great endless current of information" (see McQuail and Windahl 2015, 20).

Osgood and Schramm's model attends to one-to-one communication such as face-to-face, or via a telecommunication mode (wired telephone in Osgood and Schramm's day), and does not differentiate between sender and receiver because both parties play both roles. It sees communicators as equals and communication as dynamic and circular in development. Each party encodes into words and gestures the messages they want to send, and these are sent, decoded, and interpreted by the other party. The communication is enhanced by a continual circular flow of messages from each party to the other.

Useful principle: The element of "interpreter" stands in combination with each party's encoding and decoding functions, indicating that while decoding of the message provides data, this data also needs analyzing and interpreting for the receiving party to understand the message content.

This model is limited because the feedback concerning the message received is implied rather than identified since messages sent may or may not be specifically related to earlier messages. The model does not acknowledge the aspect of noise despite the fact that semantic noise is particularly pertinent. Semantic barriers cause miscommunication due to each party having differing background beliefs, knowledge, and experiences, so that, for instance, they may use the same term but assign it a different meaning.

> **Useful principle:** Pay careful attention to the words you use. Does the receiver attach an identical meaning?

> **Example from Nepal:** "Nepali people greet by saying *namaste*, which actually means 'to worship the divine.'" If you greet your Nepali friend, what reality of "divinity" are you each acknowledging?

Another limitation with Osgood and Schramm's model is the failure to recognize that each party may well not be communicating on equal terms. McQuail and Windahl (2015, 20) suggest, "Very often communication is, on the contrary, fairly unbalanced as far as communication resources, power, and time given to communicate are concerned."

Westley and MacLean's Model

Westley and MacLean's (1955) model tends to be applied in relation to mass communication or mass media as channels but can also, as Westley and MacLean intended (1957, 38), provoke thought about interpersonal communication. It differentiates between sender and receiver but has the environment being the provocation for a message rather than some other subjective factor. The model pays greater attention to a number of other factors that affect the communication process. These include:

- aspects of the *environment*, which give cause to the need for communication by the sender of the particular message. In the immediate physical environment these may include lighting, temperature, ventilation, and so on. For instance, during the cold of winter and with broken-down heating systems, a student sends a message to their teacher via the school messaging system; in a time of poor harvest, the farmer writes an article for the local newspaper about the need for irrigation pumps.

- the *gatekeeper,* or the person or system that controls the channel or medium through which the message is being transmitted. An example of a gatekeeper is the editor of a magazine, newspaper, television program, or institutional messaging system monitor. This person can modify or make changes to the content of the message before it reaches the receiver.

> **Useful principle:** Are we trying to communicate with someone or a group of people via a third party? Beware of the potential for misunderstanding due to third-party manipulation of the message content through a gatekeeping form of indirect communication. Accurate decoding of the original message by the receiver cannot be expected if the message has been modified according to the bias or agenda of a third party.

- *feedback* to the sender from both the gatekeeper and the receiver, and from the receiver to the gatekeeper.
- *sensory experience* by the sender in relation to the environment (or cause of the message), which moves the sender to put their message together in a particular way, so influencing the content of the message. Sensory experience (through one or more of the senses: hearing, seeing, smelling, tasting, touching) also impacts how messages are received and can influence whether the message has been interpreted correctly. For instance, the student feels stressed and uncomfortable so that he does not properly read the teacher's communication, let alone understand it.

> **Useful principle:** While feelings and expression of emotions can be noise factors for both the sender and the receiver, when handled with maturity, feelings and emotions can enhance the transparency of cross-cultural relationships that are moving into interculturality.

- *objects of orientation (sender and receiver):* the worldview, background, and subjective interests of the sender influence the message conveyed to the gatekeeper, while the worldview, background, and subjective interests of the receiver affect how the receiver interprets the message.

> **Useful principle:** The sender pitches the message in relation to their subjective interests while the receiver may be oblivious to the sender's intended meaning because the receiver is interpreting the message via subjective concerns. How aware are we of our own biases? Our biases influence the content of our message as well as how we encode it. How well do we know the person we are communicating with in terms of what they perceive as important and how they might decode the message inappropriately?

The limitations of this model lie in the fact that the gatekeeper-control effect, which shows up as bias in different newspaper corporations and mass communication via television programs, is no longer as relevant in the electronic social-media age because hidden biases and manipulative processes are not so easy to keep hidden in mass media vehicles as they were in the pre– and post–World War II eras.

Transactional Models of Communication

These models present communication as a highly dynamic interaction between two parties and for whom feedback is an expected and immediate response to messages. They communicate from a basis of some common experience with an implied understanding that communication is a transaction from which shared meaning is created from interactive experience together. The models do not refer to senders or receivers as individual elements because, like Osgood and Schramm's model, each party is seen as continuously playing both roles and all the messages interrelate.

Dance's Helical Spiral Model

Dance (1967, 296) depicts communication as a circular process that reflects increasing and increasingly complex experiences as one ages, in the manner of an upwardly widening helical spiral. Dwyer (2013, 12) writes, "The implication is that communication is continuous, unrepeatable and accumulative from all past experience. What has occurred before contributes to what is happening now with no fixed beginning, no break in the action and no closure . . . Communication is an integrated, evolving process that enhances learning, growth, and discovery . . . Communication experiences are cumulative and influenced by the past [so that] present experiences have an influence on [one's] future." As we engage with others, their feedback to our messages provides us with opportunities to expand our understanding and widen both our knowledge and outlook on life.

Useful principle: If we are unwilling to change or be flexible in outlook as we age, we are likely to miss the potential to discover wisdom and intangible riches in the outlooks and contributions of others.

Devotional comment: God can use whoever and whatever he sees is appropriate to get our attention and show us a new perspective on his grace and unfathomably loving mercy. When messages from another become difficult to receive, God is offering us a way into deeper humility and an opportunity to respond with unconditional love. Will we insist on our own perspective, or will we carefully listen to the other to discern what God knows we need to hear? God's affirmation or challenge might not be in the content of the message but in our choice of responding with a quiet and gentle spirit.

Barnland's Transactional Model

According to Barnland (1968), "Communication is not a reaction to something, nor an interaction with something, but a transaction in which man invents and attributes meanings to realize his purposes" (cited in McQuail 1984, 31). Effectively, communicators are looking to build a shared meaning of the messages they send and receive, and both parties share the responsibility to provide feedback and create understanding. This approach sees meaning created and understanding derived on the terms of community members. As Christians, we can interpret the approach as being sensitive to God's means of creativity in and through us and see the approach as a vessel for God to inspire us with insights and bring his insights through us to those we are communicating with so as to realize his purposes.

The model features recognition of public, private, and behavioral cues as key to effective interaction. Public cues are external factors such as environmental factors, while private cues are internal factors similar to Westley and MacLean's objects of orientation. Both private and behavioral cues can be verbal or nonverbal. Effective communication occurs when each party is sensitive to the cues presented or provoked during the communication process so that the cues heighten rather than hinder the encoding and decoding of messages. The model also recognizes that the cues can have different levels or degrees of effect on encoding and decoding of messages.

> **Useful principle:** We can be blessed by a fresh revelation of God's desires for our growing relationship with someone as we become increasingly sensitive to each other's behavioral cues. This brings us further along the way to interculturality and to the joy of seeing God bring new and sweet culturally relevant meaning into conversations that were previously more restrained.

CHRISTIAN COMMUNICATOR'S MODEL OF COMMUNICATION

Drawing on and building upon the principles we have met so far, consider the following figure:

We will take this model as representative of the facets that influence our communication with respondents. As we reach out with the gospel and truths of Christianity, our awareness of these facets has the potential to heighten the effectiveness of our communications. Notice how influential the perspective of subjectivity is on the potential for communicating effectively (or not!). Cultural awareness and sensitivity, adult maturity, and spiritual maturity all have the potential to heighten the Christian communicator's skill and effectiveness in communication. Effective communication requires awareness of facets of both our own background culture and that of our respondents. We need to be sensitive to what is important to our respondents and understand how their cultural preferences might impact accuracy in message decoding.

> **Important principle:** Try imagining "standing in the respondent's shoes" and considering how they might be thinking or feeling in response to our communications from their cultural perspective.

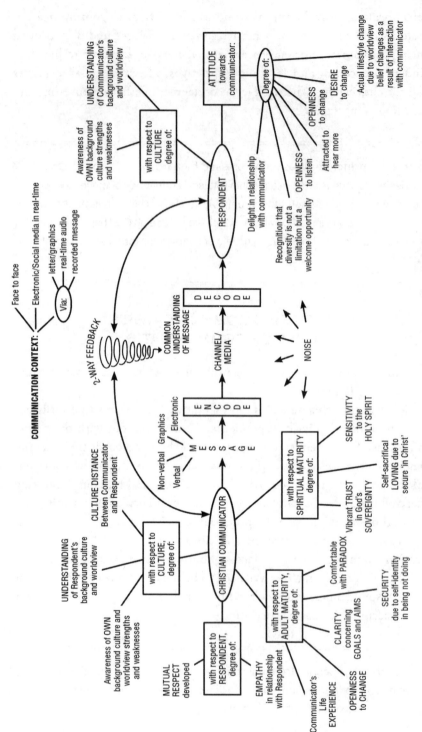

Figure 2.2: Christian Communicator's Model of Communication

We also need to be sensitive to whether the relationship is deep enough that they will trust us with ideas and concepts that seem unusual or even conflict with their worldview. As we encode messages we must engage with the recipient's degree of openness and welcoming of diversity so that our communication is both relevant and receivable. Our level of adult maturity—which is shown in relation to the extent that we are secure in being who we are and not as a result of what we have or have not achieved—also affects our communication efforts. Building relationships marked by mutual respect and empathy also requires openness to change. Above all, our spiritual maturity influences the degree to which we are willing to love our respondents unconditionally, to submit to the leading of the Holy Spirit in communication, and to live out what we communicate with a security that comes from being a child of God who trusts in God's sovereignty. Notice how increase of any of the model's items, on either the communicator's side or the respondent's side (and preferably both), heightens the potential for effective communication and increasing interculturality.

CONCLUSION

We have seen a variety of behavioral interactions that are culturally shaped and that can either heighten or hinder communication if we are not sufficiently culturally sensitive. We have also drawn out principles from early models of communication to build a communication model to aid Christians in communicating the gospel message of Christ. This communication can be either to unbelievers, to persuade them by the leading of the Holy Spirit into a relationship with God through Christ Jesus, or to believers, to encourage them in their spiritual journey.

QUESTIONS FOR REFLECTION AND DISCUSSION

1. In the "As It Happened" scenario at the start of the chapter, where do you see evidence of both low-context and high-context communicators?
2. In the "As It Happened" scenario, where do you see the potential for communication misunderstandings due to inappropriate encoding and inaccurate decoding of messages? What changes would help?
3. Which physical characteristics or commonly used items are important in your background culture? How and when might you need to be

careful to not let these biases influence your relationships with those of other cultures?

4. What aspects of kinesics (body language), haptics (touching), or proxemics (use of space) have ever caused you discomfort in communication with others? How might you overcome the discomfort in future experiences?

CHAPTER 3

Communication with Respect to Culture and Behavior

As It Happened: A British pastor was invited by a Pakistani pastor to travel to Pakistan to teach at the church's annual retreat. When the British pastor arrived in Pakistan, he was surprised to see very few people at the church. The Pakistani pastor reluctantly admitted, "You have arrived a little late." The British pastor was even more surprised because, although the church he pastored in England usually started services on time, his experience with Pakistani congregations was that they rarely started on time.

The Pakistani pastor told him, "You are always most welcome here. Actually, we were expecting to welcome you here two weeks ago." The British pastor immediately explained that his schedule and airline tickets had been organized, obviously wrongly, by his assistant in the UK. Both pastors were disappointed, but due to his cultural background, one pastor was more shocked and overwhelmed than the other.

INTRODUCTION

Background cultures shape everyone's priorities and behaviors. They overflow into communications in joyous times, in uncertainties, and with difficulty-causing differences. When was the last time you couldn't help but be surprised by or uncomfortable with the choices made by someone from another culture? This chapter looks to identify commonalities and differences between cultures and people groups so as to heighten the possibility of effective cross-cultural communication,[1] which in turn should help us

---

1. Part of the material in this chapter is based on D-Davidson (2018, 27–41).

bring the gospel message to people of other cultures. Tools are provided to help appreciate diversity and avoid potential clashes or misunderstandings as we build cross-cultural relationships with the goal of them becoming intercultural. The chapter begins by defining key terms and then describes various facets of culture as found in the literature. It also points out some of the limitations of classic contributions established in the literature and offers updates or modifications so as to rework their relevance.

CULTURE

What do we mean by the term *culture?* As briefly mentioned in chapter 1, the literature points to two approaches to culture, one "as a given and the other as a construct" (Handford et al. 2019, 163), with the constructivist understanding in reference to Holliday, Kullman, and Hyde (2017). The "culture as a given" approach (which the Willowbank report citation below follows) is criticized by Holliday (1999; 2013) and others,[2] who consider it inappropriate to assign specific characteristics to all members of a culture in a homogenous manner, dismissing the interests of individual actors. This criticism is not unfair, but pushed to the extreme, it would suggest that there are no commonly defined characteristics of cultures—only an enormous and unnavigable array of diversity.[3]

To aid effective communication, being aware of common culture patterns and life interests *is* helpful, and the discovery of commonalities and differences should be in terms of a culture's bigger-picture tendencies (or generalizations). At the same time, as will be seen, we can also recognize that individuals in specific and differing contexts may have orientation preferences that differ in degree with or fully compete with their big-picture cultural background. Both commonalities and differences then become cause for celebration and a catalyst for interactive creativity.

A helpful interculturally devised definition of culture in the literature, along with associated factors, is found in *The Willowbank Report:*

---

2. Note Berger and Luckmann (1967) brought a highly influential definition of culture into sociology from this contextual constructivist perspective (cited after Bennett 2013, 6). As mentioned in chapter 1, the constructivist perspective, along with constructionism, or putting together of social constructs according to community-based knowledge, is a factor of postmodernism.

3. See Landes (2000, 3), who, in the secular examination of culture and poverty, *disagrees* with "an economist friend, a master of politico-economic therapies [who, taking a constructivist approach, professed that] culture . . . does not permit him to predict outcomes" (italicization mine). That is, Landes prefers that culture and cultural factors as "givens" *can* permit the prediction of outcomes in relation to poverty.

Consultation on Gospel and Culture[4] of the 1978 Lausanne Committee for World Evangelization:

> At its center is a world-view, that is, a general understanding of the nature of the universe and of one's place in it. This may be "religious" (concerning God, or gods and spirits, and of our relation to them), or it may express a "secular" concept of reality, as in a Marxist society. . . . Culture is an integrated system of beliefs (about God or reality or ultimate meaning), values (about what is true, good, beautiful, normative), of customs (how to behave, relate to others, talk, pray, dress, work, play, trade, farm, eat, etc.), and of institutions which express these beliefs, values and customs (government, law courts, temples or churches, family, schools, hospitals, factories, shops, unions, clubs etc.), which binds a society together and gives it a sense of identity, security, and continuity.

We can shorten the definition as follows: Culture is an integrated system of beliefs, values, and customs, as well as the institutions that express those beliefs, values, and customs, which binds a society together and gives it a sense of identity, security, and continuity.

In line with the Willowbank report definition, Hesselgrave (1991, 100) describes culture as something we learn[5] and something that is shared, integrated, and changes. Enculturation, or learning to fit into one's own culture, comes about gradually as cultural concerns and ways are communicated to offspring and reinforced by school systems, community expectations, and peer interaction within society. The expectations of appropriate attitudes and behavior are shared and owned by those within the community so that all of the culture's varying value-driven customs, outlooks, and behaviors exist together in harmony to benefit and maintain the community's sense of identity, security, and continuity. Communication is readily understandable as members of the community live together with shared and mutually understood customs and behaviors.

Cultures are not static entities—they change as members of society create new ways of being and doing or as problems arise within the setting that need new answers.

Communicating ideas that might undermine the current sense of

---

4. Available at https://www.lausanne.org/content/lop/lop-2.
5. Edward Hall's *The Silent Language* (1959) proposed that much of culture is learned at the nonverbal, informal level by imitating models, and that, importantly, we are largely unaware of this learning.

identity, security, and continuity are not likely to be received easily. But Burnett (2002, 22) describes how when inculcated beliefs and behaviors no longer appear to help resolve difficulties, thoughtful people in a society will question traditions and traditional behavior. As a result, when influences from other societies and cultures are seen as beneficial, they are received into the culture—particularly as a means for the community to maintain security and/or continuity.

Kirk's Patterns of Culture

Kirk (2000, 86) lists the concerns that cultures usually have in common as follows:

- rites of passage and cultural practices appropriate to life stages,
- ways of categorizing differences between humans which justify acceptable and nonacceptable ways of engagement,
- acknowledgement of different kinds of suffering,
- recognition of success and failure,
- questions and answers about the meaning and purpose of life from which coping mechanisms and behaviors have evolved and are practiced, and
- standards for acceptable and nonacceptable behavior and thinking, particularly in terms of moral issues.

Communication amongst members of a society, whether large or small, is fueled by a common understanding of the associated cultural facets as well as the expected way of living in relation to each of the cultural concerns.

Worldview and Its Relation to Culture

We saw the concept of worldview included in the Willowbank report's definition of culture. What do we mean by the term *worldview?* Hesselgrave (1991, 202) boils the characteristics of worldviews down to people's basic understandings with respect to supernature (God/gods and the supernatural), nature, man, and time.[6] Hiebert (2008, 15) suggests that the concept of worldview encompasses the "fundamental cognitive, affective, and evaluative presuppositions a group of people make about the nature of things, and which they use to order their lives."

---

6. For further reading, see Kraft (1989), who, more comprehensively, gives a succinct but detailed overview of seven worldview functions and five universal worldview categories in appendices A and B, respectively.

To give practical application, we might say that "a worldview is the set of non-visible rules that are informed by deeply ingrained beliefs and values. It influences the choices people make concerning their behavior, and so that their actions and lifestyle follow the expected norms and standards of the culture. This will include following beliefs communicated and customs modeled to them since childhood because, as far as they are able to comprehend, such customs are believed to be right and appropriate" (D-Davidson 2018, 29).

Lingenfelter and Mayers advise us that personal judgments shared by many (because they are cultural customs, values, or worldview beliefs) become the judgment of that particular society, and societies tend to coerce individuals to follow its value system (2003, 114). In this way, societies can maintain identity, security, and continuity. As previously mentioned, communication of ideas that threaten the status quo can result in rejection of both the ideas and the communicator, but a change of beliefs is needed in order to change unbiblical aspects of a worldview.[7] A means of presenting new ideas in a receivable way is helped when the communicator brings an idea perceived as relevant to the receiver's current or anticipated needs. As communicators of the gospel, we must be constantly asking: Am I communicating in a receivable way, and will the content of what I am trying to communicate likely be perceived as relevant? To communicate in a receivable and relevant way, we need to understand and be sensitive to the beliefs and customs of the people with whom we are communicating. As we have seen, these people are often referred to as "respondents" or "receptors" in communication literature and in Christian communications as members of a "target group" or "those being reached out to."

Kwarst (2009, 398) claims, "Values describe what is good or best, beliefs describe what is considered to be true or false, [whereas] behavior is what is actually done." Behavior is preferred that coheres with the society or community's beliefs and values, but as Kwarst points out, this is not always the case because people can express similar behavior and hold similar values but profess totally different beliefs about them.

So when we observe people of other cultures' behaviors, we are seeing the result of worldview beliefs and values in operation. To describe how culture relates to worldview, we might describe it like looking at a tree: the visible foliage on the branches represents culture and cultural behavior,

---

7. See Hiebert (2008, 157–58) on foundationalism's interrelation of beliefs. Introducing change into the noetic structure of the underlying belief system is crucial for the sought-after change in lifestyle but without compartmentalising beliefs in a way that brings confusion and/or incoherency.

whereas the hidden roots system, trunk, and branches represent the world-view, which provides the philosophical, psychological, and emotional structure for the culture's customs, behavior patterns, and observable ways of responding to life's contingencies. Ineffective communication easily happens when we make assumptions about the behavior and underlying beliefs of others based on our own worldview and cultural background.

Generally speaking, when individuals do not follow societal expectations, they tend to be ostracized by that society. Often in missions history, the first converts to Christianity have often been those on the edges of society, and they have come to Christ because their own society rejected them whereas Christ welcomes everyone. Our first step in communication in building relationships cross-culturally is to ask God to bring to us the ones he would have us communicate with in a new culture or, alternatively, to order our steps in a way that brings us to them.

Examples of Worldview Beliefs and Values as Expressed through Cultural Behavior

Example from Japanese culture: "In my culture, being on time for meetings and other events is highly valued, so the invisible rule is that I make sure I am never late for a meeting. I believe that being punctual and even arriving ahead of time is the appropriate way to behave in my culture."

Example from Pakistani culture: "In the Pakistani culture, attention to relationships is highly valued, so the invisible rule is that even if I am working to complete a task, if someone appears and interrupts me, I stop and attend to that person. I believe that valuing people ahead of completing my own tasks is the appropriate way to behave in my culture."

Example from the Chinese culture: "In the Chinese culture, obedience to my parents is highly valued, so the invisible rule is that I never show them disrespect. I believe that showing them respect is the appropriate way to behave."

Being part of something bigger and feeling safe within it are crucial aspects of a person's self-identity, which is why communicating ideas that urge people to change aspects of their beliefs, values, or customs can bring a major psychological challenge to such respondents.

Equally key is recognizing that a person or group of people can never replace their original worldview with a completely different one. Digging up all the roots of a tree will merely kill the tree. Similarly, cutting off some of the branches won't stop the branches from eventually growing back. Something new needs to be grafted into the roots to grow a different kind of fruit in the foliage. This is why unbiblical worldview beliefs need to be addressed—not merely urging changes of behavior. Moreover, deep-rooted, long-held beliefs are not initially easily or willingly displaced by new beliefs, so, hopefully, we can see the value of inculcating Christian beliefs and values from a young age. Seeds of ideas that are communicated into young minds may well not bring immediate fruit, but even if they lie dormant for years, there is still potential for future fruition when communication from one or more new sources becomes the catalyst for growing, watering, and harvesting of seeds sown.

FACTORS THAT AFFECT THE BEHAVIOR
PROFILE OF DIFFERENT CULTURES

Lingenfelter and Mayers's *Ministering Cross-Culturally: An Incarnational Model for Personal Relationships* was a cutting-edge text when it appeared in 1986. It provided a breakthrough text to help North American missionaries better understand cross-cultural settings and prepare themselves for communication in cross-cultural ministry. The 2003 revised and updated second edition version cited below, and throughout this chapter, is still used in Bible institutes and ministry training centers in both Western and Asian settings to help students better understand and prepare for cross-cultural ministry.

Lingenfelter's experience in engaging with the Micronesian Yap people as part of an anthropological doctoral study was coupled with Mayers's facets-of-culture analysis tool. Insights from the fields of anthropology were coupled with real-life cross-cultural experience, replete with relevant examples of potential cross-cultural communication hazards.

Mayers's analytical tool described preferences of cultures in terms of polar opposites. The following section works through five of the category pairs with observations that seek to widen understanding of the issues in light of the limitations, as well as modify some of the original related perceptions so as to heighten the potential for effective cross-cultural communication.

Lingenfelter and Mayers's first "big picture" cultural difference attends to the degree of priority given by a specific cultural grouping to the issue of time in relation to the actuality and progression of events or activities. The contents of the second edition of the book are reproduced in the charts and text below. The charts describe extreme tendencies of the orientations with some minor modifications.[8]

Time Orientation (monochronism)	Event Orientation (polychronism)
1. "Concern for punctuality and amount of time expended." Avoiding wasting time is very important.	1. "Concern for details of the event regardless of the time required."
2. "Careful allocation of time to achieve the maximum within set limits." Again, no time wasting!	2. "Exhaustive consideration of a problem until it is resolved."
3. "Tightly scheduled goal-directed activities," which can mean missing out on the joy and freedom of spontaneity.	3. An "outlook not tied to any precise schedule," which can also present an unreliable or noncommitted front.
4. "Emphasis on dates," time, and timing of activities.	4. "Emphasis on present experience," undistracted by what hasn't happened yet.

Table 3.1 Modification of Table 2 from *Ministering Cross-Culturally*[9]

Factor 1: Time Orientation versus Event Orientation

Lingenfelter is a North American who, as previously mentioned, was writing to help better equip current and potential North American missionaries for cross-cultural ministry. Lingenfelter suggested that North Americans, who are often time oriented, would tend to find people who are not time oriented difficult to deal with, at least initially. Time orientation is a cultural preference tendency for many Western nations. Communication can easily be misunderstood when living amongst people

---

8. This excerpt and all following excerpts from *Ministering Cross-Culturally*, 2nd ed., by Sherwood Lingenfelter and Marvin Mayers, copyright © 1986, 2003. Used by permission of Baker Academic, a division of Baker Publishing Group. Parts of this chapter and similar charts in this chapter also appear in D-Davidson (2018).

9. Lingenfelter and Mayers (2003, 41).

of the opposite tendency if one does not consider the effect of one's preferences and resulting lifestyle.

> **Example:** An Indonesian lady commented in typically event-oriented fashion: "It's a little sad that the Western missionaries just want to rush away after the church service. It is as though they don't enjoy being with us." From this we can see that the time-oriented Westerner Christians were perhaps unaware that they were communicating disinterest to the Indonesians and that as a result she (and perhaps others) felt rejected.

Acknowledging that some cultures place more emphasis on attention to careful use of time and others less so because their emphasis is on quality of events, Lingenfelter and Mayers (2003, 49–50) advise that rather than questioning which approach is more godly, we need to acknowledge that God's approach to time is quite different from any of ours, and no culture is able to get it completely right in terms of priorities or emphasis. I suggest that, somehow, with God, the outworking of time and unfolding of activities harmonize perfectly, and it is our responsibility to adapt appropriately and communicate sensitively in step with the Holy Spirit's leading.

Observations

The time-versus-event poles are very much a reality in different cultures, but the orientation taken by an individual can also be a factor related to the individual's personality rather than merely being culture-driven. For example, I had a Japanese student in a cross-cultural communications class in the Philippines who was delighted and relieved to discover that although her Japanese culture is extremely time oriented, because of her personality, she was event oriented. She happily reported to the multiple-culture class that this new discovery explained to her why she had never felt entirely comfortable in Japan. Now she knew enough to be able to deal with the discomfort. Her new knowledge also helped explain why she felt so at one with Filipinos, whose big-picture cultural orientation is also event oriented.

In the second edition of Lingenfelter and Mayers, toward the close of the book, personalities are briefly mentioned: "Individual Yapese vary in their personalities and degree to which they conform to these orientations" (118). But the choices an individual makes relating to time/event orientation are not merely also a factor of personality; they can be because of adult maturity or development in spiritual maturity. Psychology of human development shows that priorities change as one advances in age (see Levinson 1978; and Fowler 1981). For instance, the importance of being on time and finishing on time can easily give way to new joys of lingering beyond the official finish of a scheduled event. Equally, event-oriented people are likely to discover at some point in the adult-development process that "being on time," as an earlier pragmatic necessity, can eventually become a joyful priority to get even more out of the event and interactions. In the context of personality preferences and in the interests of spiritual maturity, Mulholland (1993, 54) suggests that the spiritual maturity that comes with "human wholeness [is the living out of a] mature and discriminating ability to function with whichever side [of any of the orientation pairs] is best suited to the situation at hand." The implication is that as we are sensitive to the voice of the Holy Spirit, so we will also make and communicate God-pleasing choices regardless of any competing personal preferences.

Not unlike Lingenfelter's specific time/event pairing, Hall (1973, 153) earlier proposed two approaches related to time which he called "polychronic" and "monochronic" time. Monochronism, or having a single-focus approach to time, sees time in terms of a linear progression of increments. Monochronists make definite plans to measure out how they intend to use those increments of time, and they experience discomfort if interruptions prevent them from using time in the way they had planned. In contrast, polychronism, or having a multifaceted approach to time, is far less concerned with time as a measurement and more concerned with time as the means by which multiple aspects of life, engagement with the world, and involvement in relationships all play out together.

What to the monochronist is an interruption and potential waste of time becomes, for the polychronist, just another aspect of life coming into play with no negative associations. Time is not a series of linear increments to be guarded for best use but, rather, a collection of limitless opportunities to play one's part in the world regardless of how and when the way opens up. Moreau, Campbell, and Greener (2014, 148–49) describe how monochronists plan on the micro level, making plans for something to occur on a certain date at a specific time, while polychromic people plan "on the macro level (planting, weeding, harvesting) and plans are seen as fluid and flexible rather than rigid and fixed."

Like the time-oriented person or culture that looks forward and plans ahead, the monochronist functions most comfortably alongside other monochronists with this same outlook concerning time. Similarly, as with event-oriented people and cultures that live in the moment and are unperturbed by unexpected things happening, polychronists function most comfortably among other polychronists. Communication can be enhanced when we are aware of both our cultural background orientation and that of our respondents.

It is also important to recognize that there are different degrees of orientation from culture to culture. Japanese students have frequently volunteered that their big-picture culture is definitely time oriented. This opens up discussion on differences of degree of orientations between cultures and the potential for conflict due to lack of knowledge or misunderstandings. Is Japan, Singapore, or Hong Kong more time oriented? How many minutes late for a meeting is acceptable? Or, as in Singapore, is arrival ahead of time more the norm?

The following line diagram[10] shows a range of differing degrees of orientation from culture to culture in either direction on the spectrum:

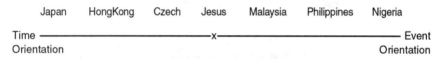

Figure 3.1: Spectrum of Degrees of Orientation: Time versus Event

Hopefully, we can see how a Malaysian's lesser approach to punctuality might communicate disrespect to Hong Kong nationals but is likely to communicate even greater disrespect to Japanese nationals. On the other hand, Malaysians might be a little frustrated by the more event-oriented Filipinos and even more frustrated by Nigerians. Similarly, while missionaries from the Czech Republic will have to make allowances when engaging with Filipino respondents, Japanese missionaries will likely find it far harder to adjust to the differing orientation.

Jesus, at the center of the scale, provides us with the perfect example of balance of the two extremes. He was event oriented in his personal life and ministry as of the Jewish culture he was incarnated into, yet he was also time oriented as appropriate for the fulfillment of God's plans—he did as the Father told him when the Father told him. As people aiming to

---

10. The details of the line diagrams in this chapter are based on my personal experience of engagement with people from other cultures. They represent anecdotal evidence, not statistical data.

witness to the love and life-changing potential of Jesus, as well as wanting to continually develop in Christlikeness, it is good to bear this in mind, regardless of our personal orientation preference. We must beware of communicating that one orientation is better than another, as this may well deny the dignity of the respondent and undermine the relationship being built.

Principles for Enhancing Effective Communication

1. In time-oriented cultures, efficiency is often rewarded (Lingenfelter and Mayers 2003, 40). I suggest that for people who are not time oriented, communicating an appropriate means of motivation at a sufficient level will help them want to meet time demands. For pragmatic reasons, people will arrive at an airport on time for their flight. Similarly, to avoid unwanted consequences (such as arriving too late for the flight) or gain positive benefits, people who are not time oriented can become motivated to make choices that display willingness to follow time demands.

Example from a Pakistani: "If you arrange an appointment with a Pakistani, then you shouldn't expect that the person will come on time. Churches in Pakistan never expect the congregation to come on time, even though they are still trying to make a strategy for change. The typical way churches do this is by opening the church and setting their service starting time half an hour or even one hour earlier than the service will actually start." The event-oriented Pakistanis are motivated to gather together sooner so that they can not only enjoy interacting with each other for a longer time before the service begins but also be in place for the actual service start time.

2. "For event-oriented people, playing the game [regardless of how long it takes] is indeed more important than winning," and in managing problems, options will be exhaustively considered with all issues being heard and deliberated over until a unanimous verdict is reached regardless of how long it takes (42). It can be helpful if it is politely communicated to event-oriented people that God (or even their community) could have other equally important events for them to be involved in today.

3. To get time-oriented people into events, give them appropriate motivation. For instance, explain who they can meet at the event and what might come of that. Get them talking and thinking about the benefits of attending the event; this will further help them to take their mind off how else they might be using the time while they are in attendance!

Factor 2: Dichotomistic Thinking versus Holistic Thinking

Dichotomistic Thinking	Holistic Thinking
1. Judgments are only black or white, right or wrong, without any gray area. Prefers decisions to be made as soon as possible rather than left unmade. Finds it easier to deal with either/or than both/and issues.	1. Is not bothered by decisions being left unmade. Sees most issues as gray and open for debate so that "judgments are open-ended. The whole person and all circumstances are taken into consideration."
2. Prefers categories with well-defined and clear boundaries. "Information and experiences are systematically organized; details are sorted and ordered to form a clear pattern."	2. "Information," categories, "and experiences are seemingly disorganized" but not to the holist thinker; "details (narratives, events, portraits) stand [incoherently] as independent points complete in themselves." This wide range of information is needed by the holistic thinker to make sense of individual situations and events.
3. Prefers rules and principles with universal application.	3. Believes that each situation is unique and is "uncomfortable with standardized procedures and rigidly applied rules."
4. "Security comes from the feeling that one is right and fits into a particular role or category in society."	4. Resists being pinned down to a particular position on an issue or to a particular social role. Can come across as unreliable and/or unwilling to make a commitment.

Table 3.2 Modification of Table 3 from *Ministering Cross-Culturally*[11]

Lingenfelter describes how dichotomistic thinking divides the object of thought into segments and considers situations or matters according to its individual parts. The particulars of a situation are considered and very

---

11. Lingenfelter and Mayers (2003, 54).

often there is a tendency to reduce each option or aspect as right or wrong, or, good or bad (53). The details of the situation are sorted out and ordered into groups of "this kind" or "that kind."

Holistic example from Dominican Republic student: "People are open to debate, and they tend to see things with an open perspective."

Dichotomistic example from a Mongolian student: "Mongolians are people who have a very direct character. We want freedom and independence. We do not want other people controlling us. That is why when missionaries come and approach us, we are suspicious and feel that these missionaries came to control us and do what they want to us."

Note the dichotomistic tone of the Mongolian example. Unlike the Dominican Republic culture, the student explained that Mongolians are very direct and take a dichotomistic approach to strangers by treating them with suspicion until they have clear proof that the stranger is not going to cause problems.

Like the time-event orientation, the preferred orientation and degree of orientation to one or other end of the spectrum is also likely to be a factor of personality as well as culture. In addition, both adult maturity and spiritual maturity also come into play. As for the time/event orientation, advancing in age sees new priorities substituted for earlier priorities so that, for instance, always "being right" becomes less important. Similarly, with spiritual development and increasing Christlikeness, one can anticipate developing a heightened sense of discernment concerning attitudes and behaviors that please God (see Fowler 2000; and Oser and Gmünder 1991) and so "grow out" of unhealthy dichotomistic judgmentalism.

Moving toward the other end of the spectrum and becoming more responsible in decision making can reflect maturation. Similarly, committing oneself to a position that pleases God but that does not reflect the expected cultural norm can be evidence of growth in spiritual maturity in the journey of life (see Misar 2010).

As for each of the cultural orientation category pairs, the labeling on the line diagram shows the orientation extremes, whereas we must be aware that the degree of orientation varies from culture to culture:

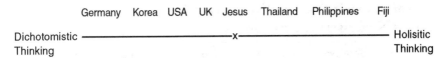

Figure 3.2 Spectrum of Degrees of Orientation:
Dichotomistic versus Holistic

Observations

I prefer to replace the term *holistic* with the term *comprehensive* since this not only gives a clearer understanding of meaning but also reduces the bias that might communicate the term *holistic* (and hence, holistic cultures) to be positive or better in contrast to the term *dichotomistic*.

Elmer (2002, 146) brings up a more specifically focused aspect of cultural difference in contrast to dichotomistic thinking but uses the slightly different term of categorical-and-holistic thinking. He attends to the Western concept of personal ownership in contrast to cultures where categorical-and-holistic thinking enjoys that "things are freely shared or given away . . . People feel free to ask of the one who has more . . . Categorical lines of yours and mine are not firmly drawn [that] cause Westerners frustration . . . Local people may ask for favors, money or objects not being used." So if a local person asks to borrow something, a nonlocal lender is likely to misread the communication as a request for a loan and expect to get what has been loaned back, but "when a loan does not get repaid or an object returned, disappointment and resentment may fester and disrupt the relationship."

Communication becomes miscommunication when cultural norms and terms are misunderstood. For effective communication, cultural awareness in relation to self-awareness is key as with each of the orientation pairs.

Principles for Engaging with Dichotomistic and Holistic Thinkers

1. Dichotomists tend to see and perceive things in black and white, and they judge their opposites as lacking principles and inconsistency; holistic (or comprehensive) thinkers, on the other hand, tend to see issues in terms of grey with no completely right or wrong response—and their opposites as legalistic and callous. Beware of judging the person on the basis of what you see. Get to know the person and then form your opinion with grace and love in mind.

2. Left-brain analytics and right-brain creativity were designed to function together; so can we, as members of the human race—and even more so as members of the body of Christ ministering together.

Factor 3: Crisis-Preventative Orientation versus Noncrisis Orientation

Crisis-Preventative Orientation	Noncrisis Orientation
1. "Anticipates crisis" but can come across as obsessive.	1. "Downplays possibility of crisis" but can come across as irresponsible.
2. "Emphasizes planning" to prevent or reduce potential future difficulties.	2. "Focuses on" current and "actual experiences."
3. "Seeks quick resolution" of problem to prevent worse things happening.	3. "Avoids taking action" until crisis actually takes place.
4. Has preplanned strategies for dealing with particular kinds of crises.	4. Pragmatic response in "seek[ing a] solution from multiple available options."
5. "Seeks [best] expert advice."	5. "Distrusts expert advice" as not necessarily relevant for the local situation. Prefers to make own decision anyway.

Table 3.3 Modification of Table 5 from *Ministering Cross-Culturally*[12]

Example from a Nepalese student: "Nepalese people sometimes prepare for incoming problems to prevent further damage." It sounds as though the choice of orientation is due to difficulties that the nation experienced in the past in some particular aspect of maintaining continuity of cultural lifestyle. What is the "damage" being referred to? Further investigation might involve asking whether Nepali people are crisis preventative in multiple aspects of life or just in selective aspects of life. Note how this clearly comes across in the next example.

Example from a Bhutanese student: "When Bhutanese know that there is a possibility of earthquake in their area, they will quickly move away from that area. But in other things we do not prepare ahead in case of a crisis—you can't prepare for everything always."

---

12. Lingenfelter and Mayers (2003, 71).

Observations

Crisis-preventative orientation versus noncrisis orientation can also be a factor of personality, and the degree of orientation is also likely to change with both adult maturity and spiritual development. A crisis-oriented person might eventually recognize that worst-case scenarios rarely occur, and so they can become less meticulous in preparing for all unwelcome possibilities. On the other end of the spectrum, adult maturity also recognizes the benefits not just for oneself but also for others, when one is more prepared for the unexpected.

Being highly crisis oriented amongst people who are not crisis oriented can unwittingly communicate tension through a desire to be in control of circumstances. In contrast, being extremely laid back and unprepared amongst crisis-oriented respondents can unhelpfully communicate either that you are uncaring or that you are irresponsible and untrustworthy.

Principles to Aid Communication for Building and Growing Relationships

1. Crisis-preventative-oriented people can be nudged to weigh whether the time, cost, and emotional energy put into prevention is justified for every single activity. Can some areas be a little less rigidly attended to?
2. Noncrisis-oriented people can be encouraged to check whether their lack of attention to preventing potential problems is causing others anxiety. Love looks to bear burdens together in an appropriate attitude of mutual responsibility.
3. Soar in the freedom of the Spirit as the Holy Spirit leads us in things of God, but let's also equip ourselves to be prepared in and out of season (2 Timothy 4:2) so that we might fruitfully touch lives in the midst of all that God has prepared for us.

Factor 4: Task Orientation versus People Orientation

Task-Oriented People	People-Oriented People
1. Prioritize tasks and "focus on tasks and principles" but, in the extreme, can appear uncaring.	1. Prioritize relationships and "focus on people and relationships" but, in the extreme, can appear unreliable.
2. "Find satisfaction in the achievement of goals."	2. Find "satisfaction in interaction" with people.

(continued)

Task-Oriented People	People-Oriented People
3. "Seek friends with similar" aims and "goals."	3. "Seek friends who are also people-oriented."
4. Accept lesser social activity and even loneliness "for the sake of personal achievements" since social interaction is not the priority.	4. Have much less difficulty putting aside personal achievements so as to be with people.

Table 3.4 Modification of Table 6 from *Ministering Cross-Culturally*[13]

Observations

By the time we had progressed this far through Lingenfelter's material in a cross-cultural communications multiple-culture class session, a young Asian student offered: "But isn't it obvious that all the Western countries are time oriented, dichotomistic thinkers, crisis oriented, and task oriented, and Asians are all the opposite?" The student was perhaps not expecting a gracious "No, that is certainly not the case." Perhaps the student was doing what we can all so easily do in cross-cultural settings: ignoring the differences being presented in favor of maintaining our expectations and long-held beliefs. This, of course, can badly hinder effective communication in any setting.

Example from Korea: Korean students have offered that, even though their culture is people oriented, the wider culture very much has a dichotomistic outlook in relation to issues of acceptable behavior. With a beautifully relevant example that recognizes the perceived difference between teachers and students, and which we will see in chapter 4 described as the concept of large power distance, one Korean student said: "In Korea, we would normally not make any statements to challenge a teacher because it would not be considered the right way to behave." He then continued with a smile: "But I think it's okay here because we're doing masters-level study, but we should always be very, very polite."

---

13. Lingenfelter and Mayers (2003, 80).

Devotional comment: The student in the example from Korea above was speaking for many of his countrymen and had found engaging with faculty members very difficult at first. This new kind of relationship could have caused debilitating culture shock, but being aware of God's calling on his life gave the student inner strength to keep pressing on in the face of obstacles and difficulties. In the face of challenging differences, we can remain secure as we find and follow God's plans for our lives and communications.

Example from Samoa: A Samoan student expressed that he had become more crisis oriented since starting studies at the seminary even though the island he grew up on didn't even have the term *crisis* in their vocabulary. This comment opened the way for a discussion on the difference between pragmatic responses motivated by necessity to meet demands and contingencies, and actual lifestyle changes due to changes in worldview beliefs. It is important to recognize that a pragmatic response is unlikely to have brought with it a change of worldview.

Key principle: As previously mentioned, worldview change comes about by the respondent being willing to change aspects of his or her inculcated beliefs and live out the results of the changed beliefs.

As with the other category pairs, one's degree of orientation to a particular side of the task orientation versus people orientation spectrum can also be influenced by personality, adult maturity, and spiritual maturity. Jesus was both people and task oriented in that he did what his Father gave him to do, and these tasks were, for the most part, centered on people and ultimately for the good of humankind. In making God-pleasing choices, task-oriented people cannot help but become aware of occasions when caring for others should be a priority. Equally, people-oriented people eventually come to a place in their adult maturity development when they realize that certain tasks must be completed to be able to help and care for others. Even the most task-oriented societies have beliefs, values, and customs related to appropriate social interaction and decision making.

Principles for Helpful Communication and Living Out the Love of God While Attending to His Purposes

1. Overemphasis on completing tasks can communicate a lack of care for people, while overemphasis on people orientation might communicate an unwillingness to be responsible in completing tasks for the good of individuals or the wider community.

2. For those who are people oriented, "failure to accomplish a task is less critical than a gain in the quality of personal relationships" (Lingenfelter and Mayers 2003, 79). They may need to see from God's perspective that achieving certain tasks at key times can open doors or maintain the means of service to him, which then impacts people, both saved and unsaved.

3. "The social life of the task-oriented is often merely an extension of work activities" (79). They will benefit from periodically doing something with no goals at all—just for fun.

4. Task-oriented people need to see the task in getting involved with people as a spiritually and emotionally healthy option and to see, as Jesus did, that people are in the task or are impacted by the task.

Factor 5: Concealment of Vulnerability versus Willingness to Expose Vulnerability

Concealment of Vulnerability	Willingness to Expose Vulnerability
1. "Protection of self-image at all cost"—unwilling to be seen to fail.	1. "Relative unconcern about error or failure."
2. "Emphasis on the quality of performance" whether or not it is completed.	2. "Emphasis on completion of event" rather than quality of engagement.
3. "Reluctance to go beyond one's known limits" to prevent failure.	3. "Willingness to try and push beyond one's [known] limits."
4. "Denial of culpability; withdrawal from activities in order to hide weaknesses or shortcomings."	4. "Ready admission of culpability, weaknesses and shortcomings."
5. Uncomfortable with and so withdraws from "alternative views and/or criticism."	5. "Open to alternative views and criticism."
6. "Vague [when asked to talk about] personal life" to prevent exposure of weaknesses.	6. "Willingness to talk freely about personal life" but may also lack discretion in disclosure.

Table 3.5 Modification of Table 9 from *Ministering Cross-Culturally*[14]

---

14. Lingenfelter and Mayers (2003, 104).

Another cultural category pair concerns the issue of transparency in life and relationships and requires us to examine how our own tendency compares with our respondents' tendency to expose vulnerability.

Observations

Regardless of one's background culture and personality, other factors may also come into play, including level of adult maturity and the limitations of one's spiritual maturity.

Preventing shame through loss of face is seen as very important in many Asian cultures, but adult maturity development and spiritual growth can also affect one's choices concerning exposure or concealment of vulnerability. This is particularly true in situations when concealing vulnerability will not please God, as well as times when exposing vulnerability will not be appropriate for the good of others. Exposing weakness can communicate a healthy humility, but it might also cause respondents to lose respect for the communicator or even cause anxiety that a similar outlook might be expected of them in return, particularly if that weakness is likely to bring shame.[15]

Principles to Help Enhance Communication in Light of Vulnerability Issues

1. To accept one's vulnerability is to be open to the strength and support of others. But we must also be careful not to communicate a casual and careless attitude concerning failure of one's self and others.

2. It will be important to expose the weaknesses of others in a loving and nonthreatening way so that what we communicate might be receivable, but as Elmer (2002, 88) reminds us: "Openness, acceptance and trust, which are important qualities in every culture, may be expressed differently in different parts of the world."

3. Whether to and when to expose one's own weaknesses as a leader needs careful attention. Having a few trusted peers or mentors, to whom we intentionally communicate our vulnerable areas and to whom we are accountable, can be the difference between ongoing stumbling and victory.

4. We must remember that God chose the foolish things of the world to shame the wise and the weak things of the world to shame

---

15. We will return to issues related to guilt and shame in chapter 4.

the strong (1 Corinthians 1:27). Humility opens the way for God to do his work both in and through us as we communicate cross-culturally.

5. Encouraging respondents to be vulnerable about weaknesses will likely only come about through building deeply trusting and caring relationships. As we will see in later chapters, such relationships are the foundation for progressing from cross-cultural interaction to intercultural engagement.

CONCLUSION

Hopefully by now we will be able to recognize the potential for miscommunication if we are unaware of the diversity within cultures. There can be a tendency, both helpful and unhelpful, to describe cultures with broad brushstrokes, but personality factors, adult maturity, and spiritual maturity may influence how individuals function (or not) as expected by their culture. This is because personality, adult maturity development, and growth in spiritual maturity can also influence decisions concerning communication and behavior when faced with various contingencies.

We should be wary of making dichotomistic or polarizing statements about people in a way that might undermine dignity. Graciousness in our thinking about others cannot help but also be the catalyst for graciousness in our behavior.

QUESTIONS FOR REFLECTION
AND DISCUSSION

1. In the "As It Happened" scenario at the start of the chapter, which of the two pastors do you think was more shocked and overwhelmed by the British pastor arriving in Pakistan two weeks late? In relation to big-picture facets of culture, why was that pastor your choice?

2. Consider your background and upbringing in relation to the facets of culture described in the chapter. Identify your "cultural profile" orientation preferences. How do they compare to and differ from the big-picture orientation of your background culture?

3. Which facets of culture and worldview beliefs that are different to your own background and upbringing have caused you difficulties in cross-cultural communications? Which principles from the chapter will you now incorporate into a change of approach?

4. Considering the benefits and advantages of the different orientations concerning facets of culture, can you identify some of the disadvantages or challenges of your background culture? How will this affect your communication and behavior from now on?

CHAPTER 4

Communication in Relation to Cultural Aspects Pertaining to Societal Structures

As It Happened: In 2003, my colleague Dr. Co and I were fruitfully ministering in the dental clinic that Dr. Co had set up in a village in a remote part of China. We were already accustomed to wearing face masks and disposable gloves in the clinic setting to maintain hygiene. With the SARS (severe acute respiratory syndrome) pandemic raging, villagers were also becoming accustomed to wearing face masks. One day we had an unexpected visit from the nearest town's local health bureau officials. These officials were part of the annual process for getting our work-visa renewal approved. We were informed that villagers who became sick or showed symptoms of the SARS virus probably would be brought by their family members to our clinic for treatment. They would not travel to a hospital in the town because there was no room for sick people with multiple family members. Although we worked in dentistry and training village dentists, we were attached to a small cooperative medical facility that also served several of the surrounding villages. The health bureau officials assured us that the villagers would be very glad to come to this medical setting because of the presence of the two foreigners—us! We were surprised and heartened by what seemed to be an appreciative affirmation. Just before leaving, the chief official told us very bluntly that no one could visit us socially from outside the district until further notice and that we were not allowed to leave the village area.

INTRODUCTION

Have you ever been in a situation where you appreciated being affirmed by someone in authority but the affirmation was followed by a harsh reminder of your tasks or obligations? How did you feel about the communication? Is it something you are used to, or did it leave you feeling uncomfortable or unhappy?

In the previous chapter we considered various aspects of culture and worldview belief that affect communication because of the behavioral differences between cultures or individuals. In this chapter we continue to look at big-picture aspects of cultural perspectives that can aid or hinder communication. The cultural perspectives we discuss in this chapter focus on orientations that affect social structure and relationships of members within the society and its immediate community. These behavioral nuances, which are often quite subtle, can relate to the understandings and obligations incurred by individualism and collectivism, social power in relation to the degree of prevailing power distance, understandings concerning patron-client relationships, as well as issues related to gender—particularly within Islamic settings. Being aware of these can help us better understand what is going on around us as we minister cross-culturally as well as how to avoid communication blunders.

CULTURE AND SOCIETY STRUCTURES

A number of factors affect the structure and functioning of societies and monoculture communities, including the existence and nature of subculture communities within the wider community. Communication can be hindered if we fail to understand the intricacies of expectations within the community concerning its component parts. Lack of understanding about the component-part subcommunities and the roles held within them can make building relationships very difficult. In some cultures, particularly those ruled by a monarchy, socioeconomic status has been ascribed according to ancestry. In other cultures, the society might recognize a hierarchy of classes or levels of authority within society based on socioeconomic or academic achievement. Other cultures have different means of distinguishing between community status levels and subgroups.

Example from Nepal: "Nepal is a Hindu country. Nepali people accept foreigners respectfully. They are very openminded, and they are easy to evangelize, especially if the foreigner is Asian. It's much harder for Westerners because they need to know there is a 'caste system' and understand the relationship of high and low class in the society. It is not the same as high and low class in the West." The Nepali is advising us that in Hindu communities, an awareness of the caste system is vital because, despite the correlation of higher and lower castes with higher and lower socioeconomic levels, the caste system is a factor of the Hindu religious system rather than an expression of achievement or exploited socioeconomic opportunities.

As we engage with members of a different culture, particularly when we are living and working within their geographical setting, we do well to work out how members of the community interact and communicate with those in their own subculture or level in society and how they interact and communicate with those of levels above and below them. Since communicating Christ is about persuasion of love and by a love that brings change, we do well to discover what else in the society contributes to decision making and impacts the potential to bring change. It will aid communication if we know about the structure of the community we are reaching out to—who is in a position to make decisions that can bring change to both individuals and the wider community?

INDIVIDUALISM VERSUS COLLECTIVISM

Moreau et al. (2014, 154–55) describe how individualism and collectivism are different vehicles for describing the self so that "in collectivist societies, the interests of the group are more important than those of the individual [whereas] individualistic societies give priority to the interests of individuals. . . . In the most individualistic countries, there is [an emphasis on self with] an interest in 'self-image, self-reliance, self-awareness, self-actualization, and self-determination,' while collectivists see themselves as members of a group and share its goals" (see also Klopf 2001, 80–81; and Fujino 2009, 22).

Example of Collectivism from Kenya: "Things are not done individually. It is a group cooperation even in raising a child."

Example of Individualism from Switzerland: "My parents wanted me to be an engineer, but I decided to be a pastor and that was that."

The dichotomistic categorization of a culture or nation as being either individualistic or collectivist misses the point made in the previous chapter; we might better consider the descriptions as depicting a spectrum on which some cultures are more individualistic or collectivist than others[1] and neither extreme would necessarily make for an ideal, secure, freedom-loving society. Extreme collectivism can cause a frustrating limitation of an individual's desire for achievement, whilst extreme individualism can cause a splintered and fractious community. As Moreau et al. further note, whilst in the past isolated tribal and rural communities were possibly able to maintain a purely collectivist lifestyle, this is rarely the case now (155). Similarly, few individualists are totally devoid of relationships with others that call for some degree of mutual care and a call for decision making for the good of the group, whether that group is a family, a sports or social club, or even affiliation to a political organization.[2] Just as the church is the body of Christ made up of many individual parts (1 Corinthians 12:12–20), so too is a secular group made up of a collection of individual members.

We might add that, conversely, even for people living in the most extreme degree of collectivism, there will inevitably be situations and occasions when individuals will make decisions with little or no need to observe collectivist principles. For example (albeit an extreme one), no authority, collectivist or otherwise, can dictate an individual's choice of inner thoughts or emotions. This can have important ramifications for communication and decision making, particularly when choices can be made in response to a gospel message that is perceived to be both relevant and compelling.

Decision Making from a Cultural Perspective

Hesselgrave (1991) makes some key points related to the issue of decision making from a cultural perspective:[3]

---

1. This section expands on D-Davidson (2018, 40).
2. See Hughes (1937) on individual responsibility within the Chinese collectivist system in relation to Confucianism.
3. This section comes from D-Davidson (2018, 40–41).

1. "Some cultures place great value on decisiveness and making up one's mind. Any decision is better than no decision. Deliberation is expected to end in closure. Indecisiveness is seen as a character flaw. Other cultures place a high value on the ability to live with indecisiveness. . . . [When options are not clear or the situation isn't seen as needing a fast decision,] it will seem better to make *no* decision than to risk making the wrong decision. . . . Tentativeness and open-endedness are aspects of wisdom" (613–14). As we will see in chapter 6, differing cultural approaches to decision making can be a major cause of cross-cultural conflict, particularly in the international business world.

2. Group versus individual decision making.[4] Group conversions to Christ as a result of cultural preferences can be a means of longer-lasting fruit than multiple individual conversions in a culture that frowns on individuals making decisions.

Hesselgrave (1991, 616) urges us to be aware of the ways decisions are made in different societies and who is qualified (according to societal understanding) to decide. Individualist societies encourage members to decide for themselves—though, ideally, the decision should be in the interest of the greater good as well. Collectivist societies make decisions as a group entirely for the good of the group. Certain individuals will be looked to as the voice or voices of authority, and their decisions will be seen as binding; the community recognizes those decisions as belonging to the group and welcomed by the group for the good of the group. We do well to identify those qualified to decide for the group as well as to be sensitive to identify those the Lord prepared to support us or be champions for us regardless of their initial underlying motives.

One key aspect of the second millennium that runs counter to the distinctives of individualist and collectivist cultural perspectives is the use of the internet and evolving cyberculture. Even collective engagement with the internet nonetheless exposes individuals in the group to ideas beyond their immediate experience and brings both individuals and groups into the globally owned realm of cyberculture. Macek (2005) writes that "cyberculture is an ambiguous . . . term describing a set of issues. It can be

---

4. See Donald A. McGavran (1980); compare with Bosch (1991, 383) who suggests that conversion in large numbers in a particular community may just be a subtle means of escaping from engaging with unwanted "dominant social issues."

used in a descriptive, analytical or ideological sense." From an ideological perspective, material presented online is available to inform, misinform, challenge, and widen perspectives both individually and collectively with little regard for the individualist or collectivist distinctives of those connecting to the internet.

Markers of Individualism and Collectivism

Individualists frequently refer to "I" and "my."

Collectivists frequently refer to "we" and "our."

> **Example:** If you ask your respondent, "Tell me about your family. Do you have siblings?" a respondent from an individualistic society with two siblings is likely to answer, "I have two siblings," whereas a respondent from a collectivist background is more likely to answer, "We are three siblings."

POWER DISTANCE AND SOCIAL POWER

In every society or communal grouping, some members are liable to be richer and able to take advantage of opportunities that are not available to those who are poorer.[5] The power that access to such advantage brings is also a means of control. As members of the society recognize this inequality, they may either choose to rebel and face rejection or follow the social protocols expected of people at different levels within recognized institutions and community subgroups, as well as within the family unit or extended family. Fukuyama (2000, 99) notes, "All societies have some stock of social capital;[6] the real differences among them concern what might be called the 'radius of trust.' That is, cooperative norms like honesty and

---

5. This and the following sections in this chapter are based on and expand upon D-Davidson (2018, 42–49).

6. Fukuyama (100) further notes that the distribution of social capital is not always good for society (e.g., the destructive power held by the Mafia in Italy). The term *social capital* is first found in Hanifan (1916).

reciprocity can be shared among limited groups of people but not with others in the same society."[7]

An associated and important facet of a society's rules of social engagement and interaction involves what Hofstede termed *power distance*, or the common understanding by members of a community that others are likely to have more power than them because social capital and thus power are not distributed equally within the community (Hofstede 1991, 46).

Regarding Hofstede's two ends of the spectrum, "small (or low) power distance" and "large (or high) power distance," Moreau et al. (2014, 166) write: "Broadly speaking, people of cultures of larger power distance believe in a social order in which each person has a rightful and protected place, in a hierarchy presuming existential inequalities, and that the legitimacy of the purposes desired by the power holders is irrelevant. . . . People in power are to be respected because they are the authorities. Therefore it is important to use titles to indicate power (such as pastor, reverend, or doctor), and to speak respectfully."

In contrast, low power distance cultures prefer minimized social inequalities, reduction of hierarchy, and no misuse of power. Showing respect for those in authority is important, but respect is expected to be reciprocated so that this mutual respect is not due to differences in social level or titles held but is due to equality being highly valued. Members of low power distance cultures value their independence according to the degree of reduced or absent power distance so that decisions are negotiated, not dictated.

The degree of power distance in the culture or community we are reaching out to affects communication. We need to be aware of what is considered appropriate communication between members of the community and be careful not to offend or embarrass others as we reach out to people. It is also important to work out how we are percieved to fit into the community structure and with the expectations of community members. Not only does power distance differentiate between those with more power and those with less power and set the understood rules for interaction, but it also affects the social distance between members of a society and therefore dictates the rules of social interaction. The greater the power distance within a culture, the less likely members are to interact in social settings with those considered to be at the opposite end of the power spectrum.

---

7. Porter (2000, 23) suggests, "The way people behave in a society has much to do with the signals and incentives that are created in the economic system in which they live." Following the social capital protocols is also a means to advance one's status in both social and economic spheres.

In small power distance settings, casual interaction with superiors is considered the norm, and casual interaction with subordinates is expected to be devoid of condescension or paternalism. However, cultures have different perspectives on what constitutes appropriate behavior and attitudes towards members of older generations, as well as in relation to whether such members are relatives or not. People from cultures with the strict hierarchy of a Confucian background, such as China, Korea, and Japan, or strict hierarchy due to a religious system, such as Islam, will be particularly concerned to acknowledge the hierarchy of roles within communities, and they are likely to feel uncomfortable when others undermine the value attached to this worldview belief.

Example from the Philippines of high power distance: "The Filipino culture is a high power distance culture—the authorities are important and dignified in our country. Filipinos have high expectations of missionaries, so it is easy for a missionary to be raised to a high position in the Filipino institutions. Also, the people will respect and follow the missionary more if the missionary will intentionally develop a good relationship with the local authorities. It will create more trust between the locals and missionaries if we see the missionaries respecting the local national authorities just as we do."

Example from Japan of high power distance: "There are great social distances between people according to their position. Pastors, teachers, lawyers, doctors are all called *sensei*, and they have to be paid a lot of respect. *Sensei* means that they have more education, experience, and Japanese people believe they deserve that respect. There are particular ways to speak politely and pay respect to those at different levels of society, and foreigners hate all that."

Example from the Dominican Republic of low power distance: "In the Dominican Republic there is no real distance between the people in the high society and the people of low status. Everyone can approach and talk to each other regardless of their social or financial status. It does not really matter if an individual is from the high class, he or she can relate, talk, and make friends with people in the lower class."

Example from Mongolia of low power distance: "Western missionaries get along well with Mongolians. However, problems arise with Asian missionaries, for example Koreans. The culture of Koreans and Mongolians is very different. First, Koreans always bow and like the respectful greeting when they meet people. However, Mongolians do not like bowing. We also do not like greeting with titles. Shaking hands, smiling, or simply saying 'hi' is okay."

Example from Myanmar: "The culture generally has a high power distance, but young people nowadays are starting to rebel."

Example from Korea of high power distance: "If you are a teacher in Korea, you are very respected because of the high power distance, but if you try to teach American children, it will be a shock because they don't sit quietly and listen. If you try to scold them, it doesn't make any difference. They will be polite but still talking all the time."

Trying to project low power distance values into a high power distance setting and vice versa is a recipe for cross-cultural disaster. However, even in high power distance settings, it is still possible and, perhaps, all the more important to interact with those in subordinate positions (or with less power) in ways that acknowledge, affirm, and cherish their dignity. This could be what makes the difference between the communicator, as an outsider, being recognized and received in a positive way, and consequently, it may stimulate openness to what else the Christian communicator has to bring and to say. Learning how to be appropriate in our communications can be the difference between being accepted and rejected.

Markers for Power Distance

High power distance expects utmost respect to be shown to people in authority. Authority figures cannot be argued with.

Low power distance expresses and expects mutual respect with no awkwardness in frank discussions with authority figures. These discussions may even include public disagreement.

RELATIONSHIPS WITHIN SOCIETIES AND
BENEDICT'S GUILT/SHAME SPECTRUM

In 1946, Ruth Benedict's anthropological studies in Asia resulted in her differentiation of cultures in which guilt brings stress in comparison to cultures in which shame brings distress. The *Oxford English Dictionary* describes *guilt* as "the fact of having committed an offence or crime" and "a feeling of having done wrong or failed in an obligation" and *shame* as "a feeling of humiliation or distress caused by the consciousness of wrong or foolish behavior; [and/or with respect to dishonor:] a person or thing bringing dishonor."

Hesselgrave (1991, 596) interprets Benedict as seeing guilt being concerned with each individual act in an additive process so that feelings of guilt increase as more transgressions of expected standards occur. It is suggested that guilt can be displaced by stopping the wrong behaviors and substituting them with approved ones. In contrast, shame is a result of falling short of cultural ideals or failing to meet expected standards. Shame brings dishonor and affects the whole self in terms of identity, self-worth, and self-esteem; guilt, on the other hand, tends to bring discomfort in relation to only specifically related aspects of self-identity.

Advances in the literature somewhat dichotomistically linked guilt with Western cultures and shame with Asian cultures. The dishonor that shame brings is very much associated with the concept of losing face, which is common in Asian cultures (but not just Asian cultures), and so causes discomfort to more than merely the individual who has lost face because it also brings shame and dishonor to the culprit's wider family.

Example from Japan: "In Japan, honor is very important. Without honor, you are shamed and your family is too."

Example from Myanmar: "When there's a problem in the community, we want to conceal shame by not showing where things went wrong. But if there are immorality problems, the guilty person should face the community and apologize publicly and submit to the decision of the leadership."

Example from Guatemala: "Foreigners should know that if they have a problem with someone in the workplace, they shouldn't talk to the person in public, but privately, so the person doesn't lose face."

Example from Samoa: "If there's a problem that affects the whole community, we gather to resolve it or help each other. But if the problem causes shame to the family, the family might prefer to conceal it."

Example from Malaysia: "*Shame* is a word that is not even right to speak about in Malaysia. When there's a family problem that would cause loss of face, we tend to protect members of the home by hiding the problem."

Example from China: "We are prone to cover up for the mistake of the other member of the family. Sometimes we refuse to even talk about it. There is a silent rule when something bad happens. If the eldest brother or the father talks about it, only then can we talk, but if they don't, we have no right to talk about it and must ignore the problem and just keep going in life."

Example from Kenya: "When we are affected by guilt in the community or in our homes, we prefer not to show that it impacts us; shame can cause longer-lasting embarrassment to families and communities."

More recent literature broadens the range and links guilt with Western cultures and shame with African, Asian, and South American cultures—in other words, it links guilt with the Global North and shame with the Global South. Yet labeling individual cultures as either a guilt culture or a shame culture (which often happens in the literature) does not do sufficient justice to differing behavior rationales. It is more helpful to recognize that all cultures have a place for both guilt and shame but that each culture may have a greater tendency toward either the guilt or shame end of the spectrum.

Understanding the cultural rationale behind certain behaviors and the different cultural contexts in which such behaviors are played out may help discern whether guilt or shame is a defining issue, but equally, one may not have enough understanding of the underlying, hidden cultural agendas (let alone the specifics of the personality or degree of adult maturity of the person or people in question) to be able to decide correctly. In such a case, rather than trying to engage with one side of the polarity, addressing areas where regret has arisen might be more helpful for resolving areas of cross-cultural misunderstanding, contention, or conflict.[8] It is important that

8. More on this is in chapter 6.

we, as cross-cultural communicators, are sensitive to what brings honor and dishonor[9] to both individuals and community groups and careful to follow the cultural rules in both verbal and nonverbal communication.

PATRON-CLIENT RELATIONSHIPS

Moreau et al. (2014, 170–71) describe the concept of social power and how this social capital can be considered to be "used as an exchange mechanism within a society . . . just as people are attracted to money and try to accumulate it, they are also attracted to social power and try to accumulate it. People who have social power and can control distribution of it in some way (granting favors, naming people to positions of social power) . . . are referred to as patrons. Those who come under their power are called clients, resulting in what is called a patron-client system."

Every culture has relationships that come under the patron-client umbrella, but the degree to which they occur and the manner in which they occur may be more subtle in some cultures. For example, parents who commit their children to the care of teachers choose to submit to the teacher's patronage; applying for a bank loan or credit arrangement makes the borrower a client of the money lender, who has agreed to become their patron. Families inevitably have relationships amongst the family members with characteristics similar to patron-client relationships as those with greater age and life experience are better placed to open the way for the younger members' benefit. Similarly, in society, people with lower social power can seek to establish a patron-client relationship with someone of higher social power. As with the building of any functional relationships, the potential client will likely have some kind of underlying agenda. The potential patron is first likely to weigh the potential value of permitting such a relationship because unlike paying back a bank loan, at which point the technical patron-client relationship is effectively dissolved, societal patron-client relationships tend to continue beyond the returning of favors into the long-term.[10]

An established patron-client relationship brings with it mutually understood obligations and responsibilities according to the culture so that Tino (2008, 322) describes it as a "friendship with strings [attached]." Depending on the particular culture and setting, benefits for the client may include being protected by the patron or protected by other clients

---

9. For some biblically based principles, see Georges and Baker (2016).
10. Cf. DeSilva (2009, 11) in the Greco-Roman world context (from where the concepts of patronage and clientele were well-established long before even the advent of Jesus).

of the patron; being part of a recognized group (namely, the associated "in-group"), which may be highly prestigious; coming into a role for which further promotion is now possible; and/or gaining the availability of information or other previously restricted resources. Other benefits and/ or obligations may be available according to the unique particularities of the context, in which case, as communicators becoming aware not only of contexts that are different to the ones we grew up in, we need to look wider than the culture's big picture patron-client relationships and be sensitive to relationship rules according to "situational specifics."[11] Being part of an "in-group" often has obligations that include preventing loss of face, dishonor, or shame to other in-group members.

Author's example of a patron-client situation in Pakistan: In the 1980's when I was based in Pakistan, there was an unspoken understanding in Rawalpindi (Northern Pakistan) that if you bought a bottle of Coca Cola from a store that was not near where you lived, as the client, you would consume the drink then and there and immediately return the glass bottle to the seller for recycling (or refilling in this case). If you bought the drink from a neighborhood seller who knew you, then it was acceptable to bring the drink home and return the empty bottle within a few days. In the much larger city of Karachi where I had missionary colleagues with several young children, it was quite acceptable for them to hold on to multiple empty glass bottles for weeks at a time because they were friends with the drinks-selling patron and were members of his in-group.

What might the benefits of being a patron include? In the example above, the benefits include income and labor—the drink seller in Rawalpindi did not have to travel to collect the empty bottles. Benefits might also include unquestioned loyalty and possibly standing against those who are not for the patron or even standing against those in the "out group." Having a large clientele can increase the patron's status in the eyes of the community (Moreau et al. 2014, 171).

How patron-client relationships become established vary according to the specific expectations and unspoken cultural rules. Some patron-client

---

11. See D-Davidson (2018, 116). In situational contextualisation, *situational specifics* are aspects of the culture that are uniquely manifested in a particular way in a particular setting and that prohibit us from applying a one-size-fits-all approach in outreach and cross-cultural communication.

relationships might be established by the potential client initiating the possibility through a planned encounter. The potential patron may then welcome the possibility or respond in a way that will be understood as refusal. As the one with the higher level of social power, the potential patron can refuse without causing cultural offence.

The potential client may bring a gift to show that they are seeking something in response. If the patron accepts the gift and responds with a more valuable gift (e.g., the patron shows willingness to use social power to benefit the client), then they will come to an understanding that further or ongoing interaction and mutual paying out of obligations are expected due to the "strings attached" to this relationship. Moreau et al. (2014, 171) also note that "this relationship is always negotiable, and either may pull away or seek to revise the relationship," but this will always be done in a way that preserves honor.

As of the potential patron's choice to receive or refuse the potential client's relationship-building initiative, any such communications, whether through words or actions, will have been communicated in a way that provides a clear meaning for both parties in their cultural context. Hopefully we can see how necessary it is for cross-cultural communicators to be able to understand and correctly interpret such behavioral cues.

Ultimately, the patron-client relationship affects social functioning in the wider community because clients of the same patron cannot help but be expected to own their common-ground relationship with each other, and this also gives honor to the patron. Being part of such groups also provides a sense of identity (273). Moreau et al. suggest that such affiliations are how people from honor-oriented cultures define themselves, but the principle also holds true for other cultures. For instance, whether they are graduates from a Global North or Global South university, wearing badges, scarves, jerseys, or other university-related apparel shows a pride in being part of a group that belongs to the same alma mater.

One of our goals as cross-cultural communicators must be to be able to identify the implications and underlying rationale of the relationships we see played out and those into which we are invited.

Key principle: When we are engaged in a patron-client relationship as either patron or client, it is of utmost importance for the sake of our integrity that we are careful not to raise expectations or make promises about what we cannot offer or might be unwilling to deliver.

This principle becomes even more critical if we are doing outreach and building relationships in a high-context communication setting where the subtleties of meaning can be easily misunderstood. Moreau et al. (273) advise that cultures attentive to saving face and thus maintaining honor are often more collectivist and may also be high-context communicators. When high power distance is also important, and patron-client relationships are not a subtle part of the society structure, it is all the more important to understand correctly how the interweaving of relationships influences the identity, security, and stability of the community. We need to consider how to shape our involvement and communication so that they might best be perceived as a positive influence by both those we are immediately reaching out to as well as the wider community.

In a cross-cultural setting we need to be aware of, for instance, the implications of invitations for meals or being presented with gifts. In strongly patron-client, honor-based cultures, some appropriate response is expected and awaited. The meal or gift could be an attempt to initiate a patron-client relationship, or it might come with an expectation that a mutually understood form of reciprocity is anticipated. Moreau et al. (274) advise that those from cultures that are not collectivist or honor based prefer not to accumulate social debt and may respond in a way that cancels out the social debt by, for instance, returning the invitation. But this may return the gift giver to the figurative starting block and completely undermine what the gift giver was trying to achieve or initiate. This can then incorrectly communicate to the gift giver that the receiver has no desire or intention to enter a patron-client relationship—or worse, that the receiver has no desire to further the relationship connection. By neutralizing the possibility of social debt, the dignity of the gift giver may well have been completely unintentionally undermined. When the gift giver then cools off any deepening of the relationship, the unenlightened cross-cultural communicator is left to wonder what went wrong following such promising beginnings. At this point the communicator would do best to seek advice about the situation from a local resident or more experienced colleague.

We need to be aware too that, as we saw in chapter 2, giving commonly used items as gifts can have different connotations in different cultures.

Example from Europe: When a man meets his girlfriend, he might give her flowers or chocolates to show his love.

Example from China: "Do not give flowers, clocks, or handkerchiefs since these all depict funerals. Also do not give pointed objects as a gift because this depicts severing of relationships."

Markers of Degree of Influence of Patron-Client Relationships

The mutually understood condition and obligations of being in a patron-client relationship have increasing potential to be manipulative according to the depth at which these relationships are understood to influence and hold society together. The greater the importance and prevalence of such relationships, the more influential and more manipulative they are likely to become.

OTHER CULTURAL ISSUES RELATED TO ROLES AND STATUS

Subcultures

Other cultural issues can affect one's role and status within the wider community, and we need to be aware of subcultures present in the community (e.g., elderly people, physically handicapped people, migrant or minority groups, etc.) as well as the rules for appropriate interaction with people of these subcultures. Nonetheless, reaching out in a countercultural way may be the means of impacting others for the gospel as they observe changed lives affecting the wider community in a positive way.

Example from Thailand: The Buddhist religion influences Thai people's lack of care for handicapped people, such as those who are blind, deaf, or physically handicapped. This is a result of the Thai Buddhist law of karma, by which people believe that bad actions in a previous life caused the person to be born into or face suffering when they are reborn into the next life. Consequently, helping and caring for these people and their needs prevents them from being released from the bad karma, and it may bring bad karma to those who are helping them.

Example from communist nations: Handicapped people are liable to be marginalized and their needs not cared for as they tend to be seen as having no use in society.

Example from Western nations: As people age and retire, they often are no longer treated with the respect of earlier years. This can be shocking to those of other cultures whose worldview beliefs include showing increasing respect as people age.

In our cross-cultural communications and interactions, we need to be aware how worldview beliefs and associated cultural practices dictate what is appropriate for interaction with those at different levels in society. For instance, domestic workers are unlikely to feel comfortable interacting socially and having fun with community members who have a higher level of employment. Similarly, those at the higher levels will likely consider it less than appropriate to interact socially with those "beneath them." It can be challenging but helpful to bear in mind what Paul wrote to the Romans: "Live in harmony with one another. Do not be proud, but be willing to associate with people of low position. Do not be conceited" (Romans 12:16).

Author's example of bringing together members of different socio-economic levels: When Dr. Co and I knew we would be moving on to another area of China the following year, we prayed about how to make the best use of our final Christmas in that area for sharing the gospel with some of the people we had come to know a little but not deeply enough to present the details of the gospel. We rented a small private mahjong gaming room in a nearby building one evening during the Christmas week and invited our neighbor living a floor above and her young son, a bank manager friend and her young son, and the man who delivered water to our home and hospital office on a fortnightly basis, along with his wife and young daughter. We invited each set of the family members to attend our Christmas party in which we would have snacks, a telling of the

Christmas story, and games for the children, all in English and Chinese. The children ranged in age from six to ten years old, and the attraction of a free English lesson by real English speakers was a big selling point, since we were the only foreigners living at the far and less-developed edge of the city. On the evening of the event, we pinned up a backdrop of Christmas cards in the gaming room showing different aspects of the Christmas story and had the children take turns reading out the Christmas narrative in English with their parents reading out sections in Chinese. We had games based on the children acting charades of key English terms in the narrative and the parents guessing the terms in Chinese where necessary. The narrative went beyond the Christmas event to include the reason why Jesus came and the effect of his death on the cross and resurrection. The evening was a great success because, although these acquaintances were from very different socioeconomic backgrounds, none of them knew each other, and they were only introduced to each other by name. The last to leave were the water-delivery man and his family. We knew him best out of the group, but we had just that evening met his wife and daughter. They lingered, showing a clear desire to keep interacting and pose questions that needed answers. Dr. Co led them through some keys to help their marriage relationship in the sight of God, while the daughter was with me and asked for Jesus to come into her heart. All this was by God's grace and leading, and it remains a matter of continuing prayer that the seeds of gospel love and truth sown would bear fruit according to God's way and timing.

Devotional comment: When we make a habit of praying, "Lord, please have me in the right place, at the right time, and with the right heart attitude to be with the people you desire me to be with for your purposes," we will find ourselves touching lives in ways beyond our hopes or expectations. They might not be the people we naturally feel comfortable with or drawn to; they may not be crowds but just a special few. As we submit to the Spirit's voice and leading, he will rise us above our limitations to rejoice from his perspective in the hope of hearing "Well done, good and faithful servant!" (Matthew 25:21). Faithfulness in what seems like service in obscurity brings us delight as we share our Master's happiness.

As seen in chapter 2, appropriate behavior related to physical touch and gestures, as well as preference for space and appropriate interpersonal distance, also need to be understood and followed both in relation to role and status and in other aspects of life. However, we must also be careful to get the right balance of observance of cultural ways without undermining biblical principles of morality, justice, and integrity. Looking to affirm and cherish dignity in the face of cultural ways that run to the contrary may very well be the means of demonstrating the love of Christ in a uniquely receivable way.

Gender

Other aspects to be aware of related to role and status in different societies include awareness of what constitutes appropriate behavior in relation to gender, particularly in Islamic settings.

In any cross-cultural setting, communicators need to be aware of the cultural rules for interaction between males and females. We need to be especially aware of what is appropriate in relation to proxemics and haptics. Coming close to a member of the opposite sex when the culture forbids it, even with the purest of motives, can leave a bad impression not only with that person but with any others watching. Making contact by touching may not merely be considered inappropriate, it might even cause danger to the caring communicator, let alone the person they are trying to help. This is particularly so in Islamic settings.

In rural and more fundamentalist Islamic settings and in light of legal requirements, men may communicate only with men and women with women and children. Where a Christian couple seeks to reach out to families, the woman might befriend the Muslim wife so that the husbands are then introduced. But even then, that does not guarantee that they will all meet together.

In deeply fundamentalist settings, Muslim women are often not allowed to venture outside without being accompanied by a male family member, and at Christian gatherings there will be a separation of men sitting on one side and women and young children on the other. As communicators amongst people in any setting that is new to us, we will do well to observe carefully the degree of proximity in which members of the opposite sex interact and what kind of touching, if any, is appropriate.

Communicating with people of the lesbian, gay, bisexual, transsexual, or queer subcultures, or those with gender dysphoria,[12] also calls for careful

---

12. Be aware that what are termed LGBTQ+ subcultures include Lesbian, Gay, Bisexual, Transgender, Questioning (including dysphoria), and those with other self-owned uncategorized or nonbinary orientations.

attention to subculture rules and degree of contexting in communication and that we be sensitive to the Holy Spirit in how to communicate with graciousness.

CONCLUSION

As we have seen in this chapter, societies and communities within societies will have their own structure based on the interaction of relationships and socioeconomic or other life concerns and desires. When we are reaching out cross-culturally, it is important that we understand the culture and cultural situational specifics within which members of the community live and pursue their hopes and dreams, whether individually or communally. We need to be aware of the implications of befriending individuals or groups of people as well as the implications of their choosing to befriend us. We need to be asking how this friendship affects the respondent's family, work situation, and community. How does power distance affect roles and status, and how are we perceived to function (or not!) in the community? Have we intentionally or unintentionally initiated or been drawn into a patron-client relationship, and what implications does that have for deepening friendships in an honorable way without compromising on integrity?

In the next chapter we will consider aspects of personality and their potential to help or hinder communication.

QUESTIONS FOR REFLECTION
AND DISCUSSION

1. In the "As It Happened" scenario at the start of the chapter, what evidence is there that we were ministering in a community with collectivist assumptions? How was power distance played out, and what patron-client obligations could you detect?
2. This chapter describes facets of culture regarding relationships within structures of societies. Which aspects correspond to your background culture concerning the degree of individualism versus collectivism, the degree of power distance, and how social power is allocated? In your background culture, are patron-client relationships subtle or obvious? What examples of these facets of culture and worldview have impacted and influenced the being, doing, and life expectations of the person you are today?

3. Of the cross-cultural interactions that you have been involved in or hope to be involved in, which aspects of society structures are either most different or most similar to your own background? Where or how might there have been or might there be difficulties for you or your respondents?

4. In the "As It Happened" scenario, how do you think Dr. Co and I responded to the health official's insistence that we were not allowed to leave the village area during the SARS virus epidemic? Why have you decided that way?

CHAPTER 5

Supracultural Perspectives on Communication, Personality, and Temperament

As It Happened: The following records a conversation between two intercultural Christian colaborers:

1: "You seem to have gone very quiet. Is something wrong? Have I upset you?"

2: "Well, actually, yes, but I'm pondering on it. I'm not ready to talk about it yet."

Thirty minutes later

1: "Are you ready to talk about it yet?"

2: "No, not yet. I'm still reflecting on what happened and how I feel about it."

Five hours later

1: "I've been thinking through the details of what's happened recently and trying to work out what might have upset you. Are you ready to tell me yet?"

2: "No, not yet. I haven't finished sorting out my feelings and how I want to talk about it."

1: "Then, until you're ready, I'll just pray for patience for me, inspired insight for you, and love-based wisdom for both of us."

INTRODUCTION

How often do we unexpectedly observe people arguing? Seeing people in disagreement can teach us more about them as individuals than when everything is going well. There are some people whom we find very easy to be with and others who easily bring out the worst in us. When we stop to consider why, we can learn more about ourselves too.

To communicate the gospel of Christ effectively, we are aiming to build intercultural relationships that are marked by empathy shown through transparency and genuineness, among other characteristics. To be genuine, we need to understand ourselves as well as those we are reaching out to. In this chapter, we will examine personality and temperament as supracultural facets of each individual's being and doing, and we will examine how communication can be either heightened or hindered in relation to these differences. To this end, this chapter examines the characteristics of personality and temperament types, preferences and priorities, and areas of potential for misunderstandings in communication, as well as means for heightening understanding to prevent or reduce the potential for conflict.[1]

PERSONALITY AND TEMPERAMENT

It is generally considered that an individual's personal style of being and behavior results from the combination of three components: (1) a God-given social style, which is an individual basic social style inherited at birth; (2) family-dynamic influences as well as input and reinforcement from the wider community; and (3) personal experience and habit patterns developed from childhood. The link between temperament and personality, or how one behaves in relation to why one behaves as they do, is not clear-cut. Social science has mulled over several key schemas, including four basic styles that date back to Hippocrates in fifth-century Greece, the sixteen types of the Myers-Briggs schema (which is based on Jungian psychology), and the Big Five personality theory.

One common factor of all three schemas of personality listed above—and one of the most distinguishing differences between individuals—is their preferred tendency toward either introversion or extraversion. Like other facets of personality and temperament, examples of people who are more introverted and those who are more extroverted can be seen in every culture. For this reason, this and other facets of temperament or personality can be considered supracultural.

---

1. The material in this chapter builds upon and extends material from D-Davidson (2018, 67–73).

Introverts and Extroverts

Mulholland (1993, 51) suggests, "Extrovert/Introvert preferences relate to where persons find their preferred focus—whether in the world outside them of persons, events, and things (Extroverts) *or* in the inner world of self and ideas (Introverts)." As with the polar categories that we saw in relation to different cultures' behavior tendencies, the introvert-extrovert preference is also a spectrum: some people sit at an extreme of either introvert or extrovert, while others will be placed elsewhere along the spectrum between the extreme position and the middle.

The simplest way to differentiate an introvert from an extrovert is to ask how the person gets drained of energy, and how they refresh their sense of vigor and energy. Extroverts are energized and refreshed by spending time with people; they would prefer to be with people rather than to be alone because for extroverts, being away from people is draining. Introverts, on the other hand, find excessive time with a crowd of people to be draining and so will eventually want to withdraw from being with people in order to renew their energy.

Each individual's preferred way of life as either an introvert or extrovert developed as they progressed through childhood to adulthood.[2] Once we know our own preference and are able to discern one from the other, we will be better able to adjust our communication for maximum benefit in building relationships. How do introversion and extraversion affect communication? An extrovert may have little problem making friends in a new environment, but are they willing to reduce their talk and listen to others? Introverts may be far more cautious in reaching out to make new friends, but they will be less likely to dominate conversations and will find it easier to listen more.

As noted, the preference for extraversion or introversion is not a fixed dichotomy but varies in degree from person to person. Extroverts typically find it easier to communicate with other extroverts, but if a Christian communicator is more extroverted than their extrovert respondent, then the communicator must be careful not to dominate the conversation because the respondent will want to talk too. If the respondent is an introvert, then the extrovert Christian communicator may drain the energy of the respondent if the communicator is too outgoing for too long. Mulholland (53) cautions us that, apart from extreme extroverts and extreme introverts,

---

2. For development of the preference through life's development stages, see Grant, Thompson, and Clarke (1983, 20–25), cited by Mulholland (1993, 52).

most people show extroverted behavior sometimes and introverted behavior at other times, and some individuals have far less difficulty moving from one to the other according to the requirements of their situation. In certain situations they know they must choose to use the less preferred side because they know that, at that time, it is the best way to deal with the particular situation. This may be due to a pragmatic but unwilling response or it may be a healthy factor of adult maturity. People are likely to prefer one side to the other. Given that people can show aspects of both behaviors, when we try to discern the preference of our respondent or respondents, we can ask which side of the introvert-extrovert spectrum he or she is the most comfortable with. As Mulholland reminds us, being introverted or extroverted is similar to right- or left-handedness: neither is right or wrong, and there will be times that we will need to use our nondominant hand (55).

When we start getting to know people of other cultures, we should beware of immediately categorizing them by their initial responses to our attempts at friendship building. Even strong extroverts may hold off displaying the fullness of their preference until they sense it might be beneficial or advantageous to them to show more of who they are. Getting to know introverts is likely to take much longer as they may not be willing to reveal too much about themselves until they have built trust. Remember that, whether introvert or extrovert, very few people are willing to confide in strangers.

MAJOR PERSONALITY TYPES

As mentioned, the idea that there are four major personality types or basic social styles can be traced back to Hippocrates in fifth-century Greece. It has since been further refined and developed with social and psychological studies correlating with the hypothesis. The four major types are termed *choleric, melancholic, phlegmatic,* and *sanguine.*

Cholerics

Cholerics tend to be looked to as natural leaders because they find it easy and appropriate to take command of situations and people and relish being in command and directing people. Being apart from people is draining and unfulfilling for them. In their efforts to complete tasks efficiently, they can come across as callous and uncaring if and when they drive people to achieve their choleric's goals and purposes. This is how and why cholerics are happy to engage with lots of people in extrovert fashion, but they also have their own agenda for how such relationships can be also used to complete tasks. Due to this, others may respond to or engage with cholerics with respect that might also be tinged with discomfort.

Example from China: One of the local Chinese people responsible for acquiring our work visas in the village setting was highly respected for achieving all the tasks he set out to achieve, but he could also come across as loud and demanding in a way that made others uncomfortable. He was a typical choleric, being and doing as he had become used to over the years to achieve the goals that were important to him. Officials that he dealt with respected him, but there were also complaints about how he would try to shortcut the task just to get it done. Villagers respected him, but some were also a little afraid of him.

In contrast:

Example from Thailand: "My father is a very good leader. He easily takes charge of situations, and people respect him even though he is not elderly. He speaks frankly but always courteously; he knows what needs doing, and he gets people doing tasks that he knows they are able to do and also that they like to do so that they complete the tasks well."

Melancholics

Melancholics tend to be particular about details and orderliness. They are quite content to work alone pondering over what material is needed to solve problems and answer the questions necessary for the task to be completed properly. They may also have the creativity associated with an artist or genius and are diligent workers. As introverts, their best work is more likely to be produced when they are alone or with just a few people. Their desires to acquire maximum resources to ensure the best answer and to complete tasks perfectly can frustrate others because of the time taken and perfection sought after.

Example from a Malaysian Chinese: "I was asked at a meeting with the academic committee why I'd make a good doctoral student. I told them I always pay attention to details and took the initiative to find relevant up-to-date resources for my masters-level assignments. Also, I always plan my work and study schedules very well, down to the finest detail. And I showed them examples of my study schedules from the past three years."

Phlegmatics

People of this type tend to be quieter, loving, caring, and people-pleasing. As introverts, they prefer small groups and talking deeply with just one or two people at a time. They dislike the tension that disagreements cause. In order to prevent discord, they may be unwilling to commit to either side of contentious issues and so can come across as unreliable.

Example from Korea: "My elder brother, who is a pastor, is very gentle with people; he always listens and avoids getting into arguments. When there's unrest, he's the one who tries to bring calm and soothing words."

Sanguines

These people are very outgoing and lively and like to be the center of attention. They like to have fun and light up the room by their extrovert presence in social settings, and this achieves their aim of being the center of attention. They will talk to anyone and everyone rather than be alone amongst people because being alone drains them. They like variety and may start projects but not complete what they started. They tend to have a short attention span, and this can cause unhelpful disruption to others in formal or serious settings.

Example of a Malaysian Indian: From a lecturer's report about a class student: "He likes to talk a lot and makes jokes. He wants the class break times to start and then extends the breaks as long as possible chit-chatting with people. He doesn't seem to want to read beyond the absolute minimum requirement and writes as little as possible too."

In contrast:

> **Example of a mature Filipina as shared in her memorial service:** "She was a lovely lady and a magnet who attracted people to her wherever she went. She would talk to anyone and everyone. Even when she was unwell and becoming very frail, she would still go and find the young people and church youth and encourage them to stand firm in their spiritual walks."

Analysis and Developments

As we can see from the above descriptions, choleric people and sanguine people tend to be extroverts, while melancholic people and phlegmatic people tend to be introverts. Both cholerics and melancholics tend to be more task oriented, while sanguines and phlegmatics tend to be more people oriented or relationship oriented. Similarly, the Myers-Briggs schema includes four different pairings of which the first, I/E, also questions a person's orientation in terms of introversion or extraversion. The Myers-Briggs second pairing is T/F for thinking versus feeling. For simplification purposes, we can take T as mirroring task orientation and F equating to people orientation, with thinkers largely using functions of the mind to process information in comparison to their counterparts processing information largely via emotion and feelings. Again, these are not merely dichotomistic designations but also recognize that individuals function at different degrees of thinking or feeling orientation and task or people orientation.

A number of authors have published materials relating to this proposal of four basic personality or temperament types but, in the analysis process, used different terms to present what are essentially the same concepts and personality attributes.[3] LaHaye (1993), for instance, emphasizes the aspect of understanding strengths and weaknesses associated with the four personality types so as to achieve Christian spiritual growth. To this end, he offers that we can expect each person to have a major and minor personality type. Smalley and Trent also distinguish between introverts and extroverts

---

3. See, for instance, Brinkman and Kirschner (1994; 2002), Phillips (1989), LaHaye (1993), Smalley and Trent (1990), and the DiSC model, which is used in secular management training as a leadership and teambuilding tool. It has its foundations in Marston (1928) to show leadership/teamwork participation styles of either Dominance (Choleric), Influence (Sanguine), Steadiness (Phlegmatic), or Compliance (Melancholic).

as well as task-oriented and people-oriented people, and like LaHaye, they recommend that each person has a major type and minor type, with the latter possibly also being a combination of the remaining types.

From this perspective we can, theoretically, see that a person who is 80 percent choleric with choleric as the major personality type, and 20 percent melancholic with melancholic as the minor personality type, could be expected to act and react differently to someone who is 65 percent choleric and 35 percent melancholic even though both people have the same major and minor personality types.[4] In the face of an unexpected crisis, the former would likely be more demonstrative and commanding in dealing with the crisis-related tasks than the latter, whereas a person who is 80 percent phlegmatic and 20 percent choleric would, as we will see, have little difficulty giving way to both of them.

My four-types personality assessment tool, not unlike Trent and Smalley's approach with character trait descriptions, can be found in appendix 1.[5]

---

4. Assigning a percentage figure is, of course, not measurable in practical terms but is used here to illustrate the point being made. Note that the potential for variation in percentage tendency of any of the major or minor personality types' characteristics is also immeasurable and so gives us a helpful clue to how it is that we are all individually and wonderfully made with no two people the same (i.e., even identical twins have different personality traits).

5. The Smalley Institute Personality Test, which aligns the four personality types with different animals, is available in a vastly extended form as Gary Smalley and Dr. John Trent's Personality Inventory from https://www.nacada.ksu.edu/Portals/0/CandIGDivision/documents/2014AC%20-%20Smalley%20Personality%20Inventory.pdf.

The charts in appendix 1 are a slight modification of those found in D-Davidson (2018, 185–86). For readers more familiar with the Myers-Briggs assessment and analysis tool (Myers, 1962), I suggest that the four major personality types are largely covered by the I/E (Introversion/Extraversion) and T/F categories (with F equating to people orientation and T to task orientation), whilst the N/S pair (ways of processing information) might be seen to be rather more related to cognitive perceptions of reality than personality, but I do also recognize that there is additional sophistication offered by the J/P pair wherein J might be described as denoting desire for order and closure, whereas P runs to the contrary. In relation to the four types schema, extrovert J describes task-completing leader-types, introvert J could be a subset of order-desiring melancholics; extrovert P could be a sanguine subset, with introvert P as a subset of phlegmatics. Hence the four types can be applied to the vast majority of people, with the Myers-Briggs schema offering the extra sophistication needed for those who nonetheless don't quite fit the basic four (e.g. they would, perhaps, be covered by any of introvert or extrovert TP or FJ). This could also be where the N/S distinction might come to the fore. Certainly, a literature review will show that the sixteen Myers-Briggs pairings, based on Jungian psychology, can be found represented in studies of multiple Western and non-Western cultures, thus suggesting the degree of universality of personality attributes proposed by Jung. This negates the view of Bennett (2004, 67), who proposes that the assumption that personality factors are universal, is merely an aspect of the minimization stage of attaining intercultural competence. I also acknowledge that the Big Five personalities schema, developed since the 1960s, appears to have met with much success. See McCrae and John (1992) for

To assess yourself, be prayerful and honest. Tick only the characteristics in the appendix 1 charts that really do apply to you and not the characteristics that you would like to have or prefer to think others see in you. Major personality type lines up with the highest score whilst minor personality type lines up with the next highest score and may be a combination of the other types where there are equal scores. If you have equal highest scores for two (or more) personality types, ask yourself whether you are more extrovert or more introvert and/or whether you are mostly more task oriented or people oriented. Get someone who knows you well to assess your scores. Be sure to score your weaknesses too as this can also alert you to areas that you did not realize might be weaknesses or temptation areas for you. Those previously unrecognized weaknesses might be hindering effective communication.

Some other helpful differentiating aspects have been described by Brinkman and Kirschner (2002, 15–18). They describe the four different personality types in terms of four intentions or desires:

a. Task-oriented leaders wanting to achieve multiple goals as efficiently as possible are cholerics whose intention is to complete each task.

b. Those who take their time as they pay careful attention to detail are melancholics, and their intention is to get the task done right.

c. Those who like to be the centre of attention and needed by others are sanguines whose desire is to be appreciated by people.

d. People-oriented carers who seek to please others are phlegmatics, and their desire is to get along with people.

To avoid unnecessary stress in relationships, Brinkman and Kirschner suggest: "Priority of these intents can shift moment to moment" (16). Moreover, "Behavior changes according to intent, based on the top priority in any moment of time. We all have the ability to operate out of all four intents. To communicate effectively with other people, you must have some understanding of what matters most to them" (21–22).

---

a helpful review. Nonetheless, I suggest that some of the aspects, such as agreeableness, neuroticism, and openness to experience, do not sufficiently allow for the change in outlook that comes with increasing adult maturity, let alone increasing spiritual maturity. See too Yang and Bond (1990) for incompatibilities of the Big Five schema with Chinese language.

Melancholic	Choleric
Introvert	Extrovert
Task-oriented	Task-oriented
Intention: Get the task *done right*	Intention: Get each task *done*
Phlegmatic	**Sanguine**
Introvert	Extrovert
People-oriented	People-oriented
Desire: *Get along* with people	Desire: Be *appreciated* by people

Figure 5.1 The Four Major Personality Types in Diagrammatic Form

Personality Types and Communication

How can we communicate effectively with people of the different major personality types when we are working on something together and in an established relationship that is beyond our control? Remember that God has allowed us to engage with each of those people for purposes that may be beyond our understanding. The experience may also help us grow in adult maturity as we seek God's leading to engage with others of differing personalities from various cultures, including our own. Personality types are supracultural. Regardless of cultural expectations for what makes for appropriate behavior, people with each major and minor personality type have similar desires and intentions even from and within different cultures' behavioral standards.

For cholerics, we need to be concise, to the point, and aware that completing the task is the priority, so focus on how we are achieving that. For melancholics, we need to attend to details and get across that we are aware of the possible options but provide evidence to support our approach to the task. For sanguines, we need to give them a sense of being appreciated, which can involve asking for their advice as we present what we are working on and communicating appreciation for their contributions. For phlegmatics, who want us all to get along well, we can communicate in a way that cares for them and their feelings as we focus on the positive effects of the project and refer to the difficulties in a way that shows people are nonetheless working well together.[6]

---

6. This paragraph provides my extension of some suggestions from Brinkman and Kirschner (49).

Major Personality Types in Combination with Minor Personality Types

We have looked at the major sides of personalities, but now let's look at the major side in combination with the minor side. It might seem strange to suggest that someone can have, for instance, a major introvert personality type and minor extrovert type when the two concepts appear to be incompatible opposites. Consider a major introvert melancholic who carefully compiles material to present at a meeting. If his minor personality type is choleric, then when the time for the meeting comes, he will feel comfortable about playing the extrovert role—especially as there will be a limit to the time he needs to take up the extrovert role. Once the presentation and discussions are completed (and as a choleric, he would like that to happen without any unnecessary time wasting), he will then revert to the major introvert type in order to refresh again. The degree to which he will be comfortable in the extrovert role will depend on his degree of introversion in relation to extraversion, or degree of major personality type in relation to minor personality type. The person who is, for instance, 60 percent introvert and 40 percent extrovert will find it less demanding to take up the extrovert role than a person who is, say, 80 percent introvert and 20 percent extrovert. Or consider someone who is 60 percent melancholic and 40 percent phlegmatic who is married to someone who is 55 percent melancholic and 45 percent choleric. They have the melancholic major in common, which will increase the potential for a harmonious relationship. The disharmony is likely to come when the minor (choleric) extrovert side sees it appropriate to spend time with a bigger group of people while the minor phlegmatic would prefer social activities involving only a few people.

When we are aware of our own major and minor personality types, along with our strengths and weaknesses, we can better understand when and why we feel uncomfortable and even frustrated with others or with the situation at hand. In courtship and marriage, it is well recognized that opposites attract, but after some time together, the interesting difference that was the catalyst for the growth of the relationship can eventually become annoying and even a source of frustration. Introverts can become frustrated with extroverts when their desire for space and time to refresh is undermined. Similarly, extroverts can get frustrated when their desire to refresh with others is undermined. When we are building friendships with respondents, we need to be especially sensitive to introvert and extrovert needs and desires if we are to see the relationship deepen.

Example of a phlegmatic melancholic from Japan: "My wife is very extroverted, and after we'd been married for some months, I felt like I just wanted to leave because I needed space. I'd try and plan ahead so I could be going somewhere else before one of her big crowds of girlfriends arrived."

Example of a melancholic choleric from Canada: "I'd get so annoyed and argue because my husband always wanted to have his friends come around. I don't mind lots of people coming sometimes, but I like some quiet too, and also they'd make the house so untidy. I always tidy it if people visit, but then I'd have to spend even longer retidying it after his friends came."

Example of a sanguine phlegmatic from the Philippines: "I find those small-group 'introduce yourself' activities frustrating when people don't want to say anything, and you're all just sitting there waiting for them to say something. I like to throw in a question to help them out."

Example of a melancholic phlegmatic from Mexico: "I find those small-group 'introduce yourself' activities frustrating when people jump in and insist you have to say something straight away. They say things like, 'Oh, just tell us whatever makes you happy.' Is it that they plan their speech faster than everyone else? Or have they already got it planned ahead? And, if so, do they even mean what they say because it's obviously not spontaneous? Is it really who they are or just what they want others to see? Anyway, I'd rather get to know people one-to-one and ask God to lead me to be with the right people for his purposes."

Example of a choleric phlegmatic from Hong Kong: "It annoys me when people don't just get on and do the obvious thing. Endlessly discussing what needs doing and holding off doing it is just a waste of time, but I'm not always choleric enough just to say that outright even though mostly I'd like to!"

> **Important principle:** Secular business management urges leaders to play to their strengths, but as Christians with both strengths and weaknesses, we cannot afford to just play to our strengths if we want to grow spiritually. Secular business managers might prefer to deny their weak areas, try to cover them up, or have others take roles that will cover the lack, but Christians help neither ourselves nor others if we do that. The weak areas due to the old self with its sinful nature will eventually slow us down and then stop our spiritual growth if we don't face up to them.

When people score themselves using the personality types' list of characteristics, less spiritually mature Christians and those with lesser adult maturity often tend to pay less attention to which weaknesses apply to them. Perhaps they are in denial due to pride, or they are truly unaware that their lives show those weaknesses. That is why it is a good idea to have someone who knows them well also provide an objective perspective on whether the characteristics they chose are realistic and which characteristics may have been omitted. This can be for characteristics related to both strengths and weaknesses. Having both husband and wife score themselves and then assess each other's results can be very revealing and even show where and why there are conflict patterns in their relationship. Similarly, for couples preparing for marriage, scoring themselves on the personality types and seeing each other's results can help them better understand each other and be prepared for areas of potential conflict in future. The same is true if groups of people working or ministering together (or intending to) score themselves so that they might become aware of how personality features, both strengths and weaknesses, can help or hinder the effectiveness of communication. This can have great benefit for communication amongst members of both monocultural and multiple-culture groups.

PREVENTING UNNECESSARY CONFLICT
AND DEALING WITH CONFLICT DUE
TO PERSONALITY DIFFERENCES

We had an initial look at task orientation and people orientation in relation to bigger picture cultural preferences in chapter 3 and saw how this major difference can affect our relationships with people whose preference is different from our own. We then saw that the task versus people orientation was not merely due to cultural background and associated worldview beliefs but also can be due to personality. Like the preferences associated with introversion and extraversion, preferences for task orientation and people orientation have the potential to cause major conflict.[7] Phillips (1989, 36–37) suggests keeping the following points in mind to prevent or reduce unnecessary conflict:

Task-oriented people:
  + tend to let their thinking rule
  + control their emotions
  + feel best when achieving a task
  + prioritize tasks ahead of relationships
But, if you are so involved with tasks that people can't get to know you or people don't like you, you create *tension* that brings mistrust and conflict. Others are likely to see you as non-caring.

People-oriented (relationship-oriented) people:
  + tend to let their feelings rule
  + they easily express their emotions
  + feel best when accepted by others
  + prioritize relationships ahead of tasks
But, if you are so involved with people that you don't accomplish any tasks, you may well be seen as shallow, unreliable, and even as just plain lazy!

By now we should be able to see why personality differences can so easily cause stress and conflict. When someone fails to recognize or ignores another person's mental or emotional priorities, the result is tension and insecurity.

Important principle: Both melancholic women and melancholic men may be driven to achieve an impossible level of perfection in completing tasks because, as for the characteristics of any of the personality types, a strength pushed to an unhealthy extreme then becomes a weakness.

---

7. Parts of this section draw from D-Davidson (2018, 71–73). See also De Dreu and Weingart (2003) for a meta-analysis of the effects of task versus relationship priorities on team relationships, and Perkins (2000, 238) for the effects on Western versus Chinese approaches to business transactions.

PRINCIPLES FOR ADJUSTING OUR COMMUNICATION SO AS TO HELP KEEP RELATIONSHIPS INTACT

We believe that God has wonderfully created every individual, and we can see the multiple unique variations in relation to each one's degree of the four personality types. All of our strengths and weakness can be vessels for God's glory through our communications as we are sensitive to his leading and as we note the following principles:

1. Choleric men may be so used to presenting themselves as the archetypal picture of indomitable strength that their exuberant desire to win in light of the possibility of failure can actually evoke a subconsciously fear-driven intensity in their desire to succeed. This can result in undermining the dignity of others as they become fodder for the seemingly emotionless and machinelike choleric. Be aware that the result of a sense of being dominated, manipulated, or controlled can't help but mark the relationship with wary dislike.

2. Women are often considered to be more emotional than men, so could it be that choleric women are subconsciously suppressing their emotions to maintain a strong appearance? Be aware that failure to recognize the discomfort that this seeming lack of empathy might cause others can result in relationships that are lukewarm and lacking in trust.

3. Melancholics do well to recognize the weakness of seeking to attain to perfectionist impossibilities and aim for realistic possibilities in which they can take pride in having done their best.

4. Task-oriented people (melancholics and cholerics) do well to intentionally practice trying to detect and notice the emotions of others during conversations and interactions. In addition, it can be helpful for them to stop and ask, "How would I feel if I were living in that person's or those peoples' perspectives?" Learning to balance the desire to achieve a task whilst also considering being gracious about the emotional responses of others can also be key to the task-oriented person also becoming more sensitive to the deeply submerged emotional side of their own nature.

5. All of us have both mental and emotional faculties, and learning to use both can be important for developing the healthy adult maturity, which brings out not only God's best in us but also the

best in others in a nonmanipulative, unconditionally loving way. For people-oriented phlegmatics and sanguines, an intentional attention beyond the immediacies of emotional response can go a long way to developing a thoughtful, rather than merely emotional, response to situations and relationships.

6. Phlegmatics do well to ask themselves, "Why am I feeling what I'm feeling, and how can I translate that into words that will be receivable by those I seem to be having conflict with?"
7. Sanguines do well to ask themselves, "Is it appropriate for me to be the center of attention right now?" and to carefully think through the implications for alternative actions and behaviors.

DEALING WITH THE DIFFICULT BEHAVIORS ASSOCIATED WITH EACH MAJOR PERSONALITY TYPE

What happens when communications seem to fail between individuals and/or groups of people so that tensions rise to boiling point and beyond? Phillips (1989, 87–88) describes how we are likely to respond at the height of such tensions in what he refers to as "back against the wall responses." He refers to those times when we are so overwhelmed by discomfort that it feels as though we have been pushed into a position from which we cannot extricate ourselves, which in turn provokes a negative aggressive or passive aggressive response. These responses manifest in various ways depending on personality type: major cholerics tend to become even more dominating, melancholics tend to withdraw, phlegmatics tend to give in, and sanguines tend to attack emotionally.

Brinkman and Kirschner (1994, 24–30) similarly describe the difficult behaviors that tend to emerge in conflict:

- The choleric wants to get the task done. So when their "back is against the wall," they become more controlling than ever because their aim is to try to take over and get their demands and directions obeyed. In order to achieve this they become *tanks*, *snipers*, and/or *know-it-alls*.
- The melancholic wants the task to be done right, not merely finished in a rush or poorly completed, so they become more perfectionist than ever. They will speak out every flaw and every possibility of potential error or negative consequence. In doing this they become *whiners*, *"no" people*, and/or *nothing people*.

- The phlegmatic, who wants to get along with people but realizes this just isn't happening, becomes more approval seeking and will sacrifice their personal needs to please others as best as they possibly can. To achieve this end they become *"yes" people, "maybe" people,* and/or *nothing people.*
- The sanguine, whose desperate desire is to be the center of attention and appreciated by people, becomes even more attention getting to force others to notice them. To reinstate themselves they become *grenades, malicious-humor snipers,* and/or *think-they-know-it-alls.*

We can combine material from Phillips (1989, 97ff.) and Brinkman and Kirschner (2002, 67–174) to look at how to communicate and interact with people when they come under pressure and act out these difficult behaviors.

Cholerics

Cholerics tend to dominate but respect those who stand up to them; when they are acting like tanks that impersonally roll over and crush anything in their way, don't back down. Instead, command their respect by standing up to them. Whatever your major personality type, communicating with courtesy while projecting a domination-resisting strength reduces the seeming invincibility of the choleric. When cholerics go into know-it-all mode and try to dominate through lengthy, well-vocalized arguments, you must talk facts that show your knowledge is equal and be assertive but not aggressive.

When cholerics become snipers, they will try to control you through embarrassing and humiliating you. Snipers, like rifle-wielding, single-shot marksmen in hiding, purposefully make unreasonable statements and sarcastic remarks in the moments when they recognize that you are most vulnerable. To counter this behavior, shift the discussion so as to get their underlying grievances to the surface and offer receivable alternatives for resolving whatever issue is at stake. Brinkman and Kirschner (74) urge that if you made a mistake, and that has been the catalyst for the choleric's dominating behavior, "admit the mistake, say what you've learned and what you'll do different next time," but absolutely don't grovel!

Melancholics

Under back-against-the-wall pressure, melancholics tend to withdraw. They need to be given space and time to think through the issues and gather the information they need so that they can make informed decisions with a degree of confidence. Communicate respect, and even if it seems superfluous to you, be prepared to fully discuss details. When they act as whiners and moan about all the negative implications and possibilities from past, present, and their projection of the future, or they become "no" people, who reject most or all of the options presented, encourage them to change perspective by becoming problem solvers. Communicate in a way that affirms they *can* be part of an excellent solution because they naturally have high standards. This affirmation helps melancholics feel useful and motivated to get involved.

When melancholics become nothing people and refuse to get involved any further, it is likely to be the impossible desire for unachievable perfectionism that stops them from producing. If they can't bring out the absolute best, then, from their perspective, producing nothing is the best option, so they won't do anything. In this case, acknowledge that there's no perfect decisions and that mistakes are helpful if we learn from them. In the face of extreme refusal to get involved, show them the negative consequences that might come about if they don't engage. Be sensitive to what kind of motivation will help them come out of "nothing" mode. Might they lose their role, the possibilities of promotion, or even their job? Encourage them to think through the potential negative consequences, but be sure to avoid bridge-burning threats. Instead, build in means by which they can quietly become engaged again—for instance, by researching to provide useful information or by locating other beneficial resources.

Phlegmatics

When phlegmatics' backs are against the wall, they tend to give in or follow a passive-aggressive tack by becoming "yes" people, who appear to agree but never deliver what they agreed to produce. Despite the frustration this behavior can cause, when it happens, communicate in a way that affirms them for who they are—people with hopes and desires and needs. Gently encourage them that their views are important and that being in disagreement doesn't equal dislike. When they become "yes" people, help them plan and commit to a specific task or a series of small, manageable tasks. When phlegmatics become "maybe" people, they are refusing to commit either way by neither completely refusing nor meaningfully agreeing. Effective communication acknowledges that there are no perfect decisions and that mistakes or poor decisions can be a means of learning for everyone. Help phlegmatics see the benefits of thinking and acting decisively and how it can be key for them to get along with others. When they become nothing people, who, like melancholics, are no longer willing to produce anything, persuade them to talk about their feelings and underlying anxieties by asking open-ended questions. If they won't respond, showing them the potential negative consequences may be a drastic last option. Although it will be painful for them, this last option can also be applied to overcome their nonproductive "yes" or "maybe" behaviors. A useful motivation for change can come by showing how the negative consequences affect relationships so that getting along with people becomes even harder, whereas positive change can strengthen those relationships.

Sanguines

When sanguines are in that back-against-the-wall place of no escape, they tend to attack emotionally. They become a grenade, suddenly exploding with an attention-catching outpouring of emotion-loaded words and accusations—effectively an adult tantrum. When it happens, don't react to their emotions by trying to speak rationally or defensively. Wait for the sanguine to cool down so that you don't get drawn into an emotionally draining and fruitless argument. The cool-down period might be hours or days, but jumping in too soon just reignites the embers. When sanguines become malicious-humor snipers, they'll come across as seeming to make funny, laughter-provoking remarks, even amidst serious discussions, but the remarks aim to bring down the adversary via embarrassment or humiliation and to get the sanguine back into the center of attention. When this happens, ask questions like: How is what you said relevant? What do you really mean? Try to bring their underlying grievances to the surface by asking questions like: Is there something important that we've missed? Is there something causing you to feel uncomfortable and how can we help you? It is vital to get the underlying grievances aired so that they can be addressed. In the scenario where sanguines project the think-they-know-it-all mode, they suggest all kinds of possibilities—some, or even most, of which are highly improbable or completely untrue. The force and enthusiasm of the sanguine personality can convince and persuade others of even the most ridiculous notions. In that case you must communicate reality by offering comments that point away from the incorrect notions such as "But I heard/read/saw that . . ." At the same time, be sure to clearly affirm the sanguine and appreciate them for the contributions they have made and that they can still make.

Devotional comment: Do peoples' personalities and temperaments change over the years? Perhaps our basic underlying personality preferences don't change, but the expressions of our temperament have the potential to change for God's glory when our hearts desire to live in Christ in ways that please God. Perhaps it is not so much that our underlying personalities change but that the way we express them becomes more Christlike as we submit to him and walk in step with the Spirit. As we increasingly—and consistently—make choices to submit our preferred will to Christ, his strength can be made perfect in our weakness in a way that glorifies him because those who have known us over the years will know that the better, more loving choices have not come from our preferred way of being and doing but because of the presence of Christ within us. That's also why, no matter how entrenched a sinful way of being or doing seems to be, there is always hope for change as we cling to the one who is our change-maker and as we thirst for deeper intimacy with him so that he then lives out through our weaknesses. Are those weak areas culturally influenced? Living in a changed, countercultural, loving, caring, Christlike manner can be a fruit-bearing witness to those of our background culture as well as to those of other cultures.

CONCLUSION

We have looked at some of the basic building blocks of personality and temperament that influence people's priorities and perceptions. We have seen how conflict can arise from personality differences and have observed principles for preventing conflict and dealing with preferences from the perspective of adult maturity. This is all part of our growth in adult maturity as well as into the spiritual growth and Christlikeness that can allow us to be the vessels for the deepening of cross-cultural relationships into intercultural relationships.

QUESTIONS FOR REFLECTION
AND DISCUSSION

1. In the "As It Happened" scenario at the start of the chapter, the two people (who are real, living intercultural missionaries) have the same major personality type in common but different minor personality

types. Which major personality type do they have in common? What do you think their different minor personality types are? What evidence did you draw upon?

2. A respondent asks you, "How do you love God?" How might you best communicate your response according to whether the respondent's major personality type is choleric, sanguine, phlegmatic, or melancholic? How would you vary the presentation of your answer if your respondent is major choleric and minor melancholic, major melancholic and minor sanguine, major sanguine and minor phlegmatic, or major phlegmatic and minor choleric?

3. Consider the ministry roles of Ephesians 4:11–12 in which "Christ himself gave the apostles, the prophets, the evangelists, the pastors and teachers, to equip his people for works of service, so that the body of Christ may be built up." Which major personality types, with their associated God-given natural abilities, might also be the preparation ground for the spiritual roles in ministry of the Ephesians verses?

4. When you assessed your personality according to the characteristics in appendix 1, which strengths were you already aware of, and which strengths did you or others notice in you that you had not been as aware of? Similarly, which weaknesses were you able to recognize, and which weaknesses are you now also aware of that have the potential to hinder effective communication or slow your spiritual growth? What do you sense that God has specifically taught you through this chapter of the book?

CHAPTER 6

Communication and Conflict Due to Cultural Differences

As It Happened: A short-term monocultural missions team goes to visit a pastor in a small town in Thailand. The team leader advises them that the pastor will expect them to remove their shoes and leave them by the door outside the building before they come inside.

Team member 1: But I have very big feet. If my shoes get mislaid, I won't be able to buy any that fit. Can I just take them off but bring them inside?

Team leader: No. That wouldn't be appropriate. You'll just have to trust God and leave your shoes outside like everyone else.

Team member 1: But I don't want to lose them. What if I bring them inside but put them in a plastic bag?

Team member 2: You shouldn't be using plastic bags because they are bad for the environment.

Team member 1: I have a paper bag I could use.

Team member 3: That's terrible. Don't you care about saving the trees?

Team member 1: But I don't want to lose my shoes because they are the only pair I came here with! I'll wrap them in my shirt then.

Team leader: No, that's not a good idea. You can't visit the pastor without a shirt on. Haven't you noticed that even poorer people in Thailand dress very tidily? We don't want to be an embarrassment to ourselves or the pastor. You should trust God and keep your shirt on.

INTRODUCTION

Isn't it frustrating when we're supposed to be united in teamwork, but peoples' personalities and priorities create a barrier to maintaining unity?

The challenge and frustrations can loom even larger when we engage with people of other cultures. When living and working among people of other cultures, cross-cultural conflict is inevitable—especially if we hope to engage with local people beyond a merely superficial level and build intercultural relationships. While conflict can be distressing, how we handle and resolve it can be the means of deeper mutual acceptance and caring transparency. Transparency is an important key to building trust, and without trust, relationships are unlikely to move beyond being merely cross-cultural.[1]

In relation to cross-cultural conflict, we also need to recognize that cultural values are concerned with "the moral principles and standards" for what could be regarded as adequate and inadequate thinking and behavior (Kirk 2000, 87). However, every culture has sins or weaknesses that conflict with the values encouraged in the Bible because every culture has common sinful aspects (e.g., deceit and judgmentalism) as well as culture-specific sinful aspects as compared with the core values of the kingdom of God. Conflict is not merely the result of cross-cultural dissonance but is also fueled by sinful tendencies and by behaviors and attitudes devoid of caring love.

We've seen the potential for poorly handled personality differences to cause conflict, particularly in relation to personality weaknesses. In this chapter we turn to other causes of conflict, including those that might be in play in any relationship and those that are caused specifically by inattention to different cultural priorities. In chapters 3 and 4 we saw how difficulties can arise when we misunderstand the rules about how cultures function and the rules the members of a different society are expected to follow in relation to one another. Now in chapter 6, we return to some of these, highlighting different ways conflict might be responded to. We then draw out some pointers and principles for heightening communication in a way that might reduce the potency of conflicts, resolve cross-cultural conflicts, and be the catalyst for these relationships to become intercultural.

---

1. Conflict is not only limited to cross-cultural engagements with local people. It also occurs amongst fellow Christian communicators. There can be an extent to which Christian communicators in cross-cultural ministry seem to project a greater tolerance for difficulties with those they are reaching out to in contrast to far higher expectations of what makes for "reasonable behavior" from their colleagues. See Turney (2013) for thoughts on increasing missionary longevity, albeit written from his North American perspective.

TYPICAL CAUSES OF CONFLICT

Conflict often occurs because one or both parties feel insecure.[2] We might even find ourselves incorrectly interpreting what we hear or see to be what we want to hear or see in order to prevent feelings of insecurity.

Discomfort manifests as either:

- Anger or kinds of destructive behavior that are actively expressed or
- Acts of passive aggression—for instance, withdrawal or lack of cooperation

> **Important principle:** With any conflict, whether in monocultural, cross-cultural, or intercultural relationships, a good deal of unnecessary further trauma can be prevented if we look to deal with the roots of problems and not merely just deal with symptoms.

Whilst differing cultural priorities, values, and goals have great potential to cause conflict, Elmer (2002, 180) advises: "Differences are not the problem when working cross-culturally. The way these differences are expressed is the problem. . . . If you show me respect in a way I am not accustomed to or not expecting, I will consider you disrespectful. The misunderstanding comes not from the value itself but in how it is demonstrated in day-to-day living." Similarly, misunderstanding any of our respondents' cultural rules related to the vehicles for communication discussed in chapter 2 (i.e., use of symbols, kinesics, haptics, proxemics, germane human/physical characteristics, use of common articles, paralanguage, or contexting) has the potential to cause conflict. The better we know our respondents and the people God has us living among, the better we can construct ways of reducing the potential for unnecessary conflict.

Misunderstanding of Cultural Rules
Misunderstanding of Symbols Used

In chapter 2, we saw how words, commonly used items, and gestures are some of the symbols people use to communicate meaning. We have already

---

2. Parts of this chapter are edited versions of material from D-Davidson (2018, 73–81).

looked at the potential for misunderstanding due to differing understanding of similar verbal and written terms as well as the potential for inaccurate decoding of gestures if the culture of both parties is not included in the decoding process. Combining symbols increases not only the potential for misunderstanding of communication, but misunderstanding that results in conflict.

Symbols example from a Colombian married to a Pakistani: "There is an obvious language barrier between us, especially with expressions which have different meanings in our cultures. For example, when we were in Colombia, he sometimes referred to my niece, who was nine months old, using the term 'monkey.' It is a common expression of love in Pakistan to call the kids 'monkey.' However, in Colombia it is an offensive expression, not a loving expression, to call kids 'monkey'!"

Symbols example of a Filipino and Westerner: "One time, a volunteer from the West was out with a Filipino volunteer in the evening. This white volunteer saw a *balut* (partially developed duck egg) vendor and bought *balut* from this old [Filipino] man. Thinking that he was helping him because he was old and out in the evening selling only a basket of *balut*, the volunteer handed him a 1,000 Pesos note [instead of the 15 Pesos price], to which the *balut* vendor took offence. He walked away angry from this volunteer because the volunteer seemed to have assumed that the vendor was poor and needy, which insulted the vendor."

Important principles: Apart from having the aim of preventing unnecessary conflict, we must be careful that any well-intentioned kindnesses do not undermine dignity from the respondent's perspective. There is no place for undermining the dignity of another if we want to love with God's love. We must be equally careful not to sow seeds of superiority or those that initiate dependency. We can avoid these errors by taking time to build trusting relationships and asking open-ended sensitive questions of people from that cultural background and in the light of their "situational cultural specifics."[3]

---

3. See D-Davidson (2018, 109, 117–23) for more on contextualizing one's approach to outreach in relation to the phrase *situational cultural specifics*.

Misunderstanding Related to Kinesics, Haptics, and Proxemics

Effective communications reflect awareness of what is culturally appropriate in relation to nonverbal body language. When we lack sufficient understanding, we can cause not only misunderstanding by other parties but also unintended offence and frustration for one or both parties.

Author's kinesics example from Pakistan: Before departing for the short-term missionary program in Pakistan, I was advised that women should not make eye contact with men unless they are related either as family or by marriage. When I returned to the UK after the two-year term was over, I found engineering job interviews very difficult because it is expected that you make eye contact with the potential employer. I had to unlearn what had become a habit in Pakistan to function appropriately in the UK and prevent potential employers from mistaking my lack of eye contact as disinterest.

Kinesics example of a Columbian and Pakistani: "We did not understand that we have different gestures of communication. For example, my [Pakistani] husband always wants me to look at him while he is speaking to me. If he is speaking, and I do not look at him, he thinks that I am not listening to him, whereas I can do other things while talking to him."

Haptics example from Japan: "Some missions groups came to Japan, and one of their strategies was to go out and give *free hugs*—but Japanese people don't hug. We hug people who are very, very close to us, but we don't hug strangers. The result was a lot of very shocked and uncomfortable Japanese people who got away from the missions workers as fast as possible."

Proxemics example from Laos: "A Westerner bought two bus tickets to travel from Luang Prabang to Vientiane so she could put her backpack on the seat next to her. But along the way the driver picked up more passengers, and some sat on her extra seat, so she was very squashed by her backpack. But that's normal traveling in Laos."

Misunderstanding Due to Contexting and Paralanguage

We do well to consider carefully whether our respondent's culture uses more high-context or low-context communication and how it compares to ours. From communicating in relation to the Chinese behavior related to giving and receiving of gifts,[4] to the frustration of low-context direct speech seemingly not being taken seriously, culture-defined paralanguage can be a huge source of tension and conflict. As we aim to build caring and trusting intercultural relationships, it will help if we can learn to recognize low-context and high-context ways of being and doing regardless of the cultural setting.

Low-context example from Mongolia: "Mongolians are people who have a very direct character. This direct character means that we are very direct in speaking. When we want to tell something, we will just speak up directly without thinking. Sometimes, we just speak up without realizing we are hurting the people that we are talking to. The problem arises when people from other nationalities [who are from higher-context nations] come and have encounters with us and get offended by our directness."

Example of high-context and low-context clashes between Filipino and German: "Multiple times, there is a conflict in communication of how a certain worker must do his job. The [German] person in charge thinks he has given a clear goal with instructions. Since the [Filipino] worker is of the shame-honor and high-context culture, he simply complies with a 'Yes' and ends up not performing well. This frustrates the person-in charge, who comes from a culture that uses extremely low-context communication. This has a negative effect on the quality of work, so it affects everyone in the company, not just individuals' relationships."

Misinterpreted Implications

Even when we are aware of the differences and commonalities of preferences between people of different nations, cultures, and subcultures, we also need to consider the implications of those preferences from the perspective of both our own and others' cultures.

---

4. See Chu (2019, 214) where he offers that older Chinese pastors are accustomed to using higher context communication than their younger counterparts resulting in misunderstanding of communications and intergenerational conflict.

Example of students from Japan and Africa: "I shared a dormitory with people from other cultures at the international seminary. One lady from Africa wanted to use my laptop, so she just picked it up from my table space. I asked, 'What are you doing?' and she said, 'I want to use the laptop.' I was very shocked because, for Japanese people, our opinion and statements are very important. More importantly, we value personal space. This means, *What is mine is mine, and what is yours is yours.* Borrowing a pen, smartphones, or any other personal thing is actually not our practice. I thought she knew this, but it didn't work out in practice."

Example from China of misinterpreted implications of power distance: "I grew up used to respecting the teacher and not speaking out in class. In graduate level studies outside China, I was told I must think critically and take the initiative to interact with the teachers. But in that lower power distance environment, I was reprimanded and told it was okay to argue with the teacher, but I must still show respect. I had to learn to interact critically and argue politely without coming across as being rude and disrespectful."

Inappropriate Expectations

Conflict can occur in our cross-cultural endeavors when we have differing cultural expectations about what is appropriate in relation to gender and perceptions of relationship building.

Romantic relationship example of Pacific Islander and Filipina: "We had a volunteer from one of the Pacific islands. Before he came to our organization in the Philippines, he graduated from a discipleship training school [in the Philippines] and made a lot of friends there, both women and men. One of those, a woman, had a close connection with him; she considered him to be a confidant and boyfriend. But later on, when this volunteer was leaving, they ended up in a fight. The woman had assumed that he liked her since he was so nice to her, and very open, and had been treating her like a girlfriend. Her expectation was inappropriate because, just like most Pacific Islanders, he was like that to everyone. This guy was so confused and did not know what he had done wrong. He only made sense of the situation when we, here in the orphanage, who are Filipinos, helped him analyse and understand the situation."

Author's example of a Western couple and Pakistan: A dear couple had long wanted to go to Pakistan as missionaries, but their pastor would not endorse them. The husband's personality is melancholic and phlegmatic while the wife's personality is hugely sanguine and constantly outgoing. They minister together in Europe very effectively, but it looked as if she would not be able to live the kind of wifely submission that is expected in Pakistan, such as walking behind the husband and being quiet in public. Even if she were very careful in public, it would likely be impossibly difficult for her to sustain a lifestyle that just didn't fit her personality. Their pastor had been to Pakistan and knew something of the culture, so perhaps that's why he wouldn't approve of their going there as missionaries.

Patron-client relationships example of Chinese and Filipino: "We went by taxi to the town [in the Philippines] as a group of Chinese. We were told by the school what the price of a taxi should cost, so when the taxi driver asked for more, we did what we'd usually do in China: bargain with the driver. The problem was that the driver got very angry with us and was shouting as we started to get out of the taxi. The local people could see and hear it all, and it was quite frightening. I never bargained with drivers after that. Apparently they have some law which allows an extra amount to be added to the fare, and it's written on a notice in the taxi, but we didn't understand that at the time."

UNIVERSAL RESPONSES TO CONFLICT INFLUENCED BY BOTH CULTURAL AND PERSONALITY ATTRIBUTES

Thomas and Kilmann (1974) identified five ways for handling conflict:[5]

1. having a win/lose mindset
2. avoidance

---

5. Thomas and Kilmann (1974), cited in Elmer (1993, 34–43).

3. giving in
4. compromising
5. carefronting

Thomas and Kilmann suggested these approaches to conflict are used by Westerners, but as we move from building cross-cultural to intercultural relationships, we will discover that people from other cultures also use very similar approaches—particularly in relation to their individual personality or temperament. For instance, those with a choleric, task-oriented personality often tend to have a win/lose mindset because their aim is to complete the task. Non-communicator/avoidance approaches can especially be seen with melancholic personalities who need time to analyze issues before they are ready to commit. Phlegmatic personalities prefer not to engage in conflict at all so they will avoid communicating; they will also tend to just give in because they don't want to displease anyone. Choleric, phlegmatic, and sanguine personalities are more likely to be willing to compromise, whereas melancholic personalities' tendency for perfectionism makes them less willing to compromise on details.

Elmer (1993, 35–42) gives some suggestions for handling these approaches. I've modified these suggestions for coherency with the four major personality types:[6]

- **Win/Lose Mindset.** It is likely that cholerics have already decided that their view is correct, so they probably will push to win what they see as a battle. It can be helpful to ask the locals for their opinions and present views as a group because it is harder for a choleric to dominate a group in opposition. Aim for a resolution in which both sides benefit. Be aware that if something affecting the wider community is at stake, but the community members do not agree with you, then you have missed the point somewhere! As for negotiating with choleric personalities, be assertive but not aggressive, and pick your battles carefully. Which issues are really crucial, and which are not? Few decisions have life or death at stake!
- **Avoidance Mindset.** Conflict avoidance is not usually a good long-term solution to a current problem. However, if emotions are running high, strategic withdrawal may be the best short-term move.

---

6. We turn to Thomas and Kilmann's fifth approach, carefronting, later in the chapter.

It is never advisable to continue arguments with people wielding offensive weapons! Avoiding conflict if the potential consequences are dangerous is very wise (39). Similarly, in the face of irrational behavior and the potential for physical violence, there may be little point in arguing. Avoiding conflict can be a sign of wisdom and maturity, but, particularly with melancholics and phlegmatics, it can also be a sign of immaturity through unwillingness to discuss important issues or unwillingness to take responsibility in aspects of important issues. Conflict avoidance results in superficial relationships. If someone appears to be avoiding you, it can be helpful to request a third-party local to come alongside you and try to uncover why the person is avoiding communication. The issue may be something completely different than the one you want to resolve.

- **Giving In.** Giving in may be seen as a way of resolving the conflict and preserving relationships (which for phlegmatics is usually more important than the details of the conflict issue), but it can also mean their forfeiting of personal values and goals. Additionally, it can be a sign of adult immaturity with an unwillingness to develop one's own opinions. Communicating disagreement does not inevitably cause dislike. Aim to build caring relationships where mutual trust frees up the other to express personal values and opinions. For other issues, choose your battles carefully—if you give in on one issue, perhaps you can have your preference on the next one.

- **Compromise.** Is compromising beneficial for both parties or merely an approach that hides the potential for further conflict? Compromise is seen often in workforce-management, political, and global-economic negotiations. It goes for a win-win result but always at a cost to one or both parties. Although the dispute appears to be solved, one or both parties walk away with some aspect of their goals, values, and/or ideals undermined. Relationships may have been subtly damaged and a hidden desire for vengeance provoked.

Important principle: When it comes to compromise, we must know what aspects of our values, beliefs, and ideals are open to negotiation but hold on firmly to those that are nonnegotiable.

PRACTICAL POINTERS AND PRINCIPLES
FOR CONFLICT RESOLUTION WITH
HEALTHY LONG-TERM RESULTS

Conflict caused by different cultural perspectives can have unwelcome consequences when building relationships. However, here are some helpful insights for handling difficulties in a way that will not only reduce the potential for aggravating interpersonal discord but also help deepen the relationships.

1. As Far as You Can, Prevent Shame, Preserve Honor, and Prevent Unnecessary Loss of Face

Elmer (1993, 54) and others have long emphasized[7] the effectiveness of saving face for achieving both short-term and long-term conflict resolution results.[8] Elmer further notes that in our communication with others, we might cause shame without realizing it. For instance (Elmer 2002, 176–78), we can cause shame and loss of face by assigning blame to people either directly or indirectly and by directly pointing out errors or wrongdoings that people have committed. Another way to cause shame is to ask someone to be or do something that they cannot be or do but are embarrassed to admit their inability. An alternative approach would be to use indirect communication to express how, if possible, we would like to achieve a particular goal or become involved in a particular issue without suggesting that they help bring about your desired outcome. This offers the person the choice to follow up and spares them from losing face if they can't or don't wish to. If helping you get involved impinges on any of their patron-client relationships, for instance, they may need time to consider the implications and perhaps offer culturally acceptable alternatives that you had not considered.

Elmer (2002) notes that being imprudent or insensitive in comparing cultures, especially to your own, can cause shame, so it is better to

---

7. For instance, see Foster (1973, 178) and Dodd (1987, 76).

8. Note that Moreau et al. (2014, 273) advise that the idea of Christ enduring shame (Hebrews 12:1–3) can be a difficult concept for those whose worldview values maintaining honor by avoiding shame. They might question how being subject to shame can paradoxically also be the means of achieving honor. But being helped to negotiate this potential stumbling block to faith by "making this connection cognitively, affectively, and volitionally will be crucial for them" to be able to connect that Christ necessarily endured shame to obey his Father. In chapter 12 we will return to the importance of obedience to God in relation to communicating about personal spiritual growth. Note DeSilva (2009, 25), who writes that Jesus "endured temporary dishonor . . . in order to gain the place of greatest honor: a seat at the right hand of God (Hebrews 12:1–2)."

downplay negative differences. Similarly, directly refusing to help when you are plied with a request can imply that the other person is unworthy and so undermine their dignity and honor. To avoid communicating rejection, Elmer (178) urges that it would be better to indirectly offer that as much as we'd like to help, we are unable to at present, and should the situation change to make it possible, we will certainly let them know. A key means of preventing loss of face is by being careful to keep communications about conflict-causing behaviors or attitudes private.

Example from Guatemala: "Individuals don't get called out publicly for high praise in the workplace as it could be misconstrued as favoritism as well as loss of face for others. Also, you should deal with individuals privately if there are problems to prevent that person from losing face publicly. It's good to not just correct them but affirm them too."

2. Become Familiar with the Basics of Face-Negotiation Theory

Recognizing that Western business-world related conflict management and decision-making principles provided little interaction with the face issues of other cultures, Ting-Toomey of Hong Kong began developing principles in 1985 for understanding cross-cultural conflict in relation to face-negotiation theory (see Ting-Toomey and Kurogi 1998). Oetzel et al. (2001, 238)[9] suggest that face-negotiation theory provides means to "resolve a conflict, exacerbate a conflict, avoid a conflict, threaten or challenge another person, protect a person's image, etc." Ultimately, the goal of face-negotiation theory is that all parties involved in a conflict might maintain face. What helps or hinders conflict resolution is the degree to which each party desires the conflict to decrease and be resolved. Some cultures are more aware of the issue of "saving face" or "giving face" than others, but the desire to be treated with dignity is a universal condition— few psychologically healthy people derive satisfaction from the humiliation that comes from one's self-worth being undermined publicly or privately. In relation to this, Oetzel et al. advise that face-related goals are intertwined with "relational, and identity issues" (239). In cross-cultural negotiations,

---

9. Note that this study concerns a cross-cultural comparison of China, Germany, Japan, and the United States.

Ting-Toomey and Kurogi (1998, 199–200) advise us to be aware of the following three aspects of face:[10]

1. in relation to self and the desire to maintain a good or respected image before others
2. in relation to other or others with concern for their image not merely one's own
3. mutual face or concern for the overall appearance of the relationship projected by the interdependency of the parties

As we might expect, members of more individualist cultures are likely to place a greater emphasis on self-face (Oetzel et al. 2001, 241). On the other hand, more relationally oriented cultures have been correlated with maintaining a positive mutual face, or interdependent face (Markus and Kitayama 1991, 227). Oetzel and Ting-Toomey (2003, 604) also saw correlation between positive interdependent concerns and concern for the face of others. We might link these correlations with the face desires of members of more collectivist cultures who try, as far as possible, to maintain harmony amongst all members. Protection and maintenance of self-face was also linked with the win/lose approach to handling conflict, while those who tend to avoid conflict were linked to the intention to maintain the face of the other or others. But as we have seen, avoiding conflict, even for the most noble of reasons such as saving the face of another, is not necessarily going to ensure helpful or healthy long-term relationship building.

Despite the differing degrees of importance that cultures assign to preventing loss of self-face and the face of others, the rules are not always followed even in strong face-saving cultures. Whilst face-negotiation theory provides some helpful insights for cross-cultural interaction, we must also recognize limitations in that individuals or groups might still seek to save or maintain face at the expense of others even in collectivist cultures. As we have seen, the degree to which people follow these cultural rules can also be affected by personality. It can be helpful to be aware that when someone causes another person to lose face, as opposed to intentionally "giving face," they may be trying to protect another relationship, perhaps with a friend or colleague or another in-group member, or to protect the relationship with their boss or elders. Colleagues who see you as a competitor may feel no shame in causing you to lose face if they do so subtly and

---

10. For further developments with face and face-work, see Ting-Toomey (2017).

to their advantage. Others who have nothing to lose by causing you to lose face and feel rejected might include:

- people who just don't like you for whatever reason (such as jealousy or personality clashes)
- community members such as institutional officials and officials designated to protect society and impersonally maintain justice along with their administrative staff
- people who see you impersonally as an unwelcome figure who is neither to be entertained nor trusted.

We do well to note that wherever people are considered as "other" due to differences in worldview beliefs, cultural practices, and/or physical appearance, there is the potential for racism, and wherever racism goes unchallenged, cultural rules about saving face are likely to disappear. When we appear to be the maligned "other," remembering that our security lies in our identity in Christ will help us to resist the temptation to respond to the hurt of rejection with more hurt.

Important principle: Persevering with consistent courtesy to build relationships in the face of aggressive opposition is key to disarming hostility and showing others that you are not a threat to their sense of identity, security, or continuity.

Author's example from remote Northwest China: When Dr. Co and I moved to a remote North China community, we were the only foreigners who had ever lived there. We were also the only non-Chinese people that a majority of the locals had ever seen in person. Dr. Co's accent, when speaking Chinese, would give her away as being an outsider, and I could not disguise being non-Chinese. To our regret, elderly vegetable sellers in the one-day-per-week market initially refused to sell us produce and would rudely shout at us to go away. Each week, we continued to go to the particular stalls that we felt God was sending us to and would quietly greet the owners with words of blessing. Eventually, once these sellers realized we were not a threat, they happily set aside for us the fruit and vegetables that we usually bought and would discuss our backgrounds in relation to their families and lifestyles. We became fascinating friends with much to share about other ways of life. Despite my pale skin and non-Asian features, one elderly lady even asked me if I was Korean—such was her limited perception of life outside the locality. We were thrilled to have these opportunities to share about the joy and wonder of living in Christ for Christ's eternal purposes in that "unploughed ground."

Important principle: Despite the importance that is assigned to saving face, there may be times when allowing loss of face—and its accompanying shame—to occur can be a catalyst for growth in adult maturity and/or spiritual growth.

Author's example in rural China: One of Dr. Co's village-clinic trainees made a major error in inappropriately treating a patient with a dental tool. Dr. Co did not want to be deceitful about the extent of the problem and had to take over and complete what had now become an extremely difficult case. The trainee inevitably lost face before the patient and the other trainees who were observing the treatment. We gathered round and prayed for wisdom and skill for Dr. Co and peace for the patient. The trainee was relieved that she could pass the patient to Dr. Co and willingly acknowledged the mistake she had made. The trainee also acknowledged the need to be less casual and more careful, and she shared that God was challenging her gently to be less self-reliant and more prayerful when treating patients.

3. If Possible, Address a Group to Reprimand an Individual

When a problem occurs for which one person is responsible, addressing a group of people rather than homing in on the individual at fault can be doubly beneficial (Elmer 1993, 46). First, it prevents shaming the individual; second, it makes the wider group aware of the issue and the specifics of the unwelcome activity.

Author's example in the village clinic in rural China: Once the clinic was set up, we bought a refrigerator to preserve the clinic's treatment materials. It was the only refrigerator in the village. Typically, villagers would preserve meat by salting it and hanging it in a cool corner of their courtyard or inside their housing facility. Shortly after we installed the refrigerator, we discovered that someone had put meat in the refrigerator to preserve it. We suspected the meat belonged to the family of one of the clinic trainees, so we began using the lock mechanism on the refrigerator. We also posted a note on the door explaining that the clinic materials needed to be kept cool and uncontaminated and that there was insufficient room for nonclinical materials. Had one person been allowed to use the refrigerator for personal items, it would have been much harder to refuse its use to other senior clinic members. Posting a note addressing the entire clinic staff resolved the problem.

Important principle: When addressing a group of people face-to-face to reprimand an individual within the group, you must be careful not to sound aggressive or overly judgmental. Remember that you are likely to be addressing the full range of personalities and combinations of major and minor personality types. Communicate accordingly.

4. Express Your Feelings Passively to Disarm Hostility from Another

Rather than assigning blame through active aggression—"When you did X, I was really Y"—we can neutralize the tension by passively expressing: "I felt Y when X happened" (Elmer 1993, 47–48). With this wording, you avoid direct accusation. The other party may find it strange when you respond in this way, particularly if they are from a different culture, but they cannot deny or dismiss your feelings. Being able to control your emotions as you communicate will also help reduce tension.

Example expanding on the Colombian and Pakistani use of the term *monkey* mentioned above: Rather than the wife saying, for instance,

"When you called my baby niece *monkey,* I was really angry because you were very offensive in my culture," she could reduce the potential for her husband to be angry or defensive in response by saying something like, "I felt really hurt when my niece was called *monkey* because that's not considered a loving term in Colombian culture."

5. Nonjudgmental Indirectness Is Less Offensive Than Direct Confrontation

If possible, tell a story to indirectly highlight the principle that is causing conflict or talk generally rather than honing in on specifics (Elmer 1993, 50).

Author's examples from China: Whilst travelling in China, many Westerners learnt to make nonaggressive comments such as "people often don't like [or 'people are uncomfortable'] when people stare at them," or tell a story about someone having lost an item that was precious to them that they were requested to lend, to illustrate that "some people prefer not to lend expensive personal items such as their camera or communications devices."

6. Be Clear That You Are Criticizing an Issue/ Action/Idea, Not the Person

Many people can find this a difficult distinction to make and so cause unnecessary offence. Members of high-context communication cultures tend to see a person's being and doing as inseparable, so they prefer to communicate about culpability indirectly to reduce the loss of face that accompanies (to different degrees culture by culture) the assigning of blame for particular misdoings. In contrast, members of low-context communication cultures prefer to address conflict directly and immediately, as it is relatively easy for them to separate the person's doing from their being. They tend to view being indirect as a waste of time or as irresponsible, noncommittal behavior, but as we have already seen in several of these conflict resolution pointers, indirectness can be beneficial as it shows care in both high-context and low-context settings. As for the previous points, Elmer (1993, 49) suggests talking in a passive voice and in an indirect manner about the conflict-causing issue can help separate the issue from the person who did wrong and therefore prevent you from appearing to condemn the person.

Author's example from Pakistan: When my Asian teammates during my time of ministry in Pakistan deemed my British style of (bland) cooking unpalatable, it opened my eyes to the reality of other peoples' tastes and expectations. I asked God for inspiration about providing food that would be palatable. Low-context style, I didn't take it personally but just understood that I needed to change my approach to cooking for the team. I much later realized how poor my offerings must have previously been to have sparked such outrage in people who would normally address issues indirectly.

Author's example from Pakistan: We were all encouraged to learn enough Urdu to be able to share our salvation testimonies, but one of the Asian teammates was very passive in initiating language learning. She very happily agreed, instead, to devote herself to prayer as another important outreach activity. This, helpfully, put the focus on the doing of activity rather than on the language-lacking being of the person, whilst also affirming her to be a prayerful lady.

7. Prevent Ongoing or Future Concern by Setting Boundaries as Soon as Behavioral Issues Arise

Boundaries define the parameters for healthy relationships so that appropriate responsibility for oneself and in relation to others is owned without destructive coercion (see Cloud and Townsend 1992; 2017). This becomes even more important in cross-cultural settings where we need to pay attention to cultural boundary considerations.

Example of Latin American ministering in Indonesia: "I knew that before you speak at an organizational meeting you are supposed to acknowledge the presence of all the key people, but I also knew that I was expected to speak very briefly, so I didn't acknowledge every leader by name, just generally. Afterwards, an Indonesian colleague warned me that the leaders were not pleased because it appeared as though I did not respect them all. After learning about my mistake, I was very careful to acknowledge every leader at meetings that I spoke at after that."

8. Where Appropriate Use a Suitable Third-Party Mediator

Example from the Latin American worker in Indonesia: Notice how, in the previous example, the Indonesian colleague warned the Latin American that the leaders were not pleased with what they considered to be disrespectful behavior. The Indonesian colleague acted as a third-party mediator to express to the Latin American that the Indonesian leaders were displeased. This prevented a greater loss of face than if the leaders had directly addressed the Latin American, and it gave the Latin American an opportunity to ask questions and discover more about the culture without any tension from those who had been offended.

Important principle: When selecting a third-party mediator, choose carefully (Elmer 1993, 76). Choose someone who is trusted and respected by both the offender and the offended party. It is also important that a third-party mediator is not likely to gossip and can be trusted to be objective in mediating for both parties.

9. Take a One-Down Position

Elmer (1993, 80–98) describes this approach as projecting a degree of vulnerability to the other party so that it looks like you are the one facing all the difficulty. The aim is to elicit a mixture of sympathy or even empathy and concern from the other party so that they will take action to help resolve the dilemma. One way of using this approach is to indirectly advise that if some particular scenario happens (or doesn't happen), you are liable to lose face (e.g., with your spouse, boss, colleagues, etc.).

Author's example of taking a one-down position: After moving to a fourth area of ministry and teaching in several hospitals in a small city,

Dr. Co and I submitted our passports for the annual visa renewal. We were informed that there was a new quota of visas, and we would have to return periodically to the visa-processing center to check if our passports were ready. The journey to the visa-processing center was lengthy, and the travelling time cut into our work hours. After several unsuccessful visits, we were waiting behind the counter when a door opened and out came a higher-level official whom we had met some years earlier. I politely acknowledged him, thanked him for his help on a previous occasion, and expressed our need for help once more: we were unable to maximize serving the Chinese people in the hospitals because we kept having to return to the visa-processing center. This made us seem unreliable in the clinics. The higher-level official then urged the officer at the counter to prioritize our passports for immediate issue of the visa stamp. Mission accomplished with rejoicing!

10. Hone Skills of Flexibility in Communication

Ting-Toomey and Chung (2012, 199–203) advise that flexibility in cross-cultural conflict requires bringing several important skills into operation. These include comprehensive attention to the other party's communication through "attending mindfully with our ears, eyes, and a focused heart" (199), cultural empathy by listening to the other party with "cultural ears," and "using language to change the way each person defines or thinks about experiences and views the conflict situation" (201). Ting-Toomey and Chung urge adopting Molinsky's cross-cultural code-switching, which Molinsky (2007, 264) describes as "the act of purposefully modifying one's behavior in an interaction in a foreign setting in order to accommodate different cultural norms for appropriate behavior."

Example from direct and indirect communication difference between Spain and Mexico: "In Spain it is a virtue to be honest and direct in communication and expression of feelings. In Mexico it is a weakness and shows little self-control and that the person is impulsive. My [Mexican] wife and I had to learn to be flexible and adapt our communication styles because our cultural ways could so easily cause conflict."

MEANS FOR RESOLVING MONOCULTURAL AND MULTIPLE-CULTURE INTERPERSONAL CONFLICTS

As listed earlier, one of the universal responses identified by Thomas and Kilmann is carefronting. Elmer (1993, 42) describes carefronting as "directly approaching the other person in a caring way so that achieving a win-win solution is most likely." Carefronting offers conditions for enhancing conflict resolution that can be applied with decreasing caution wherever relationships are growing in depth of trust. Whilst directness in communication is often not the preferred way in face-saving cultures, particularly not in business negotiations, we are not aiming to build relationships for corporate financial gain. Instead, as we seek God's leading, moving from cross-cultural to intercultural relationships for eternal results has the potential to provide the necessary framework of mutual trust that makes a mixture of direct and indirect communication possible. When face is maintained by all parties, neither side loses dignity. Achieving a win-win result to conflict can be aided by several conditions (43), which are listed below, along with my additional thoughts:

1. Both "parties come together, meet face to face and talk with open honesty." Clearly, both parties, whether individuals or groups, need to be willing to come together. This is not so easy for members of high-context communication cultures but attainable when trust has been built and as our relationships become increasingly caring and noncondemning. Growing trust and care can free people to risk communicating in new ways and thus deal with conflict in new ways.

2. "They each make a commitment to preserve the relationship and [then] . . . explain the values/goals that each party wishes to protect or achieve." This reflects an intentional acknowledgment and cherishing of dignity and, where needed, mutual face-saving, in conjunction with each party being able and willing to either explain courteously in a non-emotive manner or maintain control of emotions so that underlying agendas are brought into the open. One of the goals of love-inspired intercultural relationships is genuine transparency, which is also key for conflict resolution.

3. They look for a solution in which both parties win, "with neither having to [unwillingly] give up anything of value." This requires an openness to and acceptance of the different perspectives of others.

4. "They are both able to separate the person from the issue and speak objectively" about the issue. As we saw, this is far less likely to be the norm for members of high-context communication cultures, but the use of indirect or passive approaches to communication, as well as communication that separates doing from being, can be very helpful.

5. "Neither will be satisfied with a solution until the other is also completely at peace with it." This is a true mark of deepening relationships in which each party sees the other's interests and concerns as equal to their own. Preparation through prayer by one or both parties helps bring an eternal perspective into the conflict.

Carefronting's first condition is often seen as biblically justified because of Matthew 18:15: "If your brother or sister sins, go and point out their fault, just between the two of you." However, Elmer (43–44) suggests that "the text seems clear that direct, face-to face confrontation in a caring, loving way is the biblical approach to conflict. What is not so clear is whether this is intended to be the *only* approach to conflict, or whether it [only] represents one good approach. We must also ask whether this approach is, at least to some extent, more acceptable in some cultures than in others."

As Elmer points out (45–46), not all cultures would naturally take this carefronting approach if directness in conflict is countercultural. In some cultures, directness may only be appropriate for group insiders. Similarly, in other cultures, the preference for majority rule that we see in the Global North is not preferred because being in the minority brings loss of face. As Elmer rightly acknowledges, we need to be aware of the cultural values in play, such as shame, honor, and face-saving. I would add that we need to be aware of other cultures' perceptions concerning owning and assigning culpability.

However, in contrast to Elmer, I suggest that we must also recognize that Jesus introduced ways of behavior and societal interaction that were highly countercultural, including that we should love our enemies (Matthew 5:38–46), that the weak and marginalized should be understood to be in as much a position to be blessed by God as were the rich, accomplished, and powerful (Matthew 5:3–11), and that those respected as spiritual leaders and teachers should not necessarily be held in such high esteem (Matthew 23:1–7, 13–33). Taken from this angle, it is not unreasonable to suggest that Jesus may have been urging counterculturally that a better way to deal with conflict is through face-to-face encounter rather than continuing with indirect approaches. This can be further validated by the same principle having already been taught in the context of an offender directly engaging with someone he has offended in order to bring about reconciliation (Matthew 5:23–24).

> **Important principle:** Just as direct communicators can discover the delight of indirect inoffensiveness, so can indirect communicators discover the freedom that comes from being able to speak with unambiguous clarity without fear of offending or being rejected.

> **Example from the Philippines:** "I learned to be more direct in communication through ministering with Westerners. It was a big surprise to my family members, but I was freed from years of control and manipulation that had come through the indirectly communicated expectations of my family members, especially my brothers. When I sensed it was appropriate, they came to respect me for speaking directly. I feel my relationships with them are more whole and healed as a result because I am free to speak directly and be who God created me to be instead of being manipulated for other peoples' purposes."

ADDRESSING CONFLICT THROUGH VIRTUAL MEETINGS AND NEGOTIATIONS

When we are looking to build new relationships through electronic media as Christian communicators, we must be careful to recognize that there is no guarantee that the people with whom we are communicating are truly who they say they are. Their intentions in communicating on a website, for instance through the anonymity of a chatroom, might not reflect the purpose for which the website was set up. We need to be all the more sensitive to the Holy Spirit in how, what, and when we communicate when building online relationships. Similarly, email and text communications can be so easily misinterpreted as there is no accompanying body language, visual, or behavioral cues. During conflict, even social media's use of emojis and pictures can still be easily misunderstood. Emotional language can also be misread as indicating more than what was intended, and what is *not* written, however unintentionally, can also be the means of provoking a negative response or causing conflict. If we are preparing to send an emotion-laden communication in response to conflict, we do well to stop, pray, and hold off sending the message until we have peace that we are following God's leading and timing.

CONCLUSION

Relational difficulties inevitably arise in any ministry, not just cross-cultural ministry. Knowing that our personality and orientation preferences, along with other cultural differences, can cause conflict without us realizing ought to be fuel for prayer so that we might have wisdom when relationships seem to go sour.

In times of conflict, it is all the more crucial to hold onto the truth of God's sovereignty and the power of the Holy Spirit within us to rise us above the discouragements and trials that God is allowing to refine and mature us. In any interpersonal conflicts, whether with other communicators of Christ or our respondents, aim for building and maintaining deep relationships with a strong element of trust. It will take time to build credibility and this kind of relationship. Lean on Christ, but don't be who you are not because, in stress, who you really are inevitably comes out.

- Remember that it is not worth winning the argument but losing the relationship.
- Being gracious might have a better long-term result than being right.
- Don't be tempted to avoid conflict, but pick your battles carefully. What's worth dying for? What's really crucial? What has eternal significance?
- For leaders facing multiple peoples' expectations, resolving conflict might not be through making the "best" decision but by making the "least worst" decision.[11]

---

11. As advised by one of my cherished mentors, Rev. John H. Price, founder of Walsall Evangelistic Church, UK.

> **Devotional comment:** As Christians, our standards for Godly beliefs, values, and customs honor God when they are biblically based and when our attitudes toward others are colored by Christ's humility and unconditional, self-sacrificial love. Does this sound theoretically correct but practically impossible? Galatians 2:20 reminds and encourages us that Christ is in us and provides all we need since we are "crucified with Christ and [we] no longer live, but Christ lives in [us]."

Growing relationships always involve conflict, and when we can resolve conflicts in a healthy way, we are on our way to building intercultural relationships.

QUESTIONS FOR REFLECTION AND DISCUSSION

1. In the "As It Happened" scenario at the start of the chapter, the pastor begins to welcome the first of the team members as they enter his house having left their shoes outside. What do you think the big-footed team member did? What other options might have been suggested in order to resolve the conflict he was experiencing? What important cultural issues and priorities were at stake?

2. What other values and priorities do you suspect might cause further conflict amongst the team members in the "As It Happened" scenario? Analyze your culture's worldview beliefs concerning varying standards of right and wrong: What is seen as impoliteness? What is seen as dishonesty? How do you understand and apply the concept of integrity? What differences are you aware of in your background culture compared to the values and standards of other cultures?

3. Consider the cross-cultural conflict issues you have already experienced (or if not, where there might be potential for cross-cultural conflict based on your worldview values and resulting cultural behavior). Identify the root of the problem. To what extent might your personality have affected the degree of conflict? Consider how you might adjust your attitude and responses (whether related to personality or background culture) to bring about conflict resolution. Be sure to differentiate between values, beliefs, and ideals that are negotiable and those that are definitely nonnegotiable for you.

4. Engage with the following scenario: Christian communicators in a cross-cultural ministry have been gradually deepening the relationship with their neighbors. One evening, the neighbors' son takes their son's mountain bike, rides to a nearby store, and takes some items without paying. Police come to the Christian communicators' house, accusing their son of the theft since their son's distinctive mountain bike had been seen at the store. How should they communicate with the police officers? How should they communicate with their neighbors? What options are there for handling this conflict? Who will be affected by each option, and what values or cultural expectations might also be affected?

CHAPTER 7

Cognitive Perceptions of Reality, Truth, and Epistemology

As It Happened: Consider this conversation between a Christian communicator (C) and a Hindu (H):

> **H:** Tell me about your inner god called Jesus.
> **C:** Jesus is the Son of God.
> **H:** The sun of god?
> **C:** Yes, and his Spirit lives within me.
> **H:** The spirit of the sun?
> **C:** (Thinking, *How can I make this receivable by my Hindu friend?*) Yes, the Spirit of the Son of God, Jesus—I have knowledge of God as an inner reality.
> **H:** Inner reality? (Thinking, *I can relate to that because that's illusory—this friend is not as he appears. He must be much bigger on the inside to have the spirit of the sun inside him.*) Do you feel the heat of this spirit inside you?
> **C:** Yes, the Spirit is like a fire, and the Spirit convicts me when I do wrong things.
> **H:** It burns you up? Like spontaneous combustion?
> **C:** Well, not exactly . . .

INTRODUCTION

Have you ever been sharing the gospel or biblical truths with someone, and then suddenly midconversation you are shocked to realize that they missed the point you were trying to make? As we befriend people of other cultures and seek to deepen those relationships, we need to be sensitive not only to differences in what makes for appropriate behavioral interaction but also to the possible differences between cognitive approaches to reality and perceptions of what makes for truth. These approaches form the foundation for deriving meaning from our communications, which we hope to be perceived as relevant to the people we are reaching out to and hence attractive to them.

In this chapter, we first examine the difficulty associated with the concept of meaning and then look at theories of truth and perspectives on truth. Next, we turn to epistemology and the science of knowing, beginning with reviewing the components of epistemology's historical framework that we first introduced in chapter 1. We then discuss cognitive approaches to reality and examine the history of the literature concerning perception of and engagement with reality in different cultures. At each step, we consider the effect on intercultural communication and offer principles to avoid misunderstanding and heighten the effectiveness of communication in relation to awareness of cognitive perceptions of reality associated with people of different cultures.

THE MYSTERY OF MEANING

We face problems even pondering questions like "What is meaning?" or "What do we mean by the term *meaning?*" A philosophical answer might call into question the nature of being and existence implied in the expectation that such a concept can be explained, and even then with recourse to a series of conditions and caveats. A semantics-based answer might offer the following: *meaning* can be described as the assumed common understanding of ideas represented, for instance, through signs or symbols.

> **International example:** An internationally understood sign for toilet facilities is a symbol for a woman as a dress-clothed figure next to a trouser-wearing figure.

One reason that *meaning* is a slippery concept is because it is not easy to decide where meaning comes from or how the assumed common understanding is or should be assigned. As we have seen, postmodernism's cynicism and opposition to absolutes preferred that truth and meaning are socially constructed, but this merely produced an untenable mass of alternative, competing, and sometimes mutually exclusive perspectives. The more conservative approach, which is also not without limitations, provides three realms from which meaning might be found and assigned (see Kraft 1983, 110–15):

1. In the words or symbols used
2. In the objects themselves
3. From the subjective perspective of individuals

Meaning Found in Words or Symbols (Including Gestures)

If we consider the approach to discovering meaning by assuming that meaning is inherent in words or symbols, then we need to start by examining some semantic issues.

First, we need to recognize some different semantic modifications of the term:

- **Imparted meaning versus inherent meaning.** Imparted meaning is a reference meaning that we apply to an object or symbol. For instance, a 100 pesos banknote has an agreed imparted meaning of 100 pesos value. It can be used to buy goods up to an equivalent value of 100 pesos. However, the material of the note itself is worth far less. Inherent meaning relates to the nature of an object or symbol. For instance, the inherent value of the 100 pesos banknote is less than a centavo or one tenth of a peso.

- **Denotative meaning versus connotative meaning.** Denotative meaning refers to the agreed literal use of a word. Dictionaries give agreed-upon objective definitions of words that denote the appropriate use of each word. For instance, *cool* denotes a comfortable low temperature. Connotational use of the same word provides an implied and different meaning depending on the context of its use, which might also be local slang that changes with time. For instance, a person can be considered *cool* because of trendy clothing.

Important principle: Note the potential for misunderstanding that can come about through communication if the perceived meaning (the interpretation of what is decoded from the message) and the intended meaning (as encapsulated in the encoding of the message) are not identical.

Example from a Peruvian: "I offered my Chinese friend a craft gift I'd brought from my hometown for her, but my friend refused it. I thought that meant she didn't want it. Later I learned that I should have repeated the offer several times because Chinese people believe that if you receive a gift straight away, it shows pride as a heightened sense of self or entitlement that makes you appear to be superior to the giver. It seems that my friend didn't mean she didn't want the gift but that she didn't want to project a prideful attitude of superiority."

A limitation to this objective approach to discovering meaning is that the word or symbol used might be inappropriately considered to *be* what it is supposed to only represent. For instance, although the sun is hot, the word *hot* is not physically hot. It is only a term understood to be linked with the concept of heat. A meaning can only be inferred from descriptive words when an understood relative standard is provided. For example, the refrigerator is sufficiently cold inside to function properly when the temperature is below ten degrees Celsius; thus, the standard for *cold* is in reference to the standard for ten degrees Celsius.

Important principle: Notice that a word, term, or gesture may be interpreted in different ways by different people and cultures (see Nida 1960, 89–93, who highlights *misunderstandings* due to linguistics). For example, the concept that translates as "thank you" is considered polite by some cultures but demeaning by others. The gesture of raising a hand to attract attention may have an acceptable meaning in some cultures but be offensive in others.

Example from China: "We learn to say 'thank you' only to people at a higher level, and that's because we are obligated to them."

Personal example from China: Whilst working in a city hospital, Dr. Co and I would thank the hospital cleaning staff for their helpful work in emptying the trash bins and swabbing the floors. After initial surprise and attempts to refuse our affirmations, they eventually told us how special that made them feel because no one ever thanked them for their work. As a result of intentionally affirming and cherishing their dignity, we could tell them the Christmas story and how the low-level shepherds and high-level wise men all worshipped Jesus as equals, and we were also able to speak further and share the gospel.

Meaning Found in the Objects Themselves

This is also an objective approach to discovering meaning since we are now considering not words or gestures as symbols, but objects outside of ourselves. A similar limitation arises in that different people can have different opinions about the meaning of the same object. For instance, food leftovers found in a trash bin outside a restaurant constitute a much sought-after meal to a hungry homeless person, but to the local health and hygiene department officer these leftovers mean a health hazard as they are likely to attract rats.

Example from the Philippines: "To very devout Catholics, the robes worn by the priest mean he is covered in holiness, so the parishioners won't touch his robe because it is holy; less devout Catholics don't see it that way, and some priests even hug their parishioners. For them the robe doesn't seem to mean holiness."

Important principle: Don't assume that you and your respondents attach the same functional or nontangible meanings to different objects.

Meaning Found according to the Subjective Perspective of Individuals

This approach to discovering meaning depends purely on the meaning concocted by the individual or agreed upon by a group in community regardless of the opinions of outsiders. Meaning is not in words or objects but is created in the mind. This is not unlike the postmodern perspective, which saw meaning as being a purely subjective construction by a community yet also entitling everyone to hold to their own perspective. A similar limitation as for the other approaches applies here as well: multiple subjective meanings can disintegrate a community rather than building it up, and multiple subjective meanings reduce the potential for maintaining harmony with the wider community.

Important principle: Similar contexts and experiences may generate quite different subjective meanings either corporately or according to each individual's personal background and worldview beliefs.

Example from Thailand: "There is a great deal of transport in Bangkok all the time. My uncle drives his taxi with *serenity* however chaotic the roads are because that's the Thai way."

Example from the Philippines: "Traffic is always congested in Manila, but people just *accept* the hassle as unavoidable."

PERSPECTIVES ON TRUTH

Another cultural difference, misunderstanding of which can undermine intercultural communications, concerns differing perceptions pertaining to truth and reality in relation to worldview. Consider this fable: Three blind men are exposed to different parts of an elephant. One experiences the tail, another the elephant's trunk, whilst the third feels one of the elephant's ears. When they report their individual findings, they present three different perceptions, which leads to an argument. What they have experienced are three distinct true perspectives of the same reality. Whether communicating cross-culturally or interculturally, the appropriate mutual interpretation of language can have implications for perceptions of truth and reality. This brings us to the question of how truth might be decided upon.

Theories of Truth

There are several theories of truth, borne out of philosophical endeavor, of which the most well-known are presented below. Their reception has evolved just as confidence in modernism was usurped by postmodernism.

Nevertheless, all three theories are lived out consciously or subconsciously regardless of underlying philosophical or semantic incongruities.

The Correspondence Theory of Truth

This theory, which is ascribed to Aristotle, subjects propositions to the question of whether they "correspond" to what is the case in reality. If the propositions do not correspond to reality, then they are false. We go through our days acting out the correspondence theory of truth. For instance, if we want to sit down, we identify an object that corresponds to what we expect a chair to be and sit on it; if we want to eat an apple, we select the piece of fruit from the fruit bowl that corresponds to an apple. The theory compares the proposition with reality: the statement "the fruit I picked out of the bowl is an apple" is true if I really did pick out an apple, but if I bit into the fruit and discovered that I'd actually picked out a smooth-skinned peach, then the statement "the fruit I picked out of the bowl is an apple" would be false because the fruit did not correspond to an apple.

One commonly cited limitation with this theory comes up if we ask, "What does the correspondence theory correspond to?" since that would be a requirement for it to be a true theory. Another limitation is that this theory depicts truth as corresponding with objective reality and assumes that objective reality is perceived through subjective experience in a commonly understood way. As we saw when considering meaning, this is not always the case. Postmodernism rejected the concept of purely objective reality since we cannot separate ourselves completely from what we are examining. Experimenters influence an experiment just by being there. Only God can be completely objective. Similarly, all languages have words that are not easily translatable into another language and so cannot be expressed correspondingly, but that does not negate the truth of those terms. Ultimately, regardless of the theorists and philosophers who consider the correspondence theory of truth to be redundant, we live it out every day as we engage with objects and make choices in relation to objects.

The Coherence Theory of Truth

This theory subjects propositions to the question of whether the propositions are consistent with our other beliefs. If a proposition denies or disputes any of the beliefs we take to be true, then the proposition must be false. For instance, if I ask to see a packet of vitamin tablets in a pharmacy, I would expect to see several pieces of cohering information on the packet such as a valid brand name, a manufacturing or use-by date, and a batch-process code. If any of these were missing or the brand name were invalid, I would expect that the product is not what it claims to be because the information does not all cohere.

A limitation to this theory comes into play when we hold certain beliefs to be true but have no commonly accepted, independent, objective means to support the beliefs. For example, an evangelical who holds the Old Testament as supporting evidence may have no qualms in believing that the universe came into existence five thousand years ago, whereas a liberal or a Bible scholar more sympathetic to geological theory, carbon-dating, and so on is less likely to believe that dating since, to them, the Old Testament does not provide supporting evidence.

The Pragmatic Theory of Truth

This theory subjects propositions to the question of how well they bring about sought-after results. Beliefs that work out practically are considered to be true,[1] whereas those that do not are considered to be false.

> **Example from China:** In our second area of ministry, we were involved in community health development in remote villages in South Central China. We taught nutrition principles including that protein is essential for nourishment and healthy growth and provided bean seeds as a sustainable source of protein. Children who had been determined to be malnourished developed into healthily nourished children. As a result, the village leaders came to believe that protein is an important nutritional source for both overcoming malnourishment and ongoing healthy growth because they saw good results from the intentional introduction of protein into the diet.

---

1. Note how James (1907; 1975) linked pragmatism with instrumentality: "Any idea upon which we can ride, so to speak; any idea that will carry us prosperously from any one part of our experience to any other part, linking things satisfactorily, working securely, simplifying, saving labor; is true for just so much, true in so far forth, true *instrumentally*. This is the 'instrumental' view of truth" (34). And "you can say of it then either that 'it is useful because it is true' or that 'it is true because it is useful.' Both these phrases mean exactly the same thing" (98). See too how Dewey's approach to pragmatism and truth sees propositions as proposals from which truth is gained as judgment: "Truth and falsity are properties only of that subject-matter which is the *end*, the close, of the inquiry by means of which it is reached" (1941, 176). As seen, I prefer that, as of Biblical precepts and propositions, truth and falsity are not merely brought into being in relation to enquiry but exist regardless of enquiry or rationalistic endeavor.

A limitation to the pragmatic theory of truth arises when results are attributed to an incorrect or noncausal belief.

> **Example from China:** In a remote Chinese village, villagers worshipped at ancestral graves in the belief that this would appease their ancestors so as to make life run smoothly. Life for the villagers had both smooth seasons and difficult seasons but not because of the superstitious practices at ancestors' graves. After becoming Christians and transferring their worship to God through Jesus, they were delighted to discover that the activities to appease ancestors' spirits had never played a part in their well-being and so the activities need not be continued.

Another limitation of the pragmatic theory of truth is that one may question the degree to which a belief "works" so that relativism prevails when "some truths are more useful than others," and as postmodernists prefer, "although a proposition may be true for one person, it need not be true for everyone." This would suggest that a proposition may sometimes be true and other times be false, thus refuting Aristotle's law of noncontradiction (i.e., that a proposition may not be concurrently both true and false).[2] The loss of universal or absolute truths may be relatively inconsequential for issues such as whether or not brand X performs better than brand Y, but it has weighty consequences for questions about whether Jesus Christ truly is the only way to eternal life and whether God speaks to us through his Word, the Bible.

Truth as Revelation from an Evangelical Perspective

Christians consider truths revealed by God as found in the Bible and seen in nature to be as valid evidence of truth as principles of coherence, correspondence, or pragmatism. In the context of a multifaith world, how does one decide which "religious" revelations are true and which are false? Why or how is revelation through the Bible valid and true, but "revelation" given to Muhammad or the Hindu Vedas is not?

We can answer this by recognizing the truth that revelation from God always lines up with attributes and characteristics of God. Both God and

---

2. For a historical summary of the pragmatic theory of truth and its more recent developments including reference to difficulties with "the assumption that truth is always and everywhere causal correspondence," see Lynch (2009, 34); see also Capps (2019).

revelation from him are true, loving, righteous, orderly (not unmanageably chaotic), just, peace-loving, merciful, and so on. What sets the Bible, God's divine revelation, apart from other texts is that it proclaims the nature of God and uniqueness of Christ in the context of a historical narrative that shows the relationship between God and his people. It is both revelational and descriptive of how God developed relationship, beginning with creation and moving down through history such that the text still speaks to anyone and everyone, whatever and wherever their contexts. What raises it above any other so-called texts of "divine revelation" is that it is in its entirety a powerful dynamic Word. All other "religious texts" merely inform—they do not invite or provide for interaction in a living way with the living God. An encounter with this living Word provides us with a personal reality of truth in relation to the Bible's objective evidence, along with the subjective experience of our encounter.

Post-Reformation theology made a triad of Scripture, tradition, and reason to evaluate revelation, but we must be careful not to let tradition or reason become too weighty a means of validating faith and/or personal, devotional revelation, intuited to us through God's Word. Bear in mind the principle that Augustine (AD 354–430) advised, "all truth is God's truth," and there may well be some grains of truth in "revelation" from other religions.[3] Certainly, in our quest for truth from God's perspective, we can engage respectfully with others and do not need to fear either what they believe is true or what they believe about truth. Instead, with confidence in the God we know personally and knowledge of his Word, the Bible through which he speaks to us, we can be listening for the Holy Spirit to intuit to us the best way to engage with these befriended ones of other faiths.

EPISTEMOLOGY AND DIFFERENT
PERCEPTIONS OF KNOWING

We turn now to epistemology, which is the science of knowledge and knowing, to take a deeper look at key aspects of the historical framework that we introduced in chapter 1:[4]

---

3. See too Holmes (1979, 8), who proposes that examining anything of the world and creation has the potential to reveal truth from God's perspective since it is created by God.

4. It would not be unreasonable to suggest that this is a Western historical framework, but we must not forget that Western modernist-based education was also sought after in African, Middle Eastern, and Far Eastern nations after Western missionaries established mission schools in these nations and that the influence has prevailed in many institutions worldwide.

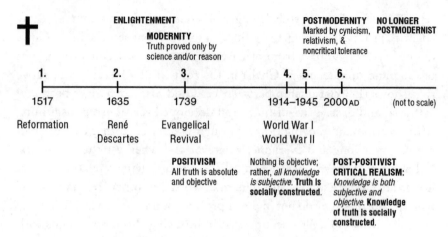

Figure 7.1 Epistemology's Historical Framework

Perceptions of Truth in Relation to the Progression of Eras
Modern Era

Positivism (or logical positivism, later called naive realism) brought knowledge through the application of science and reason and replaced superstition and magic. It was influenced by the modernist philosophical outlook in which discovery of truth was subject to the laws of science, objective testing, and analysis. The expectation was that everything can be completely known, and means needed to be devised to analyse data through rationalism and logic. Empirical results were proof of discovered knowledge and truth.

Underlying principle: All truth is absolute and objective, is believed to be deterministic in nature, and can be discovered and validated through rationalism and logic.

Application: Enquiry into natural law looked to quantitative data to prove hypotheses.

Postmodern Era (1945 Onwards)

Metanarratives were dispensed with. In other words, the following metanarrative became untenable: truth and knowledge are a bounded entity, and the increasing of knowledge improves and progressively civilises the world. Science was no longer seen as the key to knowledge. Nothing is objective; rather, all truth and knowledge is subjective. Knowledge and perceptions of knowledge are different to different people.[5] Views related

---

5. For a more detailed chart that includes other postmodern era perspectives, see Hiebert (1994, 23).

to superstition and magic may not accord with your beliefs, but others may choose to hold them.

Underlying principle: Truth is not absolute but is socially constructed so that relativism prevails.

Application: Qualitative testing methods are used to examine social phenomena, thus providing sociopsychological perspectives. Discovery in the social sciences comes by finding association or correlation between phenomena and possible reasons that link them rather than the establishment of quantifiable cause and effect preferred in the natural sciences.

Useful principle: As we have seen, postmodernism rejected the concept of quantifiable objective truth. In response to a post-modernist who prefers to deny the existence of objective facts we can point out that the date of their birth is an objective truth as is, for instance, the length of their fingernails.[6]

Postpositivist Era and Critical Realism (1970s Onwards)

Knowledge is considered to be both subjective and objective.[7]

Underlying principle: Truth is real and can be known but only approximately, and discovered knowledge can be revised.[8] Rather than truth being socially constructed, only knowledge of truth is socially constructed.

---

6. Be aware, too, of the term *post-truth*, which was the *Oxford English Dictionary*'s Word of the Year in 2016 and noted as having been around for some ten years. *Post-truth* is used as an adjective, "relating to or denoting circumstances in which objective facts are less influential in shaping public opinion than appeals to emotion and personal belief. . . . It has also become associated with a particular noun, in the phrase *post-truth politics*." Despite the ubiquity of this concept, particularly in Western settings, we do well to be careful to balance emotion-laden subjectivism with sensitive expression of fact-based, life-enriching objective truth.

7. Note that positivism looked to analyse what can be seen and engaged with whereas realism also acknowledges and searches out unseen causes of phenomena. Given the simplification here, for more on positivism, realism, and critical realism, see Payne and Payne (2004, 170–74).

Critical realism was introduced by Roy Bhaskar as a social science approach that counters the limitations of both empiricism and relativism. His earlier (1975) philosophical work described transcendental realism. This became critical naturalism in his later work (1979), which attended specifically to the social sciences. The term *critical realism* came from the merging of the earlier two terms.

8. See Porpora (2010, 89) on implications for international relations and that there "are those who consider the distinction between reasons and causes to mark a deep division between the natural and human sciences. According to this view . . . explanation is appropriate to the determinism of the natural order, whereas the understanding of reasons through what Weber (1947) called *Verstehen* is appropriate to the realm of freedom represented by the social order." As anticipated by critical realism, understandings or reasons of associations between social phenomena can clearly become modified, negated, or reconformed as studies develop.

Application: Both quantitative and qualitative research methods are acceptable in social science studies.

Personal Perceptions of Truth and Reality

Since our understanding of knowledge and reality is dependent on what we believe about reality and truth, we do well to ask how we personally acquire our perceptions of what we believe to be real and true.[9]

Kraft (1989, 18–19) suggests:

1. Our perceptions of truth and reality come to us via our upbringing—inculcated by our parents and teachers according to the norms of our culture so that "we see largely what we are taught to see."
2. Appropriate views and outlook on life are modeled by our parents, teachers, and society so that we take a selective interest in what we think about, do, and yearn after.
3. We tend to accept what agrees with what we have been taught to believe.
4. Despite our quest for knowledge, 1 Corinthians 13:12 is true of everyone: we can see only a partial and dim view of reality.

Kraft (19) believes that our view of reality is much smaller than existent reality because our perception of the fullness of reality is subject to a series of filters that limit our perception. These filters, in succession as a series of components of a person's view of reality, are:

- All that happens that we are aware of
- What we believe is possible
- What we experience of these happenings
- What we actually analyze

What is left after the filtering process is our personal view of reality, and it is much smaller than true reality.[10] Hence, Kraft suggests that our perception of reality is influenced by our knowledge of what truth and reality (and meanings associated with them) are in existence, but our perception is also conditional upon what we believe is possible and what we are

---

9. The following sections are based on D-Davidson (2018, 50–54).
10. On the same page (19), Kraft provides this information in the form of a diagram as a visual aid to show how one's view of reality decreases as it passes through each filter layer.

willing to analyze. I add that, should the result of analysis provide a new or challenging dimension to previous beliefs about reality, there is also a filter representing the degree to which we are willing to have our perceptions of reality challenged or changed.

Kraft (19–22) lists the following "factors influencing our view of reality":

1. The norms we've grown up with due to our culture and worldview.
2. "The limitations of our experience . . . our personality or temperament . . . degree of openness to new ideas." People are particularly open to new ideas when vulnerable and/or in a crisis.
3. Sin distorting one's view of reality—this might come across through rebellion, unholiness, or behavior that is lacking in love, truth, or righteousness.
4. "Our will. . . . We choose to view any given thing either as we have been taught or to view it differently. . . . The place of the will is very important in maintaining or changing one's worldview."[11] Willingness to put aside our own understandings and preference takes humility and courage.

We need to examine ourselves and ask: How willing am I to receive new ideas rather than just defend my own positions? It can help to remember that walking by faith is an act of will, and it's a choice too.

Important principle: When we are engaged in evangelism and in works empowered by God's Spirit, there is always hope where there is also faith. If people only depend on proven knowledge as the basis for what is possible, then faith or hope have no place, and we lay ourselves open to despair.

COGNITIVE APPROACHES TO REALITY AND THE EFFECT ON INTERCULTURAL COMMUNICATION

Hesselgrave (1991, 298–99) addresses culture and epistemology by pointing to views in the literature concerning how Eastern and Western ways of

---

11. See Broome (2013) on how motivation influences the will to do what we believe we ought to do.

thinking appear to follow different cognitive processes. He starts by referring back to Gulick's bisystemic perception expounded in his classic text
The East and the West,[12] which considered Western thinking and perceptions of reality to be theory based, with hypotheses drawn up and tested to
explain reality, whereas Eastern thinking was simplistically considered to
be "mythological, emotional and artistic" (Gulick 1962, 128). Hesselgrave
(300–301) then describes how Northrop's (1953) bisystemic approach
disagreed with the Western interpretation of Eastern thinking as being
largely speculative and preferred that Eastern thinking was more a case of
intuiting the reality of what is immediately concrete through its aesthetic
characteristics. In summary, for Northrop, engaging with both theoretical
and aesthetic components of phenomena at hand, complementary as they
are, would be key for his quest (and title of his book) of the meeting of East
and West.

Hesselgrave (301–2) describes how the literature evolved with reference to Perry (1958, 99–106), who cites F. H. Smith's trisystemic approach
such that, of Eastern nations and cultures, Indian ways of thinking differed
quite considerably from that of Chinese people. Smith described three different starting points for thinking:

- **Western:** Thinking begins with and progresses from hypothesised
  and proven theoretical concepts.
- **Chinese:** Thinking tends to be concrete-relational—in other words,
  engaging with the immediate and concrete in terms of relationships
  in actual situations, and by implication, a preference for concrete
  rather than abstract ideas, along with importance placed on how the
  ideas work out in experience, particularly on how they will either
  benefit or impinge on interpersonal relationships.
- **Indian:** Thinking is through intuitional or psychical perceptions that
  validate ideas on the basis of a confirmatory or intuitional experience
  from within oneself and which appears to be due to Hinduism's concept of *maya*, which is the illusory nature of the world around them.[13]

---

12. Published posthumously in 1962. See also Gulick (1914). Gulick included the Near East
as part of the West.

13. See for instance Sedlmeier and Srinivas (2016), who suggest that an object in the world is
mentally apprehended as "an object of one's [cognitive] experience but [it] is not seen as an object
of the objective world." Furthermore, "Conscious cognition needs the connection between the
intellect and . . . [the] pure consciousness." Access to pure consciousness is the means to freedom
and self-realization and is the ultimate pursuit of followers of Hinduism but pure consciousness is
"only reflected in the intellect and not recognized."

> **Important principle:** We can see how making the assumption that people all think the same way as ourselves can easily cause inappropriate encoding of the message or messages we are wanting to communicate.

Smith advised that all three types of thinking are likely to be used by people of different cultures, but one will have a bigger priority. As to the priority starting point for thinking by each of the people-types, Smith had people of the West starting from postulated and proven theoretical concepts, with a lesser priority on concrete-relational thinking, and an even lesser attention to psychical experience or intuitional thinking. Chinese people were understood to begin from concrete-relational thinking, followed by intuition, and lastly postulated concepts. Indian people were believed to begin from psychical experience, followed by concrete-relational thinking, and lastly hypothesised and proven concepts. Hesselgrave reproduces this in diagram form (1991, 303), but for Chinese thinking he follows Perry's approach (1958, 100),[14] which saw Chinese people begin from concrete-relational thinking, followed by proven concepts, and intuition or psychical experience coming last (Hesselgrave 1991, 303).

Hesselgrave (1991, 302) acknowledges Smith's suggestion that all people use all three ways of thinking and that one of the three ways of thinking will be dominant in every culture with the other two operative to different degrees. People's reasoning processes differ for more reasons than we can probably ever be fully aware of, but what's important for us as we engage with people from other cultures is to be aware of which aspect *might* be a key starting-point priority for the people we are reaching out to.

Example from Germany: "I heard the gospel in logical steps, and it made sense to me—Jesus fulfilling the law by his death was actually more appealing to me in those early days than the result that I'd be able to love people better."

---

14. Perry followed E. R. Hughes in this respect possibly in reference to Hughes (1938). See too Hughes (1967).

Example from a British national of Indian origin: "Hearing the gospel challenged my inner sense about the Hinduism I'd grown up with. I was told that the Christian God dwells in his people, and that really intrigued me."

Example from Myanmar: "The people from Myanmar are intuitional; having a power encounter with the Holy Spirit will be crucial for them to be open to hearing the truth."

Example from an Iranian: "A British woman was married to a German man, and they lived together with another couple and some local people for several years. Their lifestyle of mutual care was lived out twenty-four hours a day, and people could see the love of God for real in the relationships."

Hesselgrave (1991, 340) also warns us of the limitations of the different kinds of thinking. For instance, a Western person's excessive attention to what can be proved or reasoned vastly overrates its potential to be able to truly describe reality. I add that it also unreasonably downplays the potential to learn and grow through experience of the unexplainable. In our communication, we can include the place of living by faith (2 Corinthians 5:7) and the joy of delighting in the mystery and wonder of God's hand clearly at work in unexpected details of our lives.

Remarking on Indians' intuitional thinking, Hesselgrave warns that what is intuited is likely to be perceived as being from a divine source; hence, the words of wise teachers are perceived as though they are actually prophets. But without testing of the word, let alone practical application, it is likely that the experience becomes revered rather than the word. I add that what is needed is revelation from the truly Divine Source communicated in a way that the eyes of the intuitional thinker are opened in a new way for all time. In our communication, we can encourage with joy that God does indeed respond to those who seek him and live out that truth as the larger-than-life undeniable Spirit-within empowered reality that it is.

Regarding the Chinese starting point of concrete-relational thinking, Hesselgrave warns of the potential for idolatry, because symbols used to represent concrete ideas can easily become mistaken as being the reality of what they are merely supposed to be representing. The concrete-relational thinker can easily succumb to mistaking the world, nature, and relationship that he walks through and lives with as though these *are* the one who created them. I suggest that what is needed is a means of bridging the concrete and the invisible, communicated in such a way that the concrete-relational thinker is able to perceive (or believe in) the invisible reality *as* reality in its own right in contrast to the object or symbol being used to represent it. This is very much about helping them to cross the bridge by faith at some point in our communication and interactions concerning gospel truths and biblical principles. But we must communicate in a way that recognizes the importance of presenting ideas without undermining the implications for the respondent's wider relationships. We also need to know the respondent well enough so that the way we use language will not cause confusion or misunderstanding, particularly with respect to abstract ideas.

This presentation of three starting points for cognitive perception has referred to what was cutting-edge thought in post–World War II academic endeavor to show that one cannot assume there is a single universal way of thinking (let alone that one's own way is the best or only way). To follow up with detailed contemporary contributions to the literature is rather beyond the scope of this text, but hopefully an awareness of the phenomena will help us avoid making inappropriate assumptions when attempting to communicate about truth and reality from the biblical perspective with those of other cultures.

Subsequent developments of the trisystemic cultural outlook intro-duce facets of culture that were referred to in earlier chapters. For instance Nisbett, Peng, Choi, and Norenzayan (2001) suggest that Western thinking is more conceptual and hence conducive to abstract concepts as compared to East Asians being more holistic. They offer that this is due to individualist versus collective social systems. Navon (1977) and Kitayama, Duffy, Kawamura, and Larsen (2003) attempt to question this, but their research results are less than compelling, as they are based on response to visual stimuli. It can be helpful to note, too, that holistic thinking is often used interchangeably with the term dialectical thinking. De Oliveira and Nisbett (2017, 789) cite Peng and Nisbett's (1999) use of dialectical thinking "as appreciation of context, expectation of change, and tolerance of contradiction," whilst Peng and Nisbett (1999, 741) even suggest that "dialectical thinking is a form of folk wisdom in Chinese culture."

As we engage with these concepts and different cultural contexts, we also face the potential for making big-picture (and possibly highly inap-propriate) assumptions about cultural ways of thinking. It would not be unreasonable to suggest that although the Chinese tendency may well be to start from concrete-relational aspects, how might we decide whether intuition or proven concepts (or even something else) come next for specific respondents? The next level of influence could be a factor of a Chinese person's background. For instance, if the people are from a remote village that is alive with myth, magic, and superstitious practices, that would be more conducive to inculcation of functioning with a more intuitional worldview as the next priority. But if they grew up in a highly developed city setting and had more encouragement towards further education along with greater access to a wider range of materials and mentally stimulating ideas than their villager compatriots, then the proven concepts influence might be expected to come after the concrete-relational priority.

We should be aware too that although the trisystemic approach identified three particular perspectives on cognitive reality in relation to cultures, people of other cultures, such as Koreans in Asia and Peruvians in Latin America, have a cognitive approach to reality and truth that starts from the relational realm but finds little difficulty engaging with abstract concepts. Again, we must beware of making generalizations or assumptions concerning our respondents and, instead, get to know them by asking open-ended questions and listening carefully to how they express their accounts of life and reality.

Devotional comment: It can be overwhelming to realize how much there is to know and how little we have tapped the surface about cultural variations on perceptions of meaning, truth, and cognitive perceptions of reality and then to have to try to apply this knowledge sensitively and accurately into the relationships God has brought us into. We may be asking how much of the theory actually matches with these specific people, and are we making mistakes without realizing it so that our respondents don't seem to be getting any nearer to knowing Christ Jesus personally. In discouragement, it can help if we stop seeing our communication efforts as service *for* the kingdom of God and instead see our efforts as a love-offering *to* the King. Let's be sure to be prayerful about our communications and our relationships; deliver messages with a purpose just as we have a goal whenever we preach or teach, and as far as possible know where the respondent or respondents' hearts and lives are at so that we have appropriate objectives. Communicate in a way that ploughs, sows, waters, or harvests in step with the Holy Spirit. Be encouraged that as we cooperate with the Holy Spirit, he will do his part (in his way and timing) in bringing growth as we do our part communicating from his love and by his love.

CONCLUSION

In this chapter we have seen the hindrances to effective communication that can come from misinterpretation of language and inaccurate decoding of the communicator's intended meaning. We saw in chapter 1 that effective communication seeks to persuade in a healthy, dignity-maintaining way. We need to be not only thoughtful in our use of language but also sensitive to how our respondent might be assigning meaning and, from their cultural frame of reference, what perspective on truth and reality they are likely to derive. We can heighten communication not only by being aware of our respondent's cultural background and worldview in relation to cognitive approaches to reality but also by being aware of their personal hopes and dreams, as well as how their communications about these are affected by their individual personality. When communicating with multiple-culture groups, we should take care to communicate in such a way that all possible combinations of cognitive approaches to reality are catered for. In cooperation with the Holy Spirit, the way will open up for the truth of the gospel to become more than merely an addition to knowledge but rather an attractive reality, particularly as trust in our relationships deepens.

QUESTIONS FOR REFLECTION
AND DISCUSSION

1. In the "As It Happened" scenario at the start of the chapter, what incorrect assumptions about understanding was the Christian communicator making? How might the communicator have identified and better handled these misunderstandings?
2. Recall the essentials of the gospel message of chapter 1 (i.e., who Jesus is, what Jesus did, and why Jesus did it). When you first heard these truths, consider how you derived meaning from them either in relation to the words used, the nature of Jesus, or your subjective experience. Which aspect was most important for you and why? Discuss and compare your experience with that of a Christian from a different cultural background.
3. How might you respond to someone who tells you, "You say Jesus came to save people. Well, perhaps that's true for you, but it's not true for me"?

4. Of the cognitive approaches to reality, and taking postulated concepts, relationships, and intuition as possible starting points, from where might the thinking of the Old Testament Israelites have started? How about New Testament Jews? What might have been the preference of the Greco-Roman world, and what evidence is there of the influence that could have had on people of the territories that had been invaded? (Hint: Consider the New Testament Epistles.)

CHAPTER 8

Progress into Interculturality

As It Happened: In preparation for two years of ministry in Pakistan, I had been advised to get my ears pierced, as that's a norm for Pakistani girls and women. So I did, and one of my brothers and sister-in-law gave me a present of some lovely intricately formed gold-ball earrings. I wore them for many years until one night, on an overnight bus journey in China, I woke up to discover one was missing. The bus had driven up and down bumpy mountain roads, and the earring clasp must have worn loose. I searched the blanket I'd slept with to no avail. In my heart, I was angry and frustrated at how the bus jolted around. I was also very sad about the lost earring. Many hours later, when I had arrived at the destination and was preparing to shower, I found the earring lodged inside the jersey that I'd worn for the past twenty-four hours, but there was no sign of its securing clasp. I rejoiced at finding the earring and wore it with a clasp from another set of earrings. In a way, replacing what I'd been used to with a security device from elsewhere seemed symbolic of leaving behind security-bringing aspects from one culture and happily taking on those of another to be able to function fruitfully. Both the bus trip and the journey into interculturality were bumpy, but knowing where I was headed meant each journey had both trials and joys.

INTRODUCTION

Can you recall the anguish of losing something very precious or important to you and the relief of resolving the loss? How about the loss of something that had been a symbol of security for you, perhaps an important national identification document or bank card that then requires a lengthy administrative process to replace? The practicalities of acquiring its replacement along with the mental and emotional cost involved all involve a process.

Widening our hearts and mindsets to become intercultural and feel secure communicating with and amongst people of other cultures is also a process.

In the previous chapters we have seen different facets of culture and how sensitivity to these can heighten cross-cultural communications. We have seen how factors of personality can hinder communication even amongst monocultural relationships. We have also seen ways to counter conflict that arises due to personality clashes as well as principles for resolving conflict that arises due to cultural misunderstandings and differing cultural priorities. We have seen how cognitive approaches to reality can impact the perceived reality and relevance of the truths we seek to communicate. Our cross-cultural relationships can become deeper as we communicate appropriately in relation to all of these aspects.

In this chapter we will look at developing those cross-cultural relationships into intercultural relationships, through which the opportunities to share gospel truths and Christian perspectives have the potential to be even more effective. We begin by identifying the characteristics and implications of intercultural relationships and interculturality, particularly the crucial factor of empathy that expresses personal care. We note how engagement with need can often be the catalyst for developing relationships. We then offer principles for assessing intercultural competence and learn from insightful and challenging snippets of cross-cultural and intercultural interviews from nations worldwide. Some examples of real-life intercultural relationships follow, and finally, there are some derived transferable principles for developing and honing intercultural relationships.

INTERCULTURAL RELATIONSHIPS AND INTERCULTURALITY

We saw in chapter 1 that the terms *cross-cultural* and *intercultural* are not synonymous. Cross-cultural relationships are marked by a member of one culture intentionally communicating with members of another culture in such a way that the communicating member comes to understand the culture of the other but with little or no reciprocation. Moving into intercultural relationships shows interculturality. Nguyễn, the Vietnamese missionary, priest, and scholar, makes this differentiation: "Interculturality is a multi-directional exchange whereby both parties are enriched in the encounter; cross-cultural encounter however is one-directional communication that does not necessarily involve mutual exchange and enrichment" (2013, 36).

The literature describes interculturality from multiple perspectives. From a sociological perspective, prescriptive interculturality "is aimed at making contemporary societies more conscious about their internal diversities and more inclusive and symmetrical with regard to their so-called minorities" (Dietz 2018, 1–2). Toward this end, intercultural competency tools "are defined as functional tools and resources for increasing tolerance for, mutual understanding with, and empathy with others," particularly to reduce exclusion of minorities,[1] whilst critical interculturality[2] pursues a systemic approach to overcome historically founded inequalities (3). Dietz decries the approaches to intercultural communication that ignore or deny the power difference between communicator and respondent, which therefore remain marked by ethnocentrism (13). As Christian communicators seeking to build relationships in the global arena, the very aim of our developing interculturality and coming into intercultural relationships is so that we might gain God's perspective for loving, harmonious, and fruit-bearing relationships. Christian perspectives unashamedly and increasingly become the guiding motif of our relationships.

Deepening cross-cultural friendships into intercultural relationships happens as the Christian communicator develops in the knowledge, character, interpersonal skills, and social skills required of interculturality and develops intercultural competence. Intercultural relationships result in benefit not to only one party but, as Nguyễn encouraged, *mutual enrichment*. From a Christian communicator's perspective, I offer that interculturality provides a sense of the degree to which one has gained sufficient knowledge, developed attractive Christlikeness, and lives out the appropriate interpersonal and social skills that are marked by a delight in being a fruit-bearing vessel for God's purpose in communicating the gospel of Christ.

As Christian communicators, we look to accumulate and understand the knowledge relevant to where and how God has placed us, submit ourselves to God, and cooperate with the Holy Spirit to develop the character that projects Christlikeness. We also seek to grow in understanding and in our use of appropriate interpersonal and social skills, without the wearying that comes from striving, that enable us to function fruitfully amongst those of other cultures. Our respondent friends may not be intentionally seeking to understand our backgrounds and worldview perspectives in the

---

1. His context being within European settings.
2. Dietz refers here to Walsh (2006) and particularly in relation to Latin American perspectives.

way we seek to understand theirs, but mutually enriched relationships will be marked by a willingness—and even delight—to feel comfortable with the diversity and differences, perhaps without these friends even realizing it. This is a mark of communication that is both transforming and transformed.

What does increasing interculturality look like in practice? In our desire to communicate Christ and gospel truths, we do not need to strive to build relationships as though frantic productivity is a mark of success. Instead, as we rejoice in who we are in Christ and trust that his hand is at work in our lives, we will see him bring us to specific people and groups of people, and we will also become aware of those he has sent across our paths. The beginnings of moving from a cross-cultural to intercultural relationship are interactions marked by empathy as we engage with those specific people God brings us to and those whom he brings to us. Some people practice empathy without even realizing it. That might be due to their personality, or it might be a factor of their adult maturity and/or spiritual maturity. For these people, examining the concept can help widen understanding and potential for greater sensitivity in practical application. For others, it is important to understand what is meant by empathy so that rather than it merely being a theoretical concept, it can be a means to fruitfulness in relationships.

THE DYNAMIC OF EMPATHY

What is the difference between sympathy and empathy, and how do both impact communication? Sympathy evokes "feelings of pity and sorrow for someone else's misfortune," whereas empathy involves "the ability to understand and share the feelings of another."[3] Sympathy can include both passive and active responses to the plight of another, whereas empathy cannot help but communicate a desire to relate to and bring comfort, affirmation, or even celebration (as appropriate) into the situation of the other. As Christians, we "rejoice with those who rejoice; [and] mourn with those who mourn" (Romans 12:15).

Ekman (1999) offers six basic emotions[4] that people discern through facial expression: (1) fear, (2) anger, (3) joy, (4) sadness, (5) disgust, and (6) surprise. As we saw in chapter 2, correctly discerning the meaning of

---

3. Concise Oxford English Dictionary (2004).
4. Ekman (1999, 46) presents these as universal emotions.

nonverbal language is crucial for accurately decoding the communication of another.[5] Information related to different nuances of feeling is very often expressed nonverbally and can be difficult to decode accurately. Empathy, at its simplest, is having the "capacity [or] the ability to know how another feels" (Goleman 1995, 109). In *Social Intelligence*, Goleman (2006) broadens the topic to include practical application for awareness of emotions and heightening relationships. This is not pure theory. From a neurological perspective, the *reality* of emotional empathy or "the human ability to perceive and empathize with others' emotions when positive (cooperative) or negative (uncooperative) interactions are observed" validates the degree to which we are able to accurately decode emotions in play (Balconi and Vanutelli 2017, 105).

Goleman notes that Ekman differentiates compassionate empathy from cognitive empathy and emotional empathy.[6] Citing Goleman, Bariso (2018, 72) offers that "cognitive empathy is the ability to understand how a person feels and what they might be thinking." The attention to rationale might provoke an urge to fix problems through rational thinking but lack sympathy. In contrast, emotional empathy easily discerns, feels, and connects with the emotions of others but can result in emotional burnout for the empathizer, whereas "compassionate empathy (also known as empathic concern[7]) goes beyond simply understanding others and sharing their feelings: it actually moves us to take action, to help however we can." Significantly, we then communicate through our actions in ways that deepen interpersonal relationships, whether monocultural or crosscultural. Indeed, compassion can be a crucial catalyst for relationships becoming intercultural, particularly when we are moved by the Holy Spirit to feel something of God's emotion for our respondents.

We saw in chapter 5 how different personality factors impact human responses to situations; we further recognized how women tend to be more expressive than men in relation to emotion. However, personality differences, including task orientation, need not limit our ability to grow

---

5. See Ekman (2009, 17–18) on nonverbal communication, who reminds how difficult it is to discern when someone is lying. Küster (2020, 298) urges that a "sufficient understanding of the eliciting social context" is key to understanding another's emotional state, but this can be easily missed or misinterpreted in our cross-cultural interactions, hence the advantage of intercultural relationships.

6. Be aware too of Zaluski's (2018) preference of a nontrichotomistic approach to empathy and claims that negative motivations and self-centred aspects may also be in play.

7. From Goleman (2006, 96). Compassionate empathy is synonymous with empathic concern and action.

in understanding our emotional habits and tendencies or, importantly, in our ability to grow in empathy[8] so as to accurately understand and respond appropriately to the emotions of others. Such empathy can become developed in anyone who seeks to live by God's love and walk with the Holy Spirit, who intuits God's will to us. Learning how acts of love and care look and work out in different cultural settings and engaging with compassionate empathy are key to our moving from cross-cultural interaction to intercultural interaction.

> **Important principle:** Increasing empathy is invariably attractive to those who become respondents, and these deepening relationships are marked by empathy that is accompanied by nonpossessive warmth, unconditional acceptance of others, and transparent genuineness of who and how we are.[9]

Warmth that is *nonpossessive* generates a sense of friendly interest and focus that the other can sense lacks any manipulative or controlling tones. *Unconditional* acceptance communicates a readiness to relate to the person and their situation just as they are, without any need for them to hide or deny aspects of reality. Being genuine requires that we present who we are and how we are with *transparency*, meaning that we conceal nothing of our intent and motives. Our personalities may not immediately lend themselves to engaging with others in this manner, but just as we can grow in empathy as we walk in step with the Holy Spirit and sense what God would have us sense about the ones he brings us to, so we will discover increasing ability to be genuinely caring in acceptance of others. Relationships based on trust provide the best basis for such interactions. As our respondents, now deeper in friendship, sense our compassionate empathy, so will they also be more likely to take the risk of being transparent with us while reciprocating warmth and acceptance.

---

8. See too Balconi et al. (2017) on the benefits of cooperation over competition in relation to the brain and personality.

9. I first came across this triad of attributes in Rozell (1983) in relation to counseling but have long since realized they also mark an effective outlook for engaging with others so as to develop empathetic relationships in both monocultural and cross-cultural settings. See too Rozell (1997) and Heslop (1992, 10–11). Heslop lists genuineness, nonpossessive warmth, and accurate empathy as key attitudes and behaviors on the part of the counselor for effective counseling.

CATALYSTS FOR ATTRACTIVE EMPATHY

Now that we have some understanding of the importance of empathy for developing relationships, let's look at some of the practicalities in relation to effective communication. Compassionate empathy expresses to our respondents that we really do care about them and their concerns.

Caring can be expressed in the simplicity of enjoying times and experiences together, whether as part of work commitments or for pure fun. Caring can make an even bigger impact on relationships when we are able to not only understand and empathize with our respondents' concerns, but as we also engage with their needs. We must be aware too of the potential complications that can accompany engaging with needs, particularly if the relationship with the respondents is still only in the cross-cultural stage.

Encouraging people to come to Christ has often been associated with establishing credibility by helping meet financial need or through different kinds of community development work. At best, communication is truly transformative and results in a self-owned and self-sustaining venture by which people come to Christ in repentance that delights in forgiveness and new life. At worst, we create dependency and people only come to Christ for the perceived physical and temporal benefits. Without insights born of the growing mutual interaction that enjoys listening to and learning from each other, which are marks of interculturality, there is great potential for misinterpretation not only of the needs by the Christian communicator but also of the actions by one or both parties.

Effective and transforming communication engages need with empathy in relevant and receivable ways. This includes caring that respects dignity and does not patronize but rather promotes mutual respect. Beyond the purely physical and financial needs are those of an emotional and psychological nature. Issues that were not so prevalent in earlier decades are increasingly prevailing, such as environmental[10] and ecological concerns and issues of prejudice-provoked injustice. We need to consider how willing and to what extent we are called to engage in seeking the justice our respondents crave. To what extent are we called to battle, for instance, for ecological change or to take on other issues with them? Church leaders and church members of the Global North have tended to hold back from engaging with the outlook of the LGBTQ+ movement and questions of gender fluidity and gender dysphoria. How can we communicate into the

---

10. See, for instance, Mutua and Omori (2018).

needs of these and those of other groups who feel marginalized, oppressed, or disenfranchised? How can we communicate Christ and bring a message that is perceived as relevant in spite of, or even in the face of, such challenging personal and life-shaping issues? A helpful key lies in the concept of freedom.

Writing in the context of communicating Christ to the LGBTQ+ community, Chan (2018, 258) offers, "We might say to them 'Where you and I differ, actually, isn't on our view of gays. Where you and I differ is where we think we derive freedom, human rights and love from.'" The principle he brings out here is equally appropriate for any of our respondents who are in a place of restriction, oppression, or emotional or psychological bondage, or who sense they are unable to be who they have been created to be. Chan goes on to show that the bases for freedom, human rights, and love are in principles expounded by the Bible. We can communicate that true freedom, unconditional love, and rights that last for eternity are found only through life in Christ.

STAGES IN ATTAINING INTERCULTURAL COMPETENCE

Having looked at the concept of interculturality and implications for effective communications, we now turn to how progress into interculturality works out with attention to both theory and practice. For Bennett (2013, 12), "The term 'intercultural competence' refers to the ability to embody and enact intercultural sensitivity." Bennett's Intercultural Development Inventory is a helpful tool for recognizing the changes that come with interaction and engagement with another culture.[11] He lists the progression toward successful engagement with another culture in six stages that follow the journey from "ethnocentricism to ethnorelativism," (62) with the first three being more ethnocentric and the second three being more ethnorelative. Bennett describes ethnorelativism as being marked by welcoming cultural diversity and even seeking it out.

---

11. Bennett's inventory evolved from his Developmental Model of Intercultural Sensitivity (DMIS) (Bennett 1986; 1993; Bennett and Castiglioni 2004). Note that Earley and Ang (2003) introduced the term *cultural intelligence* (also known as CQ or *cultural quotient*), which, similarly, marks ability to relate and function effectively cross-culturally. They suggest it is influenced by cognition that builds patterns from cultural ways, motivation to engage cross-culturally, and capability of appropriate action.

Stage 1: Denial

Bennett states that in this stage, cultural differences are denied or their importance is minimized (63).

> **Author's example:** An elderly British lady, who typically considered all Asian people to be Chinese, asked me with great sincerity if I had ever met Yonggi Cho, the founder of Yoido Full Gospel Church in South Korea. For this dear lady, it was as though all Asian nations are Chinese without any cultural differences.

I add that minimizing the importance of cultural differences may occur either in the "honeymoon" stage of interaction in a new culture, when life is exciting and full of new experiences, or as one subconsciously begins trying to develop coping mechanisms for dealing with everything new and different about the culture.

Stage 2: Defence

One's own cultural tendencies are defended as being a better way than those of other cultures (65). This might be an early coping mechanism that comes into play when the excitement of the new situation has worn off and the differences have now become sources of annoyance, frustration, and even anger. This can be part of *cultural dislocation.* Hall (1976, 68) advises that "High-context cultures make greater distinctions between insiders and outsiders than low-context cultures do," and this can make initiating relationships much harder and bring the disappointment of rejection.

> **Important principle:** When cultural dislocation occurs, it can be helpful to remember amidst the frustration: "Whenever a culture 'makes no sense' to us, we must assume that the problem is ours, because the people's behavior makes sense to them" (Hiebert 1999, 378). In this time of dislocation from one's own cultural norms, much support and encouragement is needed.

Another manifestation at this stage is "reversal" or thoroughly throwing oneself into the new culture to the extent of completely rejecting one's background culture. Bennett writes of this manifestation: "However, the positive experience of the other culture is at an unsophisticated stereotypical level, and the criticism of one's own culture is usually an internalisation of others' negative stereotypes" (2004, 66). As we have seen in previous chapters, people cannot throw off their *entire* worldview and replace it with another; any attempt to do so will eventually bring the psychological distress caused by cognitive dissonance.

Author's example: I was teaching about cultural competence to American missionaries. One asked, "Then isn't it best to spend 50 percent of your time with nationals and 50 percent with people from your own background?" I replied that in a new cultural setting, there is no "one size fits all," as it depends on past experience, needs, and expectations in relation to each individual's personality and adult maturity. Some need to spend more time with those from their own background to feel safe and emotionally secure in the early days (e.g., when they are learning language), while others find great delight in spending time with local people and do not need so much reinforcement from those of their own background.

Stage 3: Minimization

Bennett writes regarding this stage: "Elements of one's own cultural worldview are experienced as universal [so that] the threat associated with cultural differences . . . is neutralised by subsuming the differences into familiar categories." However, the outsider's perceptions are still very much experienced from the vantage point of their own culture, and "one's own cultural patterns are [still seen] as central to an assumed universal reality" (66).

Example from Nepal: "Before I came to Christ, I was like every Hindu: I assumed *everyone* is subject to karma."

Bennett advises that the development of cultural self-awareness is very important to continue moving forward at this stage (2004, 67–68). Additionally, an honest awareness of one's own limitations and a means of accountability concerning the limitations (e.g., through sharing difficulties with a trusted friend or mentor) are also important for further developing intercultural competence.

Bennett suggests that the move from stage 3 to stage 4 brings a transition from "ethnocentricism to ethnorelativism," wherein "one's own culture is experienced in the context of other cultures" (68).

Stage 4: Acceptance

Cultural differences are accepted as being real and valid to those of the associated culture as one becomes comfortably aware that the beliefs and practices of one's own culture and worldview are just one set from a much larger domain of differing cultures and worldviews (68). At this stage, one becomes increasingly "adept at identifying how cultural differences in general operate in a wide range of human interactions." Importantly, this is more than merely gaining skills or accumulating knowledge about different cultural factors (69). We are starting to be able to "stand in the shoes of another" and risk considering situations from the other's perspective.

According to Bennett, "The major issue to be resolved . . . is that of value relativity" (69)—in other words, accepting that cultures have different and potentially competing value systems while maintaining an appropriate ethical stance amidst the differing value systems. We experience an urge to be committed to the values of our own worldview system alongside the call to also be neither judgmental nor ethnocentric concerning the values of others. Bennett encourages that acceptance of another culture's beliefs and practices does not necessarily include agreement with them.

> **Example from Mongolia:** "Western missionaries would also insist on doing things their way instead of listening to Mongolians about how to do it the Mongolian way. There are disagreements at times, which are discouraging for us. Missionaries do try to listen, but still, they want to do it their way. They already have an order of things to do. For Mongolians, we do not plan; we are more flexible. This is why there are disagreements."

In the above example from Mongolia, the missionaries do not appear to have reached the acceptance stage, nor do their relationships appear to be headed in an intercultural direction. In our role as Christian communicators from the worldwide body of Christ looking to share biblical perspectives and eternal values with our God-arranged friends in other cultures, we must be able to identify the culturally influenced values we hold so that we do not impose our worldview beliefs or church background cultural values on others. Equally, a spiritually healthy awareness is necessary so that unbiblical beliefs, values, and practices in both our own and other cultures are not condoned in a manner that results in syncretism.[12]

Stage 5: Adaptation

Regarding this stage, Bennett writes: "The experience of another culture yields perception and behavior appropriate to that culture. One's worldview is expanded to include relevant constructs from other cultural worldviews. . . . This shift is not merely cognitive; it is a change in the organization of lived experience, which necessarily includes affect and behavior" (70). Bennett proposes that adaptation is the necessary step toward becoming bicultural. As "culturally appropriate feelings and behavior" become habitual, this "becomes the basis of biculturality" (71). At this stage we are increasing in interculturality, and showing empathy becomes a comfortable reality as we concurrently and sensitively live from the dual perspective of our worldview and the worldview of our respondents.

Bennett offers that "the major issue to be resolved at *Adaptation* is that of authenticity. How is it possible to perceive and behave in culturally different ways and still 'be yourself'?" The answer seems to lie in defining yourself more broadly—in expanding the repertoire of perception and behavior that is "yours" (71). I advise that at this stage, it will be helpful if one's goal continues to be seeking greater intimacy in relationship with God and hence growing in awareness of what he is calling us to understand, take hold of, and put aside, which will then influence our being and doing in appropriately lived-out relationships.

Example: Paul wrote to the Corinthians: "Though I am free and belong to no one, I have made myself a slave to everyone, to win as many as possible. To the Jews I became like a Jew, to win the Jews. To those under the law I became like one under the law (though I myself am not under the law), so as to win those under the law. To those not having the law I became like one not having the law (though I am not free from God's law but am under Christ's law), so as to win those not having the law. To the weak I became weak, to win the weak. I have become all things to all people so that by all possible means I might save some" (1 Corinthians 9:19–22).

---

12. We will return to the concept of syncretism in chapter 9.

It appears that Paul, a Jew with Roman citizenship, used elements of both his former worldview and his transformed worldview to share the gospel of Christ to those enslaved by that former worldview as well as those with other worldviews.

Stage 6: Integration

Bennett describes integration of cultural difference as "the state in which one's experience of self is expanded to include the movement in and out of different cultural worldviews. Here, people are dealing with issues related to their own 'cultural marginality'; they construe their identities at the margins of two or more cultures and central to none" (72). I propose that at this stage of healthy intercultural competence, we as Christian communicators are likely to be acutely and joyfully aware that we will never be *fully* at home in the world or in any of its many cultures since we are merely pilgrims on our way to the now-but-not-yet eternal heavenly home.

Stages as a Tool

Bennett's stages provide a helpful tool for subjective analysis of our intercultural competence. They also allow us to analyze objectively the progress of others for whom we are responsible, including people we are mentoring from our background cultures and respondents from other cultures.[13]

INTERCULTURAL INTERVIEWS: MUTUAL DISCOVERY

I assigned students in my cross-cultural communications courses to interview Christians from other background cultures about their specific cultural backgrounds to discover how Christian communicators might share the gospel in a receivable way. The interviewer was required to listen carefully in order to show unconditional acceptance and to solicit transparency. In the following paragraphs you'll find excerpts from a variety of different cultural perspectives, along with comments from interviewers.[14] Appendix 2 gives a series of owned characteristics for the different cultures

---

13. See too Lustig et al. (2018) for a highly practical hands-on approach to gaining intercultural competence. Cf. Chao et al. (2017), whose research showed that those with a fixed mindset about their cultural beliefs were less likely to adjust cross-culturally.

14. This material is an amalgamation of multiple interviews from more than one interviewer per culture, slightly modified for coherent use of English in places and for coherency with context.

given by interviewees and provides context for the interviewers' comments. Transparency implies trust. But note where reduced interculturality might occasionally be present and seen as tension or defensiveness in discourses, including in the interviewers' comments.

Bhutan

Past mistakes by Christian communicators: It's hard for them to come, but some would come and not even try to share the gospel. They would build relationships and just leave.

Advice for Christian Communicators
- Try to adapt to our culture in terms of food and clothing.
- Be careful while talking to Bhutanese—don't be too close face-to-face, as this is rude. Don't touch our heads, but if you are praying for Bhutanese people, then you can.
- Be aware that there's something of the atheistic belief that Bhutanese people evolved from monkeys.

Malaysian interviewer's comments: "I was surprised at my interviewee's surprise at the classroom difference here where teachers and students interact in class."

China

Past mistakes by Christian communicators: Missionaries sometimes acted contrary to Chinese culture. Some had a colonialist outlook of superiority. Some live at a high economic level, which creates barriers with locals. Giving financial resources created unhelpful patron-client relationships.

Advice for Christian Communicators
- Know the history of Confucianism, Buddhism, and communism; most of the Chinese are ancestor worshippers.
- Know the culture by learning the language: Mandarin and also the minority language if you are called to a minority, since some elderly people do not know how to speak Mandarin.
- Start with friendship evangelism; avoid direct criticism. Chinese people will open their hearts if the communicator is able to win their trust.
- Don't talk about politics, especially the South China Sea issues, because all the islands are ours!

Korean interviewer's comments: "Korea also has territory conflicts with China, but I remained silent."

Czech Republic

Past mistakes by Christian communicators: Missionaries just did their own thing and were not willing to fathom the complicated Czech mindset to fully understand their thinking and behavior.

Advice for Christian Communicators
- Have basic knowledge of Czech history, including the communist background, because Czech people dwell on the past.

Dominican Republic

Past mistakes by Christian communicators: There is a long history of Catholicism in Dominican Republic. Protestant missionaries were like Santa Claus: they provided everything for the local church, created dependency, and did not teach how to give, including offerings, or to have a mission outlook. Therefore, the local churches learned how to receive but did not learn how to give and send missionaries to other nations. Missionaries didn't contextualize the gospel: they imposed strict rules, such as women should not wear pants and earrings. After the missionary left the country, the ministry tended to die because of lack of transition to the local people.

Advice for Christian Communicators
- Learn the Spanish language and the culture.
- Spend time with local people.
- If people see that you mastered their language, they will see your heart; but if you always use an interpreter, they will think you are lazy.
- Be careful not to be critical about the culture; don't complain about the traffic because that causes offense.
- Work with local people, train and disciple them, so that the ministry will not be something foreigners do; transition the ministry to the local people.

Japanese interviewer's comments: "They speak Spanish as their language but they are not Spanish citizens. Only in Japan is Japanese the national language."

India

Past mistakes by Christian communicators: Missionaries didn't understand the caste system; they gave money to poor people who only changed their religion for the income and status. We want missionaries who work along with the church, without breaking our national laws, and who *don't* reinforce the caste barrier.

Advice for Christian Communicators
- Build relationships so people feel respected and accepted even if you have different views or beliefs. Focus on friendship, and then people will eventually ask you about your faith.
- Don't speak against other religions or mock them. We have to present the gospel in a way that they can understand. Our task is to share the truth, not to make people angry.
- Relationships are more important than preaching. Target the head of the family or chief of the village.
- Hinduism is a very inclusive religion. There is no absolute truth in the Hindu society; they can easily believe in another god, but that doesn't mean they have repented and come to know Christ.
- Be careful with nonverbal communication. For example, don't point your finger.
- Demonstrate the love of God in the way that the people can understand, and devise strategies according to locals' needs—social work is a good tool to serve in India.
- Know that you have to work with the local church leadership.

Colombian interviewer's comments: "It was strange for me that Indians trust more in the white missionaries than their own religious leaders. Good that the outsiders must answer to local leaders."

Japan

Past mistakes by Christian communicators: Missionaries often want to do things their own way and sometimes do not cooperate with local pastors.

Advice for Christian Communicators
- Learn the language, the customs, and how to respect traditions. Smile.
- Talking in Japanese in the public bathtub is a good place for friendship evangelism.

- If you want to be close with Japanese people, you need to build up a stable relationship between you and those people before you can expect any transparency in communication, and remember that community is very important to them.
- Japanese people want to follow plans exactly, so communicate with everyone involved and make plans very carefully.

Filipina interviewer's comment: "Being naked to evangelize in the public bathtub shocked me."

Mexican interviewer's comment: "If Christian communicators can't work under the direction of Japanese pastors, then we have to pay attention to our humility."

Kenya (East Africa)

Past mistakes by Christian communicators: I had an argument regarding this question about missionaries in one of my classes: I spoke up and said that some missionaries try to impose their culture into our culture. They think they are better than us. They said Kenyan children are disrespectful, and their children are better. I told them that Kenyan children are brought up differently. We grew up that way, and if to them we seem disrespectful, in our culture we are not—we are acting normal.

Advice for Christian Communicators
- You must know the general language: *Keswahili.*
- Learn how we do things, and learn the culture. When you disrespect the culture, it seems like you are immediately judging us rather than reaching out to us; the culture will not adjust to you—you must adjust to the culture!
- Don't just stay as a group of Americans together. They come out in the daytime to minister, but they never really understand the culture and are quick to judge my culture.
- You have to earn trust by building and developing relationships.

Filipina interviewer's comments: "It was uncomfortable for me to hear that missionaries would be so direct and rude."

Mongolia

Past mistakes by Christian communicators: Missionaries came and trained the locals for leadership, but now (twenty-eight years later) some still want to maintain control. They don't allow local leaders into leadership roles. Western missionaries would also insist on doing things their way instead of listening to Mongolians on how to do it the Mongolian way. The Asian missionaries prefer to hide their feelings and do not understand that Mongolians are expressive of their emotions.

Advice for Christian Communicators
- It's harder for Asian communicators because Mongolians don't have all their honorifics and rituals. We respect elders but not like other Asian nations.
- Wear our clothing and learn the culture. Be open and be direct; don't be afraid to express what you want to Mongolians. Keeping quiet won't endear you to my people—being direct will allow you to avoid misunderstandings. Don't push us to share personal information because we'll be selective in what we're willing to share.
- Family is very important, so Western individualism doesn't work. For example, a Mongolian will not just think of himself when he receives Jesus. We don't like it if they think that we're saved but don't care for our family. Western culture seems like they don't care about the family.
- Don't just expect to do things in ministry *your* way; listen to us and flex with us!
- When you've trained up local Christians, be sure to release control and let them take on leadership roles.

Filipina interviewer's comment: "Why train Christians if you're not going to give them leadership roles?"

Korean interviewer's comment: "I think that if I ever go there, it is possible that I will be hurt by them because of their very direct character."

Myanmar (formerly Burma)

Past mistakes by Christian communicators: Missionaries haven't valued relationships as we do; also they tend to give a lot of money to the local leaders just because they want to finish the project. The gospel wasn't contextualized and only touched the lower caste, so Buddhists believe that Christianity is the religion of Westerners. The higher caste Brahmas are Buddhist and are unreached by the gospel, but they need to be because they hold political and military control.

Advice for Christian Communicators
- Learn the language of the called-to people group and value the culture.
- Eat our food and wear our clothing, as this will create an important connection, especially in the countryside. Men wear a small skirt called a *lungy*.
- Avoid touching anyone's head, as it is considered sacred; some Christian prayer practices could result in big misunderstandings.
- Build relationships and help meet social needs; you have to initiate building relationships because Burmese will not make the move. Spend time with people; if you are invited to a house, usually you will also have the freedom to share the gospel with the entire family, and they will all listen.
- Encourage the existing church leadership so that they will continue the vision that God has given them to do. It is better for the gospel to be presented by local people.
- Burmese are intuitional; having a power encounter with the Holy Spirit will be crucial in order for them to be open to hear the truth.

Filipina interviewer's comment: "The customs of respect and honor of the elderly is much like my culture."

Mexican interviewer's comment: "The interviewee was surprised our school president shook hands with him—that would be normal for me."

Nepal

Past mistakes by Christian communicators: Missionaries wouldn't follow our lifestyle of dressing and eating (sitting on the floor and using your hands). Some wore shoes in their house, which offends the locals. We value relationships very much, but some missionaries didn't want to spend personal time with our people. They usually chose to live outside the community. This affirmed the worldview belief that Christianity is a Western religion. The strong and direct nature of the Americans is also offensive.

Advice for Christian Communicators
- Seek to understand the religious practices, cultural behavioral pattern, and relationship of high and low class in the society.
- Our culture is very relational, and the missionary should be prepared to expend a lot of time with the people, talking and eating with them. Even if the local food isn't tasty to you, do not cook for yourself because it offends local people, as though our food isn't good enough.

- Learn the Nepali language.
- Always ask for the pastor's advice about whether it's appropriate to attend cultural activities. Some "interesting-looking" activities that foreigners like to go to are just evil.
- Never use the left hand in handling, receiving, pointing, and shaking because it is considered dirty.
- Clothing is very important; women should cover their full body; in prayer, women are also required to cover their heads with shawls.
- Men and women are not allowed to hold hands together or shake hands.
- Medical, education, community development, and environmental awareness programs are good for gospel outreach. Eighty percent of income is from agriculture, so agricultural programs are attractive.

Malaysian interviewer's comment: "I realized this 'living outside the local community' mentality has caused a lack of connection between missionaries and locals."

Mexican interviewer's comment: "I was challenged about missionaries wanting to join activities that seem interesting but do not realize the danger of evil that is present. How important it is to always listen to local pastors and be guided by them."

Nigeria (West Africa)

Past mistakes by Christian communicators: Missionaries often imposed colonialist values and ignored our cultural ways. They would be seen as a "money tree" and that bred entitlement.

Advice for Christian Communicators
- Since Nigeria is a very religious country and supernaturally aware, it is important to understand the worldview beliefs behind the cultural practices.
- Respect for elders is very important.
- When giving or receiving things, use the right hand, as using the left hand would be impolite.
- Taking up our lifestyle will help us feel you belong. For instance, when you as a foreigner wear our clothing and eat with your hands when you go to the villages, you'll be respected as a guest and seen as humble, showing you want to be with the people.

Filipina interviewer's comments: "Filipinos also usually come late but not as late as two hours! Also, I am still wondering why the left hand should not be used for receiving things."

Pakistan

Past mistakes by Christian communicators: The missionaries gave people a lot a financial support, but it looked like it was just to convert them. Another mistake was the lack of discipleship, and that's why many of the converts are not genuine believers. Missionaries started big projects among the communities, but they didn't pass responsibility to the people, so when they left, many projects crashed.

Advice for Christian Communicators
- It is very important to learn Urdu. Pakistanis open their minds more easily to those who use their language; serve food to build relationships; show your emotions and that you care.
- You must understand the culture and customs of Pakistan and be especially careful when doing evangelism; go to a church and learn from the leaders what is appropriate. The Pakistani government is very tolerant of Christianity, but you cannot criticize the prophet Muhammad or the Muslim culture and social system.
- Be aware that Pakistani Christians often don't consider themselves to be a part of the country, and they don't pray for the country because they don't have the sense of belonging. It's one of the causes of lack in evangelism, and why they aren't interested even to talk to Muslims.
- Help the new generation understand God's purposes for them so that they will develop a sense of belonging and develop a vision to reach their own people.

Korean interviewer's comments: "I've learnt that preparing for ministry in Pakistan surely needs much prayer and courage as well as understanding the culture."

Papua New Guinea

Past mistakes by Christian communicators: Missionaries imposed *their* culture and ideology. Some just preached the gospel without doing anything to help people's physical needs.

Advice for Christian Communicators
- Stay with local PNG folks for at least three months to learn the language; just sit down and listen to people; spend time with them.
- Talk with people in a kind and respectful way, otherwise you will invite trouble; use humor as well.
- It is very important that you should be straight and state your intentions in the community.
- Be aware: in the villages there are still superstitious beliefs.
- Be decent in your dressing with simplicity and modesty; it's better for women to wear skirts or dresses when preaching the gospel.

Chinese interviewer's comments: "It seems that a mission strategy to PNG could be similar to the strategy for Samoa—that is, the key object of evangelizing is the head of the community, and the rest of the community will follow him."

Saudi Arabia

Past mistakes by Christian communicators: Christian communicators tried to change culture by challenging beliefs rather than teaching the love of Jesus—it was indoctrination rather than relationship building.

Advice for Christian Communicators
- Understand Muslim values even if you don't agree with them.
- Don't see the people as wrong; understand that they don't know because they haven't experienced Jesus and the Holy Spirit.
- Build bridges rather than try to conquer.

Thailand

Past mistakes by Christian communicators: Foreigners especially make mistakes with the Thai language because getting tones wrong can make okay words sound like bad words. Thai people always expect that missionaries come with a lot of financial support, and that can create dependency.

Advice for Christian Communicators
- Invest time in building up the relationship first; take initiative to visit or mix with people in church and then grow trust.
- Live with the local community, learn the language, eat with them, adopt their relaxed and unhurried lifestyle, and then you can share the gospel. But don't use "Christian terminology."

- Do not touch anyone's head; respect people who are older than you; while sitting on the floor, do not stretch your legs out and point your feet toward anyone.
- Do not mock or say anything against idols or monks. As a courtesy, you must be respectful to them. Also, Thailand is a kingdom: we love and respect our king and expect the same from outsiders who come to our country.
- Know that you must only partner with churches, not lead them.

Colombian interviewer's comments: "I was amazed to learn that even if you are not a Buddhist, you must still respect the Buddhist monks as an act of courtesy."

Turkey

Past mistakes by Christian communicators: Christians were often afraid to share their faith, but Turkey has a secular form of government and many "freedoms," and religion is a very encompassing and normal part of life. Talking about faith issues and Islam, even to the point of arguing, is not "taboo" in Turkey.

Advice for Christian Communicators
- Be flexible and be relational. Making space for lengthy, relational events is an important part of Turkish life and building rapport. Be prepared to drink a lot of tea!
- Take off your shoes before you enter a home because the ground is dirty. Never put a holy book (e.g., the Bible) on the floor, as that's huge disrespect to what should be held sacred.
- If you are on public transportation, give your seat to anyone older than you.
- You may talk to those of the opposite sex and even make eye contact, but you should avoid being overly friendly.
- Talk about your faith; never forget to offer to pray in person for the one you are sharing with.

United Arab Emirates

Past mistakes by Christian communicators: Missionaries have made the mistakes of seeing people as objects rather than people and of trying to use methods that appeared to have worked in one area in another. Just because the environment looks modern and Western, the culture is not, and that trips up foreigners.

Foreigners can become influenced by materialism quickly and get drawn in by its deception. They may feel like they are being treated like a paid slave in the workplace and get frustrated.

Advice for Christian Communicators
- See them as ordinary people who need the Lord and not as people of a certain faith (like Islam) or culture to be afraid of. Genuinely reach out in friendship. Contact and friendships are made through prayer.
- Apologetics may have their place, but people respond to being accepted and loved rather than approached through religious discussions/debates.
- Be prepared to be spontaneous as they do not usually plan events.
- Be on guard against and aware of the power and subtle influence of materialism.
- Do not express physical affection with your spouse in public or offer your hand first to someone of the opposite sex.
- Dress modestly; eat with your right hand, not your left. Remove your shoes when entering a house unless told not to.
- Pray and be led by the Spirit; be willing to share your life with those God leads you to, whatever their response.

United States of America

Past mistakes by Christian communicators: People often think Americans are just white and rich, but that is not so. If they came to reach out to a people-group like Chinese or migrant workers, they didn't also pay attention to the leading cultural outlook which governed and set the laws wherever they went.

Advice for Christian Communicators
- Although Americans are usually thought of as white, there are a mixture of people from many cultures with their own subcultures (e.g., Latinos, African American), and you must communicate on their terms.
- Be on time or early. It shows you respect the values of time and politeness.
- Be countercultural. For example, Americans, being task oriented, are not used to someone who cares for them unconditionally. If you go in showing people you really care about them, it will make an impact in their lives.

Filipina interviewer's comments: "I hadn't realized that people from the cities can differ from people who live in the countryside. The white lady I interviewed told me that people from the countryside are more event oriented, more noncrisis preventative, and more community and people oriented than people who live in the cities. So you have to ask respondents about their background."

Vietnam

Past mistakes by Christian communicators: Missionaries failed to understand the Vietnamese culture and government policy. For example, when they communicated the gospel, they forgot that they were talking to atheists who had no idea about God, let alone that he heals. Also, they would provide funds, but the Vietnamese worldview belief is that if you are to have money, you have to work. Even now, some use irrelevant Western illustrations when they teach and preach.

Advice for Christian Communicators
- Prepare well. Are your target people the old people or young people? If you target the old people, then you need to know the Vietnamese language; however, the young people can understand English.
- Be familiar with the history of Vietnam; the old people are proud of winning the war, especially in the north part of Vietnam.
- In the south of Vietnam, be careful not to talk about war because they sided with the Americans. Start talking about life and business.
- You should know about evolution theory and atheism because it's part of the communist worldview. Always remember that the people have an atheist mindset. Vietnamese still worship idols and burn incense, but it's not religiosity, just rituals for selfish motives.
- If you go to the countryside, do a project with the farmers before communicating the gospel. If you are in the city, think of practical projects like coming up with an English club in order to earn their trust.
- Building friendship is important. Avoid being manipulative with the gospel. Be interested in people's lives and in the community. After doing projects with your target group, slowly share the gospel.

Filipina interviewer's comments: "I was surprised and felt anxious that Vietnamese are more dichotomistic thinkers and that you are only seen as either a friend or an enemy."

EXAMPLES OF INTERCULTURAL RELATIONSHIPS

Irish wife and Mainland Chinese husband: "We've been married seventeen years and have two children. Chinese people don't really work on their marriages. I had expectations about saying sorry and forgiveness, then realized my husband's way of saying sorry was to do something nice for me,[15] not talk about the issue. It's taken a long time to get to resolutions on issues, and we're not completely there yet. Getting to know each other's personality is really important."

Spanish husband and Mexican wife: "Although we spoke the same language (Spanish), the cultural differences were very significant. We had many misunderstandings in our communication when we were getting to know each other. What to me was a matter of common sense caused my wife to get really angry at me because relationships with others were affected. We had to keep persevering."

Japanese wife and Taiwanese husband: "Language was an early struggle to communicate fullness of meaning. Now I struggle more in communicating with Japanese people because they expect me to respond in the Japanese way, but I have changed through being married to my Taiwanese husband, especially as he is not at all time oriented."

White British wife and Nigerian husband: "In the early years of the relationship after we had moved to Nigeria, there were many cross-cultural differences: the treatment of women and children and the way his family felt they could make demands of him set up a struggle of loyalty for him. What helped our relationship become deeper was becoming Christians; living as Christians with good Christian friends and the activities of the church we attended became a unifying focus."

---

15. See too Gary Chapman (1995) on five different love languages. The Chinese husband's way of saying sorry appears to correlate with "acts of service."

IMPORTANT PRINCIPLES FOR
DEVELOPING AND HONING
INTERCULTURAL RELATIONSHIPS

In the previous two sections we have seen individuals advising about communicating with people of their own culture, followed by insights from spouses in intercultural marriages. Their examples put flesh onto the concepts described in the chapter, from which are derived the following transferable principles that will help us put intercultural theory into practice:

- Developing intercultural relationships best occurs when people are open to learn about each other's culture.
- The initial encounter may seem unplanned, but what occurs after friendship has been offered needs to be intentional. Be prayerful throughout the relationship-growing process.
- Intercultural relationships deepen when both parties seek and offer forgiveness. Getting to this point requires transparency and vulnerability. Apart from personality differences, forgiveness encounters can work out differently depending on the culture.[16]
- Listening is an important part of acceptance and empathetic communication, as is persevering to understand each other.
- Be willing to offer yourself and the time that is God's gift to you; be flexible and open to the Holy Spirit's leading.
- Growth in interculturality cannot help but change us, as we replace old ways with unifying new ways that become "normal" ways by God's grace.

Devotional comment: Growing in interculturality requires us to put aside, even lose, some aspects of our background culture's outlooks and lifestyles. Have we discovered the wonder of the truth that in losing, we win? Being willing to come prayerfully to the cross is the comforting, refreshing means of once again finding our identity and sense of self-worth in being God's precious children. He brings us into gain from loss as we see what unconditional love and acceptance of others looks like from his perspective. He gives us the promise of sufficient grace and empowerment as we

---

16. See Fujino (2009) on how independence of individualists can contrast with the interdependence of collectivists in relation to the area of cross-cultural forgiveness.

rest in him in our being and doing in these relationships. As a result, we become more than we were—not only in Christ but also in his purposes for us, as transforming communications bring forth the fruit of intercultural relationships.

CONCLUSION

Transformed and transforming communications are a mark of intercultural relationships, and empathy is an important factor for developing these communications and growing in the interculturality that builds intercultural relationships. Our communications in sharing the gospel have the potential to be most effective as our respondents trust us and are moved by our expressions of empathetic care.

QUESTIONS FOR REFLECTION
AND DISCUSSION

1. What does the scenario in the "As It Happened" section at the start of the chapter tell you about God's grace to me during and after the bus trip?
2. Of Bennett's stages in attaining intercultural competence, between which two stages is it probably the hardest to transition? Why?
3. Which interviews in the chapter seem to reflect high power distance nations? Which nations seem to have low-context communicators? Check your choices with the full interviews in appendix 2.
4. Read the Papua New Guinea interview in appendix 2. Based on the interview content given, do you agree with the interviewer's comment in this chapter? Why or why not? From a technical perspective, which Bennett stage might the comment be reflecting?
5. In relation to current or potential future relationships, what is God saying to you personally about the reality of loss and exchange in interculturality?

CHAPTER 9

Christian Communicators and Contextualization

As It Happened: A Filipina related the following about an event with her Christian family:

> We were moving into a different house, and my mother wanted to go ahead and bring rice into the house first. She said she wanted to be sure to prepare the house so that God would always bless us with provision there. She also said we may not sweep the floor in the evening as that would sweep the blessing out. I said to her, "Mama, that's not biblical; we don't need to bring rice in first—it's like trying to manipulate God. It's just a superstitious practice and not how God wants us to relate to him." So she didn't do it, but it seemed like she wasn't very happy about not doing it. Sometimes she still speaks about not sweeping the blessing out in the evening, but I urge her to trust God and pray her concerns to him. I don't know where she got these ideas from.

INTRODUCTION

"We are not human beings having a spiritual experience. We are spiritual beings having a human experience."[1]

We will most likely already have begun to discover some of the mysteries of our respondents' beliefs about causes and effects, both seen and unseen, as our relationships become increasingly intercultural. They may have spiritual worldview beliefs quite unlike our own. We may meet beliefs

---

1. This quote is frequently referenced as a translation from writings of the French Jesuit priest Pierre Teilhard de Chardin (1881–1955).

and systems for reinforcing self-identity and a sense of security that vary from comforting and pleasing to incredulous and bizarre from our perspectives. But we dare not dismiss the beliefs of our respondents out of hand if we are to honor their dignity and cherish them as friends.

Three decades after World War II, in recognition of the difficulties and challenges faced by then-contemporary missionaries, missionary statesman Tippett (1975, 16) wrote: "The greatest methodological issue faced by the Christian mission in our day is how to carry out the Great Commission in a multi-cultural world with a gospel that is both truly Christian in content and culturally significant in form." The challenges we face today are the same that Tippett faced.

To communicate a relevant and receivable message, we need to consider both the cultural context of the people we are reaching out to and also the situational specifics of the local people and their setting. What bore fruit with respondents in one location may not be repeatable in another, even amongst people of the same background culture. To communicate the gospel message and biblical truths effectively, we need to be aware of the local current beliefs and practices, and contextualize the spiritual truths of Christianity while being careful to avoid syncretism. Syncretism is the combination of unbiblical praxis with Christian principles, and it can also come about if the message of the gospel and what it means to be a Christian aren't properly understood. Syncretism results in an outlook that is neither truly Christian nor biblical.

Example of perceived syncretism given by a nonindigenous Australian: "The Aboriginals drink a lot of alcohol and get drunk. It's a normal cultural behavior for them. When they become Christian, the Holy Communion services in denominations where wine is used just seemed like a justification to keep drinking alcohol."

Example of perceived syncretism from America: "I once visited a church in Tucson [Arizona] where they broke bread during the service with coffee and donuts. It seemed rather strange to me because coffee isn't fruit of the vine, and the minister didn't explain the reasoning behind it."

Example of perceived syncretism from Nepal: "Some missionaries used red wine during Communion, but the Nepalese wouldn't drink it because they would never drink cow's blood. Cows are sacred to Hindus; the red wine the missionaries used for the sacrament looked like cow's blood."[2]

At this point, we also need to be clear of the implications of differing perceptions of how the gospel and the reality of culture relate to each other. This chapter attends to these issues and provides principles to ensure spiritually healthy contextualization of the gospel message with a resulting Christian lifestyle with the potential to be culturally significant.

THE GOSPEL AND CULTURE

Hiebert (1999, 381) writes: "It is not always easy to distinguish between the gospel and human cultures, for the gospel, like any message, must be put into cultural forms to be understood and communicated by people." As we saw in chapter 7, different cultures follow different thinking processes to arrive at understanding, and for effective communication, we need to be aware of the situational preference of those we are reaching out to.

At this point, we must consider the relationship between Christ and culture in general.[3] Sorting out our own stance increases the potential for effective communication in intercultural ministry, particularly when we are ministering alongside those of other cultures and working together even when we have differing perspectives. It is important for us to be aware of which principles we are willing to compromise and which are nonnegotiable.

Niebuhr's *Christ and Culture* (1951) has long been the classic text for examining the relationship between the gospel and culture. He offers the following types of relationship:

- Christ against culture—but this type separates believers from the world in which they are to be salt and light

---

2. The examples of possible syncretism above are all focused on the elements of the Communion service, which is referred to in different ways according to denominational churchmanship (e.g., as breaking bread, the Lord's supper, or Holy Communion). Notice that the description used is not necessarily defined by culture or particularly used in relation to certain cultures.

3. This section reflects material from D-Davidson (2018, 113–15).

- Christ of (or within) culture—but this type can either intentionally or inadvertently lessen the importance of Christ's divinity so that the gospel is reduced to self-reliant humanism
- Christ above culture—but this type either intentionally or inadvertently downplays Christ's humanity and also dismisses the reality of evil and sinfulness in the world
- Christ and culture in paradox (or tension)—but this type can't help but bring a separation between the kingdom of God and the kingdom of the world, although, unlike the Christ against culture type, the believer knows he cannot escape from the world
- Christ the transformer of culture—this type sees culture transformed by the power and presence of Christ lived out in the world

Carter (2006, 111) questions Niebuhr's typology and brings an alternative perspective. Carter urges that the situation in which Niebuhr wrote "presupposes both the existence and legitimacy of Christendom. However, both his criticism of Christ against culture type and his endorsement of the Christ transforming culture type lose their cogency in our post-Christendom context. Not only does he assume that the church should make the compromises necessary to retain influence within the culture, he also assumes that the wider culture is ready and willing to be transformed by Christians." Carter makes some valid points since, at the time that Niebuhr wrote, the demise of Christendom was already being declared, and it accelerated rapidly from the 1960s.[4]

Further, Carter suggests that the church was always under cultural pressure to compromise biblical principles and that "Niebuhr's approach . . . leads to Christians accommodating themselves [by way of compromising biblical principles]" to the surrounding society. Carter not unreasonably questions the assumption that the wider culture is ready and willing to be transformed and, on the contrary, suggests that the Christ against culture type has rather more been replaced by a culture against Christ outlook. We can certainly see this in the rise of militant Islam atrocities worldwide.

Carter also suggests that the church in the days of Christendom has had no qualms about sponsoring violence to achieve its own ends in coercion with the state—from the church of the fourth century all the way through the colonialist era. As a result, he champions a resistance to such temptation, and his non-Christendom typology reflects this. He rewrites

---

4. See McLeod and Ustorf (2003).

three Christendom types that, in line with his hypothesis, accept violent coercion. In contrast, he then offers three non-Christendom types that reject violent coercion. These are:

1. Christ transforming culture—for all society but [unlike the Christendom version] should not be imposed by force, but preached by word and deed.
2. Christ humanizing culture—for the church only, but motivates loving service to society.
3. Christ separating from culture—for the church only. (112–13)

Carter's perspective ultimately boils the issues down to the ethics of violence (or not) in the name of the gospel, particularly "the use of violence in promoting Christianity" (185). As a result, Carter prefers that Christians should not engage in modern war (196). He urges us that regardless of worldview ideology or cultural tendencies, even when we engage a resistant and hostile culture, we should aim to bring the gospel in a peaceable manner.

Carter's work has certainly shaken the traditional ground broken by Niebuhr, but his distinction of Christendom types being marked by coercion to violence in contrast with his non-Christendom types is remarkably dichotomistic. It is unreasonable to suggest that a norm of violence marked the entire church-backed missionary effort from the fourth century through the colonial era and onward. Equally, to suggest that this is not so of post-Christendom missionary activity naively dismisses the potential for violence inherent in any activity founded on impure motives.

Niebuhr's analysis and typology are reliably descriptive and invite the reader to be aware of alternatives in choosing one's stance. In contrast, Carter's typology, notable for its attempt to move us on from Niebuhr's classic text, is the vehicle for a very noble underlying polemic but ultimately comes across as directive and with a rather shallow call to the field of ethics literature.

Boa (n.d) writes, "Perhaps the major problem was Niebuhr's assumption of culture as a single, unitary reality whose relation to Christ and the church could be defined in one way. In an increasingly multicultural world, we must now ask about Christ and *cultures*: How does Christ relate to the diverse cultural traditions and expressions in our world? And how do these diverse cultural traditions relate to one another in Christ?" Before we turn to Boa's answer, we should note that the world was no less multicultural in Niebuhr's day, and taking a singular assumption of the concept is not necessarily problematic in the way that Boa implies. Niebuhr's approach to gospel and culture can equally be imposed upon the concept of Christ and cultures. As an alternative to Niebuhr's five types, Boa prefers "that the relation between Christ and our plurality of cultures may be understood from at least three perspectives. First, Christ is the *Reconciler* of cultures—he is the one who can bring people of different cultures together. Second, Christ is the *Redeemer* of cultures—he brings wholeness and hope to people of all cultures. Third, Christ is the *Ruler* of cultures—he is the one who establishes the standards by which all cultures are ultimately to be judged."

If we examine Boa's perspectives, we can see that all three are part of Niebuhr's fifth type, Christ as transformer of culture, in that transformation has the potential to bring reconciliation between different peoples (Galatians 3:26–28); transformation manifests as the redemption of those ways which were previously incompatible with kingdom of God principles (1 Peter 1:18–19); and transformation brings a transferal of submission from unbiblical worldview-priority allegiances to love-based submission under the lordship of Christ both individually and also collectively as united members of the body of Christ (1 Corinthians 12:12–13) of which Christ is the ruling head. Boa's perspectives nonetheless also give us some key issues to factor in when we communicate about the nature of the relationship that deciding for Christ will bring our respondent into. Prior to that, we need to be prayerful about how we contextualize the gospel message.

CONTEXTUALIZATION OF THE GOSPEL MESSAGE

Contextualization of the gospel message is essentially communicating its truths in such a way that the respondent can receive the truths without the Christian communicator compromising on any aspect. We facilitate this by getting to know our respondent so we can interact in an appropriate way. We need to know where the respondent is along the journey toward coming to own the gospel of Christ for themselves. For some respondents, message communication requires preevangelism, which involves getting them used to the truth of God's existence. There is little point in introducing truths about Jesus as God's Son if the respondents don't believe in the existence of God. First, we need to be aware of their background beliefs about God and, if they have religious beliefs, be careful not to assume they share our understanding of the term *God* or other Christian terminology.

Example from China: In the school system, communism teaches that there is no such thing as God and that religion is merely a manmade idea. According to Karl Marx, "Religion is the sigh of the oppressed creature, the heart of a heartless world, and the soul of soulless conditions" and hence "the opiate of the people."[5] What do opiates do? They dull the mind and senses to the pain in which people live. They provide for a less uncomfortable but purposeless existence of surviving but not living the celebration that is life. Despite this being part of the communist manifesto, Chinese culture includes a variety of religionlike practices that seek to honor or appease essences in the unseen spiritual world, including veneration of the spirits of the dead. Unholy though such spirits are, it does give a bridge to common-ground concerns for issues related to the spiritual realm.

Example from Mongolia: "Mongolians think that Jesus is a foreign God. So missionaries need to share who God is as a creator first and then introduce Jesus. If they introduce Jesus first, then the locals reject the gospel."

As Christians, we know God as the almighty Creator who is omnipotent, omniscient, and omnipresent; we know that he is a God of righteousness, truth, and love, all of which work out through his justice-upholding nature. Inquiries into our respondents' beliefs or the pervasive beliefs in their culture can help us decide whether we need to begin by helping them recognize the presence of God. We can do this by modeling in our relationships our awe of God's transcendence as well as our joy at his immanence. We can show how we live moment by moment in delight of God while seeking his direction for our lives. We can offer to pray to God for their needs, perhaps initially out of sight but later with them present. We can show them that we believe God orders our lives and does all things well. Whenever it is appropriate, we can show them truths in the Bible— preferably in their heart language. They already may have had spiritual seeds sown that we can water.

But don't forget: if our respondents do have a concept of God, they may

---

5. Usually ascribed to Marx's 1843 but unpublished in his lifetime *Critiques of Hegel's Philosophy of Right*. See Marx (1970) in the Bibliography for a translated version.

perceive the concept in terms of a great many other attributes, including some that are incompatible with the Bible.

> **Author's example from Syria:** While I was completing doctoral studies, I was living in international students' accommodations in the UK for a few months. In the communal kitchen I met a Muslim lady, Eliz,[6] who was studying the history of the growth of Christian missionary work in Syria. As part of her research, she had visited several Catholic churches to see what the missionaries believed. I asked her if she would like to visit a Protestant church, knowing that, although I had preaching ministry at churches most Sundays, I had a free Sunday coming up. Her PhD supervisor agreed, and Eliz and I went to one of my ministry-supporting churches. There was vibrant praise and worship, heart-inspiring preaching, and a prayer ministry time at the end of the service. As we drove away from the service, Eliz kept saying, "You *love* your God, but I don't love my God." It was clearly an astonishing experience for her to see and feel the love lived out amongst Christians in that service, and her heart and mind were astounded at this major difference. She kept emphasizing the word *love* and how she didn't love her God. Of course, with great delight, I then related to her how she could come into such an experience through Jesus.

CONTEXTUALIZING EVANGELISM AND THE ESSENTIALS OF THE GOSPEL

Communication to facilitate contextualized Christianity likely has its best beginnings in contextualized evangelism. Wright (1998, 453) defines *contextualized evangelism* as "presenting the uncompromising gospel of Jesus Christ in the sociocultural, ethnic, and linguistic context of the hearers so they may respond and be discipled into a church." We have seen the importance of trying to "stand in our respondents' shoes" to sense how they might be decoding and interpreting our communications through their worldviews and cultures. We saw too how getting to know our respondents and identifying their needs are key to empathy that builds on attitudes of nonpossessive warmth, unconditional acceptance, and genuine transparency in relationship with them.

---

6. To maintain anonymity, this was not her actual name.

We need to communicate the truths about Christ and the salvation that belief in him brings in ways that our respondents see as relevant in relation to their cultural beliefs. The term *salvation*, for instance, may have no relevance at all to followers of other religions, let alone communicate the concept of a loving relationship with a spiritual being. Identifying where our respondents' religion has limitations that impact their existence can be a means of communicating in an appropriate way about, for instance, the freedom that knowing and loving Christ brings. We saw the essentials of the gospel in chapter 1, and that communication is most effective when we refer to each essential truth only as respondents are prepared and ready to receive them. Prayer is an important part of our outreach at any stage so that we might be attuned to what our respondents are ready to hear, receive, and respond to favorably. We need to be sensitive to which aspects of the gospel truths fill deficiencies in the respondent's religious system or system for coping with life, such as fear of death, an oppressive lifestyle, hopelessness in relation to fate, inability to escape from control by evil forces, lack of means for forgiveness or release from guilt or shame, or the inability to be freed from karma or similar bondage imposed by the respondent's religious or political system.

To those whose religious systems lack a means for the forgiveness of sin or removal of shame or guilt, we can explain what Jesus did to achieve these by his death on the cross that overcomes sin and removes guilt and shame. Johnson (2015, 18) suggests that for those whose religious systems depend on gaining merit, we can communicate what Jesus did when he died on the cross in terms of vicarious merit-making for our sakes.[7] We can communicate why Jesus did what he did in terms of the freedom that faith in him brings from fear, including fear of death. Faith in Jesus also includes deliverance from oppression, including the oppressiveness of karma and the weight of the evil intents of worldly ways, as well as deliverance from personally distressing ways of being and doing.

Key to these gospel truths becoming receivable and liberating truths to our respondents is our communication of the difference between religion and relationship: as Christians, we do not follow a religion, but rather we come into a relationship with God through Jesus, and as we come into the reality of his love for us, we seek to pursue intimacy in relationship with him. We no longer follow rules according to a religious structure but seek

---

7. See Johnson (2015) for an insightful account of contextualizing the gospel for Thai Buddhists.

to live according to the truths commanded by Jesus in order that we may grow in love with God concurrent with developing the relationship and way of life so as to delight and please God.

In communicating the gospel essentials of who Jesus is, we can then communicate the nature of God's desire for us to be reconciled with him on the basis of new birth and a loving, thanksgiving relationship with Jesus. As we live out the reality of this relationship, we must also communicate the reality of his presence within us so that our respondents are made aware of both the objective and subjective components of God's compassion-laden, reconciliation-bringing strategy.

Important principle: It is never enough to merely communicate truths *about* God or Jesus; we must communicate so that our respondents understand that they may come into a personal relationship with God through Jesus and that the Spirit of Christ comes to dwell in the hearts of those who are in such a relationship.

CULTURAL CONSIDERATIONS IN THE SPIRITUAL HARVEST OF DECISION MAKING

As we saw in chapter 4, some cultures prefer being decisive over leaving situations open-ended and lacking closure (Hesselgrave 1991, 613). People from such cultures do not appreciate indecisiveness, and they perceive this as an uncooperative nature, which reflects on the indecisive person's character. Other cultures have no problems with decisions being left unmade, particularly if there's any possibility that a wrong decision might be made. In such cultures the waiting process and even failure to make a decision can even be a sign of wisdom.

Conversion and Decision Making as a Point and Process

Hesselgrave (617) notes that some people see the journey into a deepening relationship with God as a process following a single, discernible decision, whereas others view it as a process marked by a series of decisions and decreasingly immature choices. Certainly, Christian growth is a process in which one must continue to choose appropriate responses to the challenges that come. In both individual and group conversions, point and process are involved. If one can't discern the point of conversion, it is all the more necessary to make provision for the different stages of genuine conversion and provide appropriate encouragement at each stage:[8]

- **Discover.** The person or people discover that Jesus was sent by God to pay the price for sin and restore relationship with God, and these truths have been communicated with appropriate contextualization.
- **Deliberate.** The person or people deliberate over whether to change from their current way of being and doing and follow this different way (the way of a follower of Jesus).
- **Determine.** The person or people decide that, yes, they do want this new way of life, so they choose to believe in Jesus and follow the commands of Jesus as they become increasingly exposed to them in the Bible.
- **Dissonance.** When trials and difficulties come, which may include family or community hostility, they are challenged to decide whether to remain in the faith or go back to their former way of life with the cultural ways and community ties that had kept them feeling secure. This is where the questions of Hiebert's "Flaw of the Excluded Middle" become pertinent (see further below).
- **Discipline.** They purposefully choose to become part of a church and be that member of the body of Christ that is their calling. This is a key factor in the decision to submit to the authority and lordship of Christ.

It is important to note that people will change only if they perceive that the anticipated reward makes paying the required price worthwhile (Hogbin 1958, 57; cited by Hesselgrave 1991, 624). So the people we reach out to weigh what they understand of our message and, consciously or unconsciously, think through the cost involved versus the potential gains that might come of responding positively to the message.

Iyadurai (2015, 239) provides a conversion process model that includes the hostility faced by the new convert in an Indian context. He offers that whilst encounter with the divine is "the central event in the conversion process," social-psychological and religious practices dimensions constantly interact to influence or prevent evolvement of the conversion process into

---

8. This section follows D-Davidson (2018, 100–101). What follows is my modification of the stages that can be found in diagrammatic form in Hesselgrave (1991, 618), figure 46.

transformation from previously followed Indian religious practice to a new Christian outlook.

> **Important principle:** We dare not reduce the price to make the gospel easier to accept, and we must also be on the lookout for unsound motives so that our outreach does not merely produce what has, in earlier times, been referred to as *rice Christians*.[9] Very often our local friends are most vulnerable and open to gospel truths during times of crisis or amidst difficulties that their worldview and cultural practices cannot help resolve. We must communicate truths with love in a way that neither condemns nor condones unsound motives but points people to Christ, who sees and knows the deepest motives of people's hearts. By grace he brings conviction, not condemnation, as the spiritual journey unfolds.

The Process of Deciding for Christ

Through the stages in the conversion process just described, as we are led by the Holy Spirit, we help our friends to discover the truth of Jesus. We must then give them time to deliberate on the issue before they decide to move forward and take a step of faith. They must not be pushed, crowded, or manipulated into making decisions. If their conversion is not a personal act of mind, heart, and will, then when difficulties come and the dissonance stage arises, they will be more likely to fall back into their old ways.

As we would do with any people being led in a salvation-seeking prayer (e.g., what is often termed a *sinner's prayer*) or a prayer with the aim of entering into relationship with God through Jesus, we must then ask what they thought happened by and through the prayer. This is a helpful way to discover what and how much the one being led in prayer has understood about the event. It also provides an immediate opportunity to clarify points wherever necessary. Where the answer suggests that people only appear to have made a decision for Christ or have prayed just to please us, we must make it clear that the focus is on pleasing God, not us. When the answer shows there has been misunderstanding, this is the time to gently

---

9. A term that historically refers to people who made decisions for Christ based on unsound ulterior motives such as to get food, medicine, or some other material benefit. Preston and Preston (2010, 279) write of William Dampier's views (circa 1689) of French Catholic missionary work among the Tonkin people: "In the first English use of the concept, Dampier believed that many of their converts were rice Christians [since] 'alms of rice have converted more than their preaching.'"

clarify matters until the feedback confirms that we have communicated sufficiently and lucidly.

We are likely to find ourselves communicating with people who appear to be making the "right" responses when we bring up Christianity, but they might be familiar with Christian terminology and not necessarily have a true understanding of the implications of being a Christian. One helpful way to move forward can be to show them or ask them to read a verse like Galatians 2:20, in which Paul wrote to Christians who had clearly also not grasped some key truths: "I have been crucified with Christ and I no longer live, but Christ lives in me. The life I now live in the body, I live by faith in the Son of God, who loved me and gave himself for me." We can then ask to what extent this is also their experience. As we listen to their response, we can ask the Holy Spirit to show us how to address any misunderstandings about the gospel. For instance, have they understood the difference between living by faith, which is by God's grace, and trying to build a bridge to God through works? If their words are full of taking up the cross and living sacrificially to attain to salvation, then we can show them Ephesians 2:8–9: "For it is by grace you have been saved, through faith—and this is not from yourselves, it is the gift of God—not by works, so that no one can boast."

For some it can be an enlightening truth that the Spirit of Christ comes to live in those who trust in Jesus Christ for forgiveness of sin and new birth by his Spirit. Can they say by faith that, yes, Christ lives in them? If not, they might know a lot about God and Jesus Christ but not know him personally. They may have a relationship based on God's transcendence but lack the experience of God's immanence and the presence of Christ within. They may have made a ritualistic commitment to Christ as savior but not surrendered themselves fully to the lordship of Christ in every area of their lives. Our response can be to pray with them and delight with them as they enter a new depth in love and knowledge of God in Christ.

We may encounter people who turn down the opportunity to know Christ as Savior and Lord. Where people prefer to say no to the opportunity to invite Christ into their lives, we need to be sure they are not saying no to an inappropriately communicated message or have not misunderstood what we were trying to get across. In that case, they weren't refusing God or Jesus but just a very poorly communicated message! Openness to God's Holy Spirit for what, how, and when to speak is of the utmost importance. Developing openness and sensitivity to God's voice comes as we grow in intimacy with our Lord and Savior. Some of our most fruitful times can be when we seemingly spontaneously grasp the unexpected and unplanned moments to interact with those sent our way by God for his timely purposes. Similarly, when times of dissonance come for these believers, we can look to God for the inspiration that provides the uniquely crafted, loving, and appropriate response.

HIEBERT'S "THE FLAW OF THE EXCLUDED MIDDLE"

We saw above, in the stages of the conversion process, that believers—either those newly born again or those showing signs of growth—may face a time of dissonance when they face trials after turning to Christ and then have to decide whether to keep following him and his ways or return to their old ways and coping mechanisms.

What Hiebert (1994, 196) labels the "excluded middle" is the realm between religion and science where cause and effect are believed to be the result of gods or spirit forces in communities where the spirit world is a key part of the worldview belief.[10] These middle-ground questions are "the questions of the uncertainty of the future, the crises of present life, and the unknowns of the past" (197). The West largely only has answers for religion-based questions that deal with the ultimate questions of life and death and for issues where science or practical experience can be used to provide answers that explain natural world phenomena. Hiebert's point was that the Western approach is less able to answer "middle-realm" questions related to life's practicalities such as "How can I be sure of a prosperous harvest?" or "How can I ensure my daughter has a healthy baby?" when respondents' cultural ways *had* provided certain rituals to supposedly bring such assurances.

Tempting as it may be to dismiss other cultures' beliefs and coping mechanisms as simplistic, childish, groundless, or irrational, we must not ignore the importance to the local people of these worldview beliefs and resulting behavioral practices.

Example from Malaysian Chinese culture: "If you are reaching out to Malaysian Chinese, do not tell them ancestor worship is not biblical straightaway, as they might feel very offended. This is the way the Chinese

---

10. This section uses excerpts from D-Davidson (2018, 103–6).

show their filial love and respect to their ancestors. You will just put them off the gospel."

At some point respondents need to be exposed to challenging truths, and our part is to pray and be sensitive to God's timing. When middle-realm issues arise, we dare not back away from them. Hiebert warned that if we do not have credible answers to middle-realm questions, Christians from settings with nonbiblical coping mechanisms might just go back to whatever magic, superstitious rituals and practices, or coping mechanisms they engaged in previously, or they may find whoever they used to go to for answers. Similarly, when new Christians or even maturing believers face times of dissonance, if we are unable to communicate believable and receivable means of maintaining Christian faith, these people may find returning to the old ways a more helpful option.

Hiebert was writing about middle-realm questions in the context of what used to be called "primitive" or "tribal" people, particularly those whose lifestyle and livelihood were in close proximity to nature and dependent on the forces of nature to maintain security and continuity. We need to recognize too that people at all levels of the socioeconomic spectrum grow up with cultural coping mechanisms to deal with whichever middle-realm questions are pertinent in their settings. In times of difficulty, they are likely to return to engaging with the coping mechanisms with which they grew up, regardless of the changes of environment.

Example: Someone from a low socioeconomic rural setting might excel academically and rise to a much higher level in a city setting, but when he faces difficulties that he has no immediate means of resolving, he may well go back to his animistic or superstitious practices of earlier days, even if in secret. During a difficult time, he would be returning to what gave him a sense of security, regardless of how incongruous it might appear to others.

People at every socioeconomic level grow up with coping mechanisms for dealing with life's contingencies, such as throwing rice when entering a new house or going to a temple and following certain rituals.

> **Important principle:** Once people have become Christians, if they are not given credible and convincing answers as to how to deal with their middle-realm questions, they may see a welcome option in returning to former coping practices, perhaps secretly.

One of our best approaches can be modeling trust in God's sovereignty and helping new believers grow in trust that God is in control and knows what's best for his children at all times; we can help them believe, know, and experience, as we do, that he loves us so much that he'll only allow what is best for us. With new believers, it is important to get at least a mental assent that God is sovereign as early as possible. As the spiritually young believer grows in intimacy with God through growing familiarity with his Word and through an active relationship of prayer and conversation with him throughout the day, the heart agreement inevitably catches up, as does the believer's experience. If and when things do seem to fall apart, it can be helpful (if possible) to get mature believers of the convert's cultural background to share their experiences and encouragements too.

In practical terms, the convert is used to *doing something* to answer the middle-ground issues' needs: to assure a good harvest, to guarantee a healthy baby, and so on. What can we offer for them to *do* instead? The obvious and most sensible activity is to pray with them and acknowledge the activity of bringing the issue before God. When we pray with them, we should model appropriate prayer—prayer that is looking not to manipulate God inappropriately but to cooperate with him, prayer that expresses the desire to trust him as sovereign, whatever happens. Rather than telling new believers what they should or shouldn't do in their cultural context, we expose them to the truths in God's Word and ask the Holy Spirit to inspire them and bring them conviction of what is appropriate in order to maintain a spiritually healthy and growing relationship with God.

> **Example from rural China:** When I was teaching about discovering spiritual gifts, I asked the Christian villagers when they were most aware of spirits in the villages that were not the Holy Spirit. In one breath they replied it was during the annual grave-sweeping festival when families would go up to the ancestors' burial sites. There, by custom, they would

worship the ancestors by bowing down, burning (fake) money, offering fruit and other offerings, and clearing away the foliage around the grave. When I asked what the believers did on that day, there was some embarrassed shuffling. One young man volunteered that he would go up to the grave with his family and praise God aloud, thanking him for the ancestor who allowed the young man to have been born. In praising and worshiping God, he would declare God as his only object of worship, and while he would join in tidying around the grave, he would not make any other offerings, but he would continually thank God for the ancestor. After he shared his approach, the other believers had an excited discussion about how they could do the same from then on.

From the example above, we see the healthy fruit of allowing local believers to discern the appropriate ways to live as Christians in their specific settings. Helping believers of another culture to grow in love with God and be led by his Word requires that we put aside any desire to direct how they live out Christ. They know their customs and related worldview beliefs far better than we ever will, and giving them the opportunity to discover the Holy Spirit leading them forward is not only honoring their dignity but also an important part of helping them grow spiritually.

COMMUNICATING FOR INDIGENOUS CHRISTIAN CONTEXTUALIZATION AND CONTEXTUALIZED CHRISTIANITY

In the 1912 book *Missionary Methods: St Paul's or Ours?* Roland Allen (1912; 1962) famously criticized the missions approach in which missionaries depended on their own cultural and socioeconomic background and, unwilling to believe that the Holy Spirit could also work in local believers, delegated authority in the planted churches reluctantly. More than a century later, this is still an important book for contemporary missions and Christian communicators. As we engage in communicating Christ worldwide, we should be alert to whether the people becoming Christians and the churches being planted merely reflect the churchmanship of the missionary communicator or whether the churchmanship is on local peoples' terms and according to what they perceive as culturally appropriate.

> **Devotional comment:** Roland Allen's challenge remains: As we communicate Christ, are we trusting the Holy Spirit to work in the local believers' lives so that they can grow and be the means of growing the work, or are we Christian communicators still directing all the work? Part of letting go is recognizing that the local people have a better perspective on how to reach out appropriately so that, although we begin as "teachers," we become interactive intercultural "learners." This requires humility: just as there is always more of God for us to discover as individuals, so too is there more to be discovered as intercultural Christians learning from each other.

Pursuing God's leading requires us to be sensitive to our intercultural Christian friends' perspectives and anticipate that they can be sensitive to the Holy Spirit and will have answers to cultural issues that we may not even have been aware of. In previous chapters we noted the importance and effectiveness of developing intercultural relationships while communicating a relevant and receivable message so that people of other cultures respond positively to the gospel message. Now we will examine what contextualized Christianity looks like and how appropriate communication can be the catalyst to facilitate it.[11] Ultimately, contextualized Christianity will see the establishment of a body of believers functioning as a church that is appropriately planted, meaning it fits in the local context, is devoid of syncretistic leanings, is not dependent on outside resources, reaches out of its own accord in a way that makes it an attraction within the local context, and so acts as a catalyst for healthy transformation of the local and wider community. This has long been recognized as church planting that results in indigeneity.

Indigenous churches traditionally have been recognized by the following principles: (1) self-governing, (2) self-financing, (3) self-propagating, and (4) self-theologizing. In other words, they are able to grow and develop without being dependent on those who began the work, particularly if it was through cross-cultural ministry, and they are in the process of deciding on biblically sound approaches to theology and praxis as necessary due to the circumstances of their setting. It is the antithesis of Smalley's (2009, 497) observation: "It may be very easy to have a self-governing church

---

11. This remainder of the chapter brings out excerpts from D-Davidson (2018, 144–46).

which is not indigenous. . . . All that is needed is to indoctrinate a few leaders in Western patterns of church governance, and let them take over." Here Smalley is criticizing Westerners, but Christian communicators from any cultural background ministering interculturally need to be careful that we are not seeking to impose our national or denominational background churchmanship.

The first three principles of self-indigeneity (self-governing, self-financing, and self-propagating) arose from the West through Henry Venn and Rufus Anderson in the nineteenth century, and they have long been taught to and applied by Global South missionaries with varying degrees of success.[12] The fourth principle, self-theologizing, also came from Western missiology.[13] A fifth principle, "self-missionizing," was introduced from the Global South by Lazarus Chakwera at the Africa Assemblies of God Alliance (AAGA) meeting in Tanzania in 1998.[14] Chakwera called for churches started by missionaries to demonstrate their autonomy by becoming missionary-sending churches. In some respects, the concept of self-missionizing could be considered an expected extension of self-propagation, as the local church body is envisioned to reach out beyond its immediate setting by following the Great Commission of Matthew 28:18–20.[15] Part of our role as Christian communicators is to encourage believers to seek God's vision for their ongoing ministry both near and far.

Newberry (2005, 113) proposes adding "a sixth 'self' to a contextualized African model of indigenous principles," that of self-caring in relation to social concern. Again, that could be considered a key means of self-propagation.[16]

Gilliland (1989, vii) urges those in the early stages of outreach to be aware of two equally spiritually unhealthy extremes in cross-cultural communication of Christ that apply equally to intercultural ministry: At the one extreme "you end in obscurantism, so attached to your conventional ways of practicing and teaching the faith that you veil its truth and power from those who are trying to see it through very different eyes . . . [and at

---

12. See Hastings (2003, 24) on the incongruity of the self-governing aspect of the three-self principle in Africa even into the twentieth century.

13. See, for instance, Bosch (1991, 452).

14. See Chakwera (2000) in which he introduces *The Eleventh Hour Institute* to provide missions training in Malawi and across the African continent.

15. See too Wagner (1976), who describes mission work as the four stages of a "full circle" and completed when the planted church is sending out missionaries.

16. On a more helpful note, local church attention to social concern can also be a means of reducing the dependency-outlook, which was one of the original catalysts for the indigenous church's three-self principle.

the other extreme is] syncretism [which] compromises the uniqueness of Christ and [delivers a false gospel]."

Newbigin (1994, 67) confirms these two extremes and further warns us:

> There are always two opposite dangers . . . between which one must steer. On the one side there is the danger that one finds no point of contact for the message as the missionary preaches it, [so that] to the people of the local culture the message appears irrelevant and meaningless [whilst at the other extreme] is the danger that the point of contact determines entirely the way that the message is received, and the result is syncretism. Every missionary path has to find the way between these two dangers: irrelevance and syncretism. And if one is more afraid of one danger than the other, one will certainly fall into the opposite.

As Christian communicators, we need to take care that our engagement with cultural practices is a prayer-fueled balance that neither undermines biblical principles nor causes offence or confusion for our respondent friends. Every setting and context will have its own situational specifics, so we cannot assume a common timing or action for the issues communicators face worldwide. But we can get guidance from those who have gone before us as well as through prayerful fellowship with contemporaries in other settings.

Critical Contextualization to Avoid Syncretism

Hiebert (1985, 184–90) suggests three possible ways for missionaries and local people who become Christians to deal with their traditional cultural beliefs, values, customs, and institutions: (1) denial of the old (rejection of contextualization); (2) acceptance of the old (uncritical contextualization); and (3) dealing with the old (critical contextualization).

Complete rejection of contextualization is likely to result in a group of local Christians becoming a nonindigenous church because, with none of their own cultural ways included, they are liable to be ushered into an approach to churchmanship that is a reflection of the churchmanship of those who communicated Christ to them. Urging the local believers to reject all their cultural ways and beliefs effectively separates them from the rest of their community and communicates rejection of and to the wider community. Taking this "Christ against culture" approach fails to communicate that new life in Christ is still lived *in* the world but just not according to nonbiblical worldly ways. Hiebert points to another danger of completely rejecting all the old ways: believers might prefer to maintain links with their cultural ways and former relationships and so practice a syncretistic mix of Christian and non-Christian beliefs in secret.

> **Example of rejection of contextualization from Myanmar:** "Most missionaries rejected our culture and attempted to change our culture. They taught us, 'Your culture is not important, and Christ is more important than anything else such as culture.' Yes, this is true, but culture can be renewed so as to glorify God and promote his purposes."

Hiebert (185–86) identifies two major faults of the second approach, uncritical contextualization. First, "it overlooks the fact that there are corporate and cultural sins as well as personal transgressions." We need to communicate that the aim of the gospel is to bring about not only individual change but also societal change. Second, uncritical contextualization provides no means of preventing syncretism.

Of the third approach, critical contextualization, Hiebert (186) suggests that worldview beliefs and resulting cultural practices should be examined in relation to biblical principles before they are accepted, rejected, or appropriately modified.

We who are communicating with people of other cultures must be aware of not only the various cultural forms or practices lived out but also their function in holding the community together. We must discover— and be sure we correctly understand—why the local people follow specific practices and what the associated underlying worldview beliefs are. In this light, we aim to separate practices that have deep religious significance (or practices with underlying beliefs that run counter to biblical principles) from practices that are merely a matter of aesthetics or practicality (such as the design of clothing that is worn or utensils used for eating). For instance, Inuits wear thick furs to keep warm, and Chinese people usually eat with chopsticks, whereas Filipinos eat with a spoon and fork.

If we are unsure what worldview beliefs are associated with particular cultural practices, the best way to discover them is by asking local people whom we have come to know and trust.

The Critical Contextualization Process

Hiebert (186–87) provides several steps for the critical contextualization process:

1. "An individual or church must recognize the need to deal biblically with all areas of life," which is "one of the important functions of leadership in the church."
2. Local church leaders and the missionaries must encourage the congregation to meet and analyze their cultural ways.
3. "The pastor or missionary leads the church in a study of Scriptures related to the question at hand."
4. "The people corporately critically evaluate their own past customs in the light of their new biblical understandings and make decisions regarding their response to their new-found truths." Hiebert rightly recognizes the importance of nonlocal missionaries allowing the locals to make the final decision because, once they are familiar with relevant biblical teaching, they are in a better position than the missionary to critique local beliefs and customs. At the same time, the missionary may need to raise questions because local people might fail to see how their own cultural biases or assumptions run contrary to Scripture.
5. "Having led the people to analyse their old customs in the light of biblical teaching, the pastor or missionary must help them to arrange the practices they have chosen [to keep, where necessary and/or preferred] into a new ritual that expresses the Christian meaning of the event."

Hiebert further advises that in addition to rearranging old practices, local believers need to incorporate new ones. Where the local leaders choose on behalf of the people, they must also be willing to stand behind these choices and enforce them. They and their church congregation need to be willing to reject the practices that compromise the integrity of the local church in relation to living out biblical principles.

Perhaps not unreasonably, Hiebert puts the responsibility of critical contextualization onto local church leaders in cooperation with the missionary or missionaries involved in planting the church. However, going back to the example of the annual grave-sweeping event, we can see how the young villager came to the conclusion for himself after having been exposed to God's Word; it was not a result of either Dr. Co or I telling them that

God is the Christian's only object of worship. He had sought God for how to deal with the annual grave-sweeping event and had been inspired to alter his outlook and activities accordingly. It was a precious answer to our prayers to have a believer from that village setting work out a way forward that would not compromise his beliefs, biblical principles, or relationship with God. The suggestion was based on his experience with God and desire to honor him, and it provided the necessary indigenous response that was far more credible to his fellow believers than Dr. Co or I merely directing them. By offering a means of dealing with the nonbiblical practice in a way that was deemed culturally acceptable, he was self-theologizing, which, as we saw earlier, is one of the marks of an indigenous body of believers and a contextualized church.

Important principle: For Christian communicators in any setting (whether cross-cultural or not), a *balance* is needed in communicating information and providing tools for spiritual development, churchmanship, and evangelistic and outreach activity without being *overly prescriptive* in how the related activities should look in practice. How they work out in practice is, ultimately, best decided by self-theologizing local believers.

On a practical note, we should probably recognize that few churches in any part of the world are likely to have a congregational majority keen to "do theology," so it might be more helpful to change *self-theologizing* to something that more reflects self-contextualizing or "biblically appropriate and culturally acceptable for the setting" and help growing believers to recognize the need for this. This means seeing the local believers continue to work out which beliefs and practices need rejecting or modifying and how to incorporate new beliefs and practices, as well as prayerfully considering how the spread of the gospel and their culture best fit together.

CONCLUSION

We have seen how important it is to contextualize our communication of gospel truths from the beginnings of evangelism all the way to helping local people establish themselves as part of the worldwide body of Christ by functioning as a church on their own terms. Whether for each believer's spiritual nourishment, for members of the indigenous church engaging in discipleship, or for engaging in self-theologizing, development of faith, and life in Christ as members of his body requires an appropriate means of engaging with God's Word. That is the focus of the next chapter.

QUESTIONS FOR REFLECTION
AND DISCUSSION

1. In the "As It Happened" scenario at the start of the chapter, where do you think the mother might have learned those syncretistic ideas from? How would you advise the daughter? Who might be in the best position to advise the mother, and what do you think that person might say?

2. A Samoan student offered: "One of the biggest mistakes that missionaries have made in Samoa is to try to impose Westernism in Samoa. For example, they introduced and insisted on the use of a [neck] tie as a symbol of holiness. This comes from a theology greatly influenced by Western culture. It's a big problem that missionaries do not let Samoan Christians create their own theology." In this example (which appears to have been generalized to the whole of Samoa), what might be considered a form of syncretism? Where have biblical principles become confused with cultural ways? What is the Samoan Christian's biggest complaint, and how might it be addressed?

3. If you were asked to advise an indigenous church that followed a custom of burning paper outside a new home in order to symbolically ensure God's cleansing of the building, how might you use Hiebert's five critical contextualization steps to address the issue? Which biblical texts might be included in step three?

4. What are the major universal obstacles to Christ transforming culture or cultures? How might Christians of different cultures interculturally be part of transforming culture for God's glory?

CHAPTER 10

Communication in Relation to Biblical Interpretation

As It Happened: An American missionary was doing a Bible study with Thai students. They had read the narrative of the miraculous catch of fish in Luke 5:1–11. The missionary asked: "In verse 8, why did Simon Peter say to Jesus, 'Go away from me, Lord; I am a sinful man'"? One of the students replied, "Simon Peter acknowledged he was a sinful man because he had killed so many fish." The missionary was a little shocked since this was not the answer he was expecting, but he realized that the student's interpretation was based on the worldview beliefs of his background in Theravada Buddhism, which includes beliefs in karma and reincarnation, and the bad karma that would come from killing living creatures.[1]

INTRODUCTION

Growing in relationship with God involves engaging with and learning from his Word, the Holy Bible. What happens when people interpret Scripture in ways that we feel really are not appropriate? For instance, how would you have reacted to the answer given above by the Thai student? We tend to interpret the meaning of Scriptures according to our own understanding and experience of terms and scenarios and, quite unhelpfully at times, assume our interpretation is correct and complete, but perceptions and insights can vary from culture to culture and from individual to individual within cultures. We have seen how different theological perspectives influence the approach taken to engaging with the Bible and the extent to which it is seen

---

1. Johnson (2015, 4). See too (Davis 1998, vi–viii) for how John 3:16 may be inappropriately interpreted by Theravada Buddhists, since a God who loves also shows weakness and desire whereas, for Buddhists, desire should not be entertained but rather, overcome.

as authoritative. For our purposes, we will continue viewing the Bible from an evangelical perspective, which takes the entire Bible's content as authoritative.

In this chapter we begin by acknowledging linguistic concerns when engaging with Bible text cross-culturally and then examine the potential for syncretism in relation to views of culture and of the Bible. We then offer a brief overview of how approaches to biblical interpretation have attempted to engage with cultural factors and their influences within Scripture, and we discuss means for helping our respondents understand and apply Scripture in their own lives and cultural settings. Finally, we will examine the question of worldview from Jesus' perspective and identify key biblical principles for living as a follower of Christ in any cultural setting.

VIEWS OF CULTURE AND SCRIPTURE IN RELATION TO THE POTENTIAL FOR SYNCRETISM

We saw in the previous chapter how important it is that our respondents can grasp God's intentions for themselves in relation to their cultural context, the particularities of their worldview beliefs, and the situational specifics of their setting. When we have developed an intercultural relationship with a respondent, the respondents are more likely to be transparent about their views and perspectives, and we can enjoy a level of trust that allows them to receive and consider alternative perspectives. Christian communicators who are not from that same setting, or whose worldview beliefs run contrary to that of the respondents, must be sensitive to the aspects of their own background culture and worldview beliefs that color their approach to interpretation of Scripture.

Nida (1960, 33) introduced the SMR structure of communication: "the source [S], the message [M] (the actual form of what is communicated), and the receptor [R]."[2] His "Three Language Model of Communication" (46–47) further assigned the SMR structure to each of these three: the language and communication of the biblical times, the language of the missionary (or Christian communicator), and the language of the receptor (or respondent). Nida's model and examples not only focus on linguistic forms but also highlight the need to acknowledge that three different cultures are involved in engaging with the Bible: the Bible-era culture, the sender (communicator's) culture, and the receptor (or respondent) culture.

In relation to linguistic differences, Nida famously dismissed Bible

---

2. Nida first described this theory in 1952.

translation that sought semantic-equivalence or correspondence of words of another language with Bible text terms, proposing dynamic equivalence of terms as a more helpful alternative.[3] As we seek to communicate biblical principles to people of other cultures, we must not forget that we have been on the receiving end of communication by others and may well have taken for granted what we received as accurate and correct interpretation of the Bible texts.[4] As we have seen, intercultural relationships are marked by mutual acceptance of difference, but that should not be used as leverage to attempt to manipulate our respondents to live out Christianity and churchmanship amongst people of their culture as we have been taught to live in ours.

Important principle: Let the Bible be our means of evaluating our cultural assumptions first before we consider how to communicate Bible-related messages to respondents in another culture.

Our perspectives on the authority of the Bible and our view of the concept of culture can influence the form of Christianity that respondents take on board, for better or for worse. Difficult though it may become, since every setting will have challenging issues and questions, our aim is to help respondents into contextualized Christianity devoid of syncretism.

A helpful earlier contribution to the issue comes from McGavran (1974), who valued how the Bible has universal appeal and application so that "the Spirit of Truth helps us to discover *from the written record* the new light we need for our own day and our own culture" (55). McGavran presents four standpoints from which views of the Bible and views of culture might interact in relatively helpful or unhelpful ways for communicating Christ and biblical truths into differing cultural settings.

Before we engage with the nature and implications of McGavran's four standpoints, we will unfold the meaning of some of the terminology he uses regarding a high or low view of the Bible and a high or low view of culture.

---

3. Nida (1964, 120) urged: "We must analyze the transmission of a message in terms of a dynamic dimension. This analysis is especially important for translating, since the production of equivalent messages is a process, not merely of matching the parts of the utterances, but also of reproducing the total dynamic characters of communication."

4. Richards and O'Brien (2012) give pointers to understanding of relationships in Bible-era times, whilst Richards and James (2020) point out that unlike the individualist cultural background of early and Western protestant missionaries, the biblical text largely came about through collectivist cultures with importance attached to kinship and patronage.

He describes having a high view of the Bible as believing that the "entire Bible—the canonical Scriptures of the Old and New Testaments—is the Word of God. It is authoritative and demands faith and obedience to all its declarations" (52). He writes of this view, "As the Lord, the second person of the Trinity was truly man and truly God, so the Bible is truly *the words of men* and truly *the words of God*" (66). In light of these beliefs, people with a high view of the Bible see the Bible as being of utmost authority in matters of ethical, moral, idealistic, and practical lifestyle. In contrast, for those who have a low view of the Bible, "The Bible has little authority . . . in fact, the low view provides a convenient philosophical base for a high view of culture," (56) guided as it is by the supposition that other "religions also have much truth in them" (61). This high versus low view of Scripture comes across as a typically Western dichotomistic outlook of either/or, and McGavran's four standpoints reflect this. In reality, a Christian communicator's view of Scripture may sit along the spectrum, either more toward a high view or more toward a low view, but not necessarily in a way that can be specifically measured or quantified.

Turning to perspectives on culture, McGavran supposes that "competent missionaries throughout the ages have tended to take a higher view of culture" (67) than their nonmissionary counterparts. This was perhaps not so much the case in the earlier centuries of colonialist missionary activity, but it became more of a reality when anthropological insights came to the fore and were considered to be an important tool for cross-cultural engagement. A high view of culture places high value on cultural particularities and serves to protect and preserve cultural ways—albeit colored by the anthropologist's fascination for the "other" beliefs and resulting practices rather than for the effects on building relationships with people. In contrast, a low view of culture sees little or no importance played by the role of differing worldview beliefs and cultural ways in preserving the identity, security, and continuity of groups of people, let alone sensitivity in respecting peoples' desires for preservation and continuity. As with one's view of the Bible, one's view of culture may sit somewhere along a high-low spectrum that tends toward one end or the other in a nonmeasurable way.

McGavran's four standpoints can be described as follows:

1. **Bible: high view; culture: low view.** The communicator has a high view of the Bible that shows great respect for the authority of Scripture and belief that people should trust and obey all its declarations. But the communicator also has a low view of culture. When Christian communicators hold this position, it can result

in a body of believers with a nonindigenous Christian lifestyle that is strange to the wider community, and churchmanship similar to that of the communicator's. At the extreme there may also be a fundamentalist approach to Scripture and potential for legalism in churchmanship and lifestyle.

Example from Myanmar: "Missionaries preached the gospel but didn't put it in the cultural context. Christianity is considered to be more of a Western idea. Missionaries changed the names of the local people and kept the converts in Bible schools to prevent them from backsliding."

2. **Bible: low view; culture: high view.** The communicator's high view of culture aims to respect the cultural ways so as to preserve the peoples' traditional way of life. On a positive note, this may also serve to uphold their dignity, but combined with a low view of the Bible, a body of believers may not even emerge, and if it does, it has a strong potential to be syncretistic. This scenario might be associated with communicators who are also liberal Christian anthropologists.

Example from church-planting work amongst Muslims: In attempts to contextualize the Christian faith in an acceptable way amongst Muslims,[5] some Bible translation organizations have proposed a translation of the Bible that would retranslate all references to Jesus as the Son of God since that concept provides a major stumbling block to Muslims. While these translators may have a high view of the rest of the Bible, removing references to Jesus' deity as the Son of God for the sake of preevangelism intentionally takes a low-view of divinely inspired Scripture as to the nature of Jesus.

---

5. See Travis (1998, 407) for the C spectrum of church-planting amongst Muslims. See Williams (2007, 62) in relation to Massey's amendment of the spectrum but in which the C4 "maximal contextualization" description (and, inevitably onwards to C5 "total contextualization") could just as well be read as "maximum potential for syncretism." See too Williams (2011, 339) in which he not only points out the spectrum's inattention to folk Islam but also that both C1 and C5 groups are essentially tied by background traditions. A link (342) is made with Hiebert's steps for critical contextualization (which we saw in chapter 9) showing the potential for syncretism not only for C5 groups holding onto all traditions but also for C1 members when the old ways being completely rejected cause the group member or members to engage in syncretism, albeit secretly.

3. **Bible: low view; culture: low view.** In this scenario, any emerging body of believers is likely to be neither indigenous nor particularly vibrant Christians. The aim of the communicators may be more in line with liberal developmentalism seeking to "improve" the community in the realms of healthcare and education rather than concurrently facilitating development for eternal spiritual results.

Example from Africa: Albert Schweitzer (1875–1965) worked in the, then, French colony of *Lambaréné* and won a Nobel prize in 1952. Researching Schweitzer's view of culture, Harris (2016, 1107) "places him within the context of medical missionizing. Although he worked in Africa for over fifty years, Schweitzer was strangely indifferent to the continent's culture. Unlike his fellow missionaries, he never learned native languages, and his service was primarily grounded in a Nietzschean rejection of European conventionalities and a desire to develop his unique 'ethical personality.'" Schweitzer's low view of the authority of the Bible is seen in, for instance, his view of "the historical Jesus" (Schweitzer 2001, 478): "The Jesus of Nazareth who came forward publicly as the Messiah, who preached the ethic of the kingdom of God, who founded the kingdom of heaven upon earth and died to give his work its final consecration never existed. He is a figure designed by rationalism, endowed with life by liberalism, and clothed by modern theology in a historical garb. This image has not been destroyed from outside; it has fallen to pieces."

4. **Bible: high view; culture: high view.** McGavran urges that this standpoint is most appropriate for Christian communicators. Hesselgrave (1991, 120) points out, "By 'high' view of culture McGavran means that each culture is *reasonable* given the specific circumstances in which it has developed."[6] But that does not mean all aspects of a culture can be considered to be right according to biblical criteria, "only that, provided we understand the situation in which [the cultural components] developed, they can be regarded as *reasonable*." However, once a person becomes a Christian, what was previously considered reasonable may no longer be so. Hesselgrave prefers

---

6. Here Hesselgrave cites McGavran (1974, 67). Note that this also rather begs the question of who decides what the criteria are for fulfilling the concept of 'reasonable' . . .

that "[McGavran's] *clash* is not between Christianity and culture" but between Christianity and *aspects* of specific cultures. While McGavran suggests that this standpoint is the ideal, it is something of an impossible venture. At some point the Christian communicator will have to decide whether a scriptural truth takes priority at the expense of a cultural preference or whether the cultural way is given priority over a biblical principle. In contextualizing Christianity and Bible truths amidst a culture's *unreasonable* or questionably *reasonable* preferences, Scripture and culture cannot be taken to hold equal authority. If the communicators actually have a higher view of culture than their view of Scripture, they may be unwilling to give Scripture the priority, and syncretism can result, albeit in a subtle way. In this scenario there is the potential for communicators who hold a strong evangelical Christian anthropologist mentality.

Example from Nepal: "Missionaries can be a bad witness by what they do. Sometimes they want to be very adventurous and visit beautiful places that have been offered to the gods. Very devilish things have happened in these places: people die in the rivers although they are not deep, but that is because of the diabolic activity. There are places that have been built for the gods. Even the inks to put on the forehead are offered to the gods. The festival of color is dedicated to demons, but it is very attractive to visitors. Missionaries agree to participate in these things because they believe it is culture but do not know the background. My recommendation for missionaries is always to ask for the pastor's advice about whether it's appropriate to join in activities."

Important principle: Wisdom is needed in any setting to know how to project a suitably high and appreciative view of culture without also appearing to condone unbiblical beliefs and practices. Keep referring to and applying the critical contextualization steps.

In addition to McGavran's four standpoints, it might be helpful to include a fifth standpoint taken by many evangelical Christian communicators: those who hold a high view of the Bible and have undertaken training to have some appreciative awareness of the importance of respect for culture. They also gain understanding of generalizable principles for contextualizing the presentation of the gospel along with principles for living a Christ-honoring lifestyle as found within the Bible according to the specifics of different cultural settings.

WHAT MESSAGE AND WHOSE PERSPECTIVE?

The essentials of the message we must communicate concern God as love, the person and nature of Christ as God's Son, and salvation into new life that comes through faith in his death and resurrection. We need to communicate the message in a way that is understandable and relevant to the respondents. Following new birth, deeper biblical teaching is needed.

As evangelicals, we take an approach to biblical interpretation that first looks to discover the intention of each Bible-book author in the Bible-era time and setting who was inspired by God to speak or write and then consider whether and to what extent the author's intended meaning has changed for our time and settings, followed by how we might apply the principles discovered in the Scripture. We need to examine the content of Scripture verses in relation to each other and their wider context, as well as both the historical and literary context of particular Scriptures before we discern their meaning and application for our context.

> **Important principle:** When we examine a text, we should never propose a new meaning that is not actually taught in Scripture or could not have applied to the people of the era in which the Scripture arose. Fee and Stuart (1983, 26) advise that "a *text cannot mean what it never meant*," or as Fee expands in later editions, "a *text cannot mean what it could never have meant for its original readers/hearers*."[7] Since the biblical author's intention reflects God's intended meaning, we may not impose a meaning on a text that could not have applied to those of the Bible-era.

---

7. See, for instance, Fee and Stuart (2003, 64) and later editions, and for video presentations of the material (Fee, Strauss, and Stuart 2018). Note the caveat (Fee and Stuart 1983, 26) concerning the question of whether "a text [could] have an additional (or fuller, or deeper) meaning, beyond its original intent. . . . In the case of prophecy, we would not close the door to such a possibility [since] with careful controls, a second or fuller meaning is possible." The perennial difficulty lies in the potential for inappropriate subjectivity in proposing additional meanings and the question of how, and by whom, suitable criteria might be set that could evaluate the validity of alternative "possible" meanings.

> In other words, if a meaning is proposed that the Bible-era author could not or would not have intended, then that same meaning also cannot be applied to readers of the Bible in any later era.

The traditional approach to communicating about God's Word involved the interrelation of (1) the author, who was God's vessel to produce the text, (2) the text itself, and (3) the communicator, who is both searching for and wanting to communicate God's intended meaning. A fourth element includes the audience or respondent(s), who are best served by being encouraged not only to receive input from the communicator about God's Word but also to engage with God's Word themselves. We must differentiate too between devotional reading (i.e., what the Scripture means for me in my personal circumstances, the meaning of which is likely to be taken well out of its original context) and reading for instructional study of the Bible that seeks God's intended meaning as expressed through the inspired biblical authors. The latter is the material for preaching and teaching, whether formally or informally, and in our preparation for preaching or teaching, our approach to interpreting God's Word influences our interpretation. In the letter to Timothy and Titus, Paul urges these influencers of others that sound doctrine must be taught, so it behoves us to pay careful attention to what is involved in biblical interpretation.

APPROACHES TO INTERPRETING THE BIBLE

As recognized through Nida, Bible interpretation has long struggled with the difficulty of translating the meaning of oracles and events recorded by those in Bible era times into equivalent meaning for those in later eras. Elliot (1993, 7) urges that due to issues raised by scholars (such as linguistics), as well as time and context-specific influences, we need to study "not only the social aspects of the form and content of texts but also the conditioning factors and intended consequences of the communication process . . . [along with] the manner in which this textual communication was both a reflection of and a response to a specific social and cultural context."[8]

Christian communicators face the difficulty not only of reaching back

---

8. See Newell (2016) for examples of cross-cultural engagements throughout the Old and New Testaments which show settings with manifestation of more than a single social and cultural context.

to those former cultures appropriating meaning for themselves but also of communicating to respondents in a way that the respondents can also gain appropriate meaning from the Bible for their own setting. Awareness of the difference between Bible-era cultures and later cultures, including ours, has been described in terms of horizons (see figure 10.1).

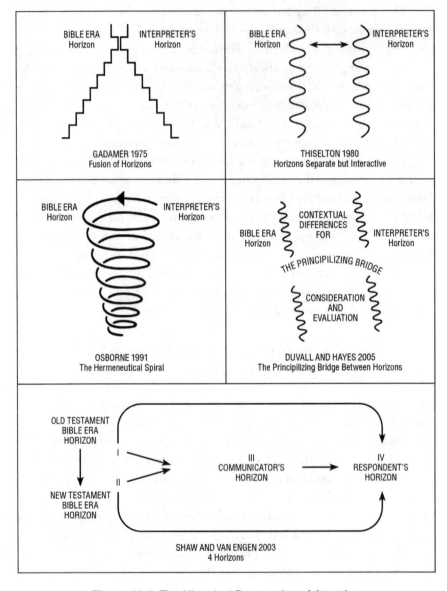

Figure 10.1: The Historical Progression of Attention
to Horizons in Biblical Interpretation

Summary Explanation of the Progression of Horizons in Biblical Interpretation

Gadamer (1975; 1976) saw the need for a fusion of the Bible-era horizon and the later-era interpreter's horizon to facilitate cross-era understanding. While such a fusion lends itself admirably to philosophical reflection, it is highly impractical. Thiselton (1980) suggested that although the horizons must be separated, the interpreter can consider them as being interactive to aid interpretation of Scripture. Osborne (1991) presented his perspective on engaging with the two horizons through a hermeneutical spiral in which depth of understanding of the author's intended meaning has the potential to increase as interpreters begin with the biblical text in relation to their initial understanding, reflect on the text from the perspective of those in the Bible-era context, and through continuously engaging with the text from the perspective of their own context and returning to the Bible-era horizon, allow a new and deeper perspective to be brought into their own context. This involves gaining increasing insight and "spiralling nearer to the text's intended meaning as I refine my hypotheses and allow the text to continue to challenge and correct those alternative interpretations, then to guide my delineation of its significance for my situation today" (6). Osborne urged that engaging with the two horizons in this manner has the potential to bring the interpreter increasingly into a deeper understanding of the text from the perspective and horizon of the Bible-era respondents and from which the later-era interpreter might draw more insightful implications for the interpreter's horizon. While diagrams depicting Osborne's spiral tend to see the spiral direction indicating increased understanding as the spiral widens, I prefer to take the reverse approach and see understanding and perception decrease the distance between the two horizons as the interpreter becomes more deeply aware of the Bible-era contexts and, from those increasingly insightful perceptions, the implications and significance for the interpreter's horizon. In other words, I see more insightful understanding as the spiral narrows.

Osborne's spiral approach sought to overcome the difficulties associated with the earlier purely objective historical-critical approach to biblical interpretation, which was followed by overemphasis on subjectivism associated with reader-oriented approaches.[9] Overemphasis on reader-oriented

---

9. This somewhat simplistic description of the developing nature of hermeneutical approaches can be supplemented by Osborne's attention to structuralist, poststructuralist, reader-oriented, deconstruction, and mediating positions in appendix 1 (1991, 366–96).

approaches risks losing the distinction between devotional reading and instructional study.

An expansion from two horizons to four horizons followed as scholars recognized that the Old Testament and New Testament were interdependent horizons in their own right. Shaw and Van Engen (2003) presented an approach to Bible interpretation from the perspective of four horizons in relation to communication theory and linked this with the use of an inference model of communication for communicating Scripture cross-culturally. Duvall and Hayes (2005, 23) describe the concept of "crossing the principlizing bridge" so as to evaluate differences between the Bible-era horizon and later-era interpreter's horizon in relation to differing contextual aspects such as culture, language, time gone by, the scene of the particular Scripture, and the covenant in place at that time, among other elements, and from this derive principles for providing meaning and application for those of the horizon of the interpreter's era. I include a fifth horizon, that of the Holy Spirit, which provides a uniting feature for the other four horizons. Just as the Bible-era authors were inspired by the Holy Spirit to produce the Bible texts with meaning and significance for those of the Bible-era horizons, so we too, as later-era horizon interpreters, are intuited to by the same Holy Spirit through our relationship with God. As we engage with horizons and seek to draw inferences as to the authors' intentions, we can also seek Holy Spirit intuition concerning the significance for our own situations. In addition, we can seek intuition concerning how best to communicate in a way that encourages our respondents to also seek "the relationship between meaning and significance" (Osborne 1991, 12) for their own cultural contexts. This combines objective and subjective elements of biblical interpretation but with the expectation that even differing subjective perceptions of meaning—for instance due to seeing alternative emphases within texts and application of truths discovered—will never violate the fundamental law of loving God and loving each other if they are truly intuited by the Holy Spirit. Where disagreements about meaning of texts arise, our best response is to "agree to disagree" with humility and grace and through love-fueled graciousness that maintains unity without condemnation (Klein, Blomberg, and Hubbard 1993, 151).

Shaw and Van Engen's Approach to Communicating Bible Truths

Earlier approaches to exposing respondents to Scripture rightly had the respondent receiving from both the communicator and the Bible text, but these often included a less helpful underlying assumption that respondents would understand the text in the same way as the Christian communicator. Shaw and Van Engen (2003, 84) present a less simplistic approach that ultimately seeks to engage the respondent with both the communicator and the Bible from the perspective of the respondent's context and world-view. They present "4 horizons or viewpoints, of meaning [which] seem to inform the Christian understanding of what God has said [and these 4 horizons are]: (I) God's context-specific intended meaning in revelation found in the Old Testament, (II) God's revealed intended meaning in the New Testament that involves a new understanding of the Old Testament, (III) the gospel communicator, and (IV) the contemporary respondents."

D-Davidson's Five Horizons United in the Holy Spirit

As mentioned, I add a fifth horizon to Shaw and Van Engen's approach: the Holy Spirit. The Holy Spirit provides the means of uniting all the horizons since the Holy Spirit inspired the biblical text authors to be vessels bringing forth God's Word in horizons I and II, and for horizons III and IV of the Christian communicator and respondent respectively, the Holy Spirit brings divine intuition to further aid understanding (see figure 10.2).

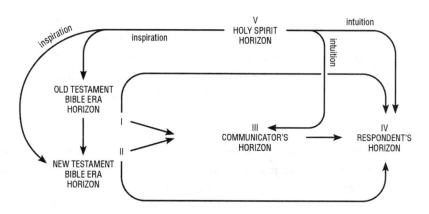

Figure 10.2: Five Horizons United in the Holy Spirit

Key principles from Shaw and Van Engen, which equally apply to my Five Horizons model, include:

1. As we build relationships with our respondents, we must both watch and listen so as to discover how they engage with and understand their world. In other words, we should become aware

of the worldview rules underlying the culture that govern how our respondents understand and interact with the world. From this we can then decide how to communicate in such a way that enables respondents to move toward an understanding of horizons I and II (91).

2. As we interact with respondents whose contextual horizon is different than our own and try to see horizons I and II from the perspective of the respondents, this causes us, as communicators, to reconsider our own understanding of horizons I and II. We do this with an expectation that the Holy Spirit seeks to help us by intuiting to us an awareness of fresh insights from a divine perspective.

3. We must look wider than the perspective of our own horizon to understand and even anticipate the questions of people from other cultures and lifestyle contexts. We tend to process the questions and perspectives of others in relation to our own experiences, uses of symbols, and perspectives of reality and so might also miss the implications for understanding that arise from the perspectives of our respondents. We must not forget that just as we know God from the perspective of our own contexts, so will our respondents be relating to God from the perspective of their own context since in any new context, "God is known and understood in new ways" (91). As communicators, we must avoid merely teaching what we already know about the Bible to respondents without bearing in mind the respondents' different cultural context because it is important that our respondents engage with the Bible and understand it on their own terms.

4. Our aim should be to help respondents who become Christians to be able to engage with the Bible and not only reap the benefit of what we, as communicators, know but also hear God's voice for themselves in his Word as intuited to them by the Holy Spirit and communicate that to others (92).

5. As Christian communicators, we can and should expect to learn from our respondents. They can bring us new perspectives and insights about the meaning of Scriptures as they relate ways of being and doing of people in Bible-era contexts to their own contexts. We can be further built up in God's Word as we present Scripture and listen to our respondents' responses (97). At the same time, we can also carefully address or dismantle misunderstandings.

Devotional comment: As we discover more of how our respondents hear from God through his Word, it can also widen our appreciation and stretch our anticipation and expectation for so much more that God desires to communicate to each of us through his Word. Just as different perspectives of God's nature and presence can be discerned in different settings, so too when we have taken up the call to communicate Christ to those in different cultures, the settings and people within them can be the very means he uses to communicate with us in new ways and draw us into deeper intimacy with him. In those times when life is sweet, we may find new faith-raising, delightful experiences of his joy; in troubling times of trial and stress, the fresh revelation of his presence with us and for us may, all the more, enable us to persevere in maintaining an attitude of rejoicing at all times, praying continually, and giving thanks in all circumstances that is God's will for us in Christ Jesus (1 Thessalonians 5:16–18).

6. When we become aware as communicators that the information in a Bible text assumes understanding of concepts and circumstances that are different to what the respondents can relate to, then we must provide the information needed to help them understand. Shaw and Van Engen describe this in terms of helping the respondents draw suitable inferences in relation to the author's intention with "understanding based on assumptions" (111).

Example from rural China: As the villagers' witness expanded to the town and to other villages, several small groups were set up and led by teams of two or three of the emerging leaders. We taught them principles of biblical interpretation and preaching on a genre by genre basis, and each week they would take turns preaching after we had first checked their prepared content and application with them. When we were teaching these emerging leaders about preaching from prophecy and the book of Jonah, we found that the villagers had no experience of an expanse of water as large as a sea. The Chinese name for a lake some distance away translated the lake as a "sea." I had to explain that the term *sea* refers to water that surrounds land and not an expanse of water within land. I also had to explain that when, like Jonah, one is far away from land on the sea, all that you can see in any direction is the horizon. That gave them a better mental understanding of the context of the story of Jonah.

Important principle: None of us, whether communicators or respondents, should bring meaning to texts in a way that disagrees with or violates New Testament teaching. Rather than suggesting that different cultural perspectives bring completely different and even competing meanings to a text in ways that might even disagree with New Testament truths and teachings, it can be more helpful to suggest that differences of perspective are more about emphases on details that are less relevant to the overall meaning of the text.

Example from rural China: In another seminar, I was teaching emerging leaders about the structure of parables and principles for preaching from texts containing parables. I began reading the parable of the sower from Matthew 13:3–8. When I got to verse 4 and some seed "fell along the path," one of the young men cried out, "But no one sows like that!" From his perspective and experience, sowing seed was carefully and purposefully done. One didn't waste the precious commodity of seed by letting it fall away from the prepared ground. As much as I tried to say that seed was sown in Bible-era times by broad casting, he indignantly kept insisting that this could not be the case because "No one sows seed like that!" Eventually a Christian sister villager quietly said, "But if the Bible says that, then that must be what happened." The young man had become focused on details of the parable purely from the perspective of his own cognitive environment. The overall meaning of the parable in relation to the rest of the chapter appears to show that the size of harvest is in God's hands,[10] not ours, but I had to change where the teaching session was going with this particular part of the chapter and attend to what was important for the villagers' context—the young man wanted to focus on the different kinds of ground for fruitful sowing.

---

10. Hagner (1993) on Matthew 13:1–13 in Word Biblical Commentary (CD version).

MODELS OF COMMUNICATION AND COMMUNICATION OF SCRIPTURE

We are familiar with the horizons or perspectives that should inevitably influence our interpretation of the meaning of different Scriptures. Now we will see that how we communicate to our respondent about the meaning of Scripture requires more tools than we usually use for communicating on a day-to-day basis. We will review the code model of communication, which has been our tool so far, and the inference model and its additional benefits for effective communication of issues related to Scripture.

1. **The code model** (which we saw in chapter 2) borrows from the science of communication. It involves the communicator encoding a message, which is transmitted to the respondent, who then decodes it into the meaning most appropriate to their understanding. "The emphasis is on the presentation of the message," and communicators aim to mirror the meaning of the content of the message as accurately as possible by making the encoding as helpful for the respondent as possible. But "less emphasis is placed on how the message is actually received" or how the respondent is affected or influenced by what they have rightly or wrongly understood (2003, 109–10). Two-way feedback is important to counter this.

2. **The inference model** recognizes that we are unable to get feedback from Scripture authors and therefore cannot check the accuracy of our perceived understanding but, instead, bring out inferences of meaning and "draw understanding based on assumptions" (111). The model aims to provide for appropriate contextual information to be supplied to the respondent as the respondent attempts to decode the communicator's message about the Scripture author's intentions (110). Scripture's human authors made certain assumptions so that their Bible-era audience could understand their meaning, and consequently, the communicator makes assumptions about the author's intended meaning and draws inferences based on those assumptions. The desired outcome is that the respondent might correctly understand and draw accurate inferences from the communicator's encoded message, which is based on assumptions

about the Scripture author's intended meaning. When intent matches the respondent's inferences, "relevance"[11] of the message has been achieved. Relevance theory engages with the concept of one's cognitive environment. "A cognitive environment is merely a set of assumptions which the individual is capable of mentally representing and accepting as true" (Sperber and Wilson 1995, 46). Higgins (2010, 190) adds:

> Thus cognitive environment includes a person's current and potential matrix of ideas, memories, experiences, and perceptions. New assumptions and thoughts that occur in the communication process might reinforce existing assumptions, or could lead to changes in the receptor's cognitive environment ... [so that according to relevance theory] accuracy in communication is described as an increasingly shared cognitive environment. Note that one of the implications here is that in communication both communicator and receptor will have their cognitive environments changed, and the goal implies a process of increasing understanding.

Five Horizons Inference Model of Communication

Shaw and Van Engen (2003, 111) provide a diagram with components pertinent to an inference model of communication, which is reworked to include D-Davidson's fifth horizon as seen in figure 10.3.

Ultimately, the communicator should be helping the respondent come to the place where they no longer need help from the communicator but are able to draw appropriate inferences concerning Scripture authors' intentions for themselves. Until then, successful decoding and understanding of the message by the respondent "requires that a communicator has a deliberate intent to convey information from which respondents are able to bring out the intended meaning while using contextual information available to them" (111). This requires that, as communicators, we become aware of what contextual information our respondents are lacking as well as what they have available to them and how they might use it in light of the following principles.

---

11. See Sperber and Wilson (1986).

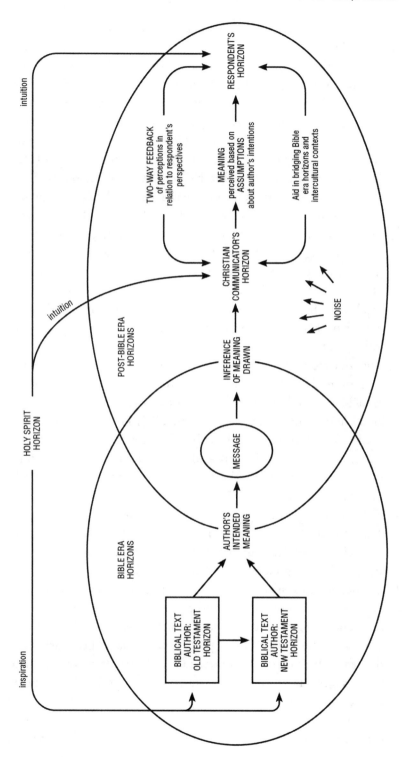

Figure 10.3 Five Horizons Inference Model of Communication

Important Principles Concerning Communication of Scripture in Relation to the Inference Model

1. "Communication does not focus on the forms and meanings used to present the message. Rather it concentrates on the thought processes necessary for communicators to ensure that respondents understand the scriptures' intent as clearly as possible. . . . The focus is on presenting a message so that the respondent is able to discover and apply the intended meaning of the author as" inferred in the Bible text (112). As communicators we need to become aware of the respondent's cognitive environment in relation to the message being presented.

   Of Bible translation, Gutt (1991, 99) claims, "The view that the main problem in translation is that of finding the right way of expressing the content in the receptor language has tended to obscure the problem of the communicability of the content itself." The inference model of communication intentionally attempts to deal with those context-bound aspects of texts that would otherwise have been incommunicable or misunderstood by people of other contexts.

2. The code model can be used effectively for exegesis of Bible content as it attends to what God has said. In comparison, the inference model "is more hermeneutical (context-oriented with respect to God's intent)" (Shaw and Van Engen 2003, 112). Both models are needed for interpretation of the Bible to be appropriated and communicated relevantly in cross-cultural and intercultural settings. As a simple comparison, the code model "is more content-based," whilst the inference model "is more context-based" (113).

3. If the forms and meanings communicated are clear to the respondents but don't help them in inferring the author's intent (as far as is possible), then "they are not faithful to the message of Scripture and may lead respondents into heresy" (114).

4. The acknowledgement of the Holy Spirit horizon provides validating criteria for respondents' and communicators' inferences since there should be no contradictions or incoherency in relation to the Bible as a whole. The Holy Spirit inspired the biblical authors so that the Bible's contents are noncontradictory. If there appear to be passages whose meaning seem to infer opposition, it is likely due to our or our respondents' lack of sufficient understanding or lack of contextual information, in which case we do best to reserve judgment until further light can be shed on the problem.

Areas of potential contention are unlikely to be of doctrinal or eternal significance in relation to the essentials of the gospel.

> **Important principle:** We may never assume our respondents have understood both the meaning and implications of what we have tried to communicate. Incorporating continuous feedback into the communication process is crucial for our respondents to get beyond forms and meaning, and implications of the inferences, so that appropriate application might also be made.

Application of the Five Horizons Inference Model to John 4:4–30

The code model is used for exegesis of the passage content in conjunction with the inference model's attention to the context of the Bible era in relation to the context of the respondent. Applying the inference model in its simplest form, we look into the text, identify assumptions the author might have been making in relation to the Bible-era audience, and then identify the aspects of the narrative's context for which the respondent is likely to need explanation. Having provided this contextual information, we then bring out some potential inferences related to the message based on the identified assumptions so that its significance can be applied into the lives of Christians and, specifically, into the setting and lives of our respondents. Asking our respondents for suggestions about application of inferences heightens the relevance of the Scripture to them. In this example, application is given to needs in relation to the social, emotional, and spiritual realms. What follows is a brief example of application of the inference model of communication.

Important assumptions that the writer of John 4:4–30 might have made about the audience could include:

- Knowledge of the relationship of relative enmity between the people of Samaria and Jews in Jesus' time. We can explain to the respondent that in horizon I times, Samaria was the capital of Northern Israel. When Assyria invaded Northern Israel in 722 BC, the Assyrians distributed people into Northern Israel that they had captured through invading other nations. When local troubles appeared to indicate that these deportees did not know how to worship the supposed local geographically denoted deity, an Israelite priest was returned to Samaria to instruct these captives in the law of Yahweh. As a result, subsequent generations born of the non-Israelite captives worshiped Yahweh but were looked down upon by Jews for not being of pure Israelite heritage. This brings enlightenment as to the incredulity of the disciples in horizon II.

- That the audience would have been surprised that Jesus would talk to a woman.
- Knowledge and experience that the use of a well as a water source was a normal aspect of lifestyle.
- Knowledge of the use of a particular vessel as a means of drawing water from a well.
- The relevance of the time of day at which Jesus sat down and the Samaritan woman appeared.

Consider which of these contextual assumptions need to be made known to the respondent. Hopefully we can see that respondents who are accustomed to drawing water from wells in their own culture and geographical setting are at a distinct advantage to those who are city dwellers and have never given serious thought to where water comes from before it gets to the faucet.

As we examine the content-unifying message of the narrative, we can see water referred to, initially, in a literal sense, but Jesus also refers to water in a spiritual sense, as the water Jesus gives wells up to eternal life (v. 14). The woman did not appear to understand what Jesus was offering her and was surprised by his knowledge of her life situation. In response she became open to spiritual truths, and we see a heart that appears to have been ready for truth. In retrospect, we can appreciate the spiritual truth about Jesus as the provider of living water, and to expand on this aspect of Jesus' nature, we can also turn with our respondent to the narrative of John 7:37–39, in which Jesus cries out, "'Let anyone who is thirsty come to me and drink. Whoever believes in me, as Scripture has said, rivers of living water will flow from within them.' By this he meant the Spirit."

Potential inferences based on assumptions and potential applications include:

- **Social needs:** Jesus wasn't prejudiced and neither need we be. What personal application is the Holy Spirit intuiting to us concerning people around us?

- **Emotional needs:** Jesus knows the state of our hearts and lives and comes to refresh and deliver us, not to condemn us. Do we sense this as a reality, or is it merely a mental assent?
- **Spiritual realm:** Jesus is the source of life who draws us to him to worship in right spirit and right understanding. He is consistent and generous in supplying resources to keep us revived and encouraged, and he renews life in us that we might spread this good news to others. Are we seeking the Holy Spirit's leading on a regular basis so that we are poised and ready for those ordained moments and opportunities to touch lives?

WORLDVIEWS AND THE BIBLE: IS THERE A CHRISTIAN WORLDVIEW?

We have seen the helpful implications of acknowledging different horizons when communicating Scripture. Our aim is to help our respondents and intercultural friends to learn from God's Word, deepen their relationship with him, and live fruitful and transformed lives. All of us can expect to see transformation as our priorities shift from selfishness to selflessness in Christ and as we are open to worldview beliefs being accordingly challenged and transformed. This inevitably provokes the question: Is there a Christian or a biblical worldview that we should expect to take on?

Kraft (1989, 81) writes, "It is misleading to use a term such as 'Christian worldview.'" Kraft bases this assertion on three main arguments. First, when people become Christians in any culture, they "still look and think more like the other members of their society than like Christians of other societies. . . . It is obvious that not even all Christians of a given society act their Christian principles in the same way. This would suggest that there is not a single Christian worldview" (81), but rather, that Christians live culturally-shaped lives following biblical principles that have replaced non-biblical cultural ways of life.

Second, though people who become Christians may need to make significant changes in their worldview, their beliefs don't all need changing, and they can never entirely replace their original worldview with another one. As we saw in chapter 3, a tree's roots can never be completely dug up and replaced without the tree dying, but some root limbs and branches may be lopped off and new sections grafted in. As Kraft writes, "If God were advocating a [single] totally Christian worldview, the implication would be that there is one divinely endorsed set of assumptions, values, and commitments designed to compete with those of every cultural worldview" (81).

Third, Kraft points out that when a person first becomes a Christian, certain worldview beliefs will very clearly need to change, but many cultural ways that do not have religious significance will not need to change. As new believers grow in their relationship with God and are open to the voice of the Holy Spirit, they will likely become aware of other aspects that need changing. From this we can see that worldview change, like spiritual growth, is a process.

Based on these assertions, Kraft (103) concludes that terms such as *biblical worldview* and *Christian worldview* are imprecise and misleading since they "could easily be misconstrued to imply either that there is only one cultural worldview in the Bible (which there isn't) or that God endorses one or another of those worldviews as normative for everyone (which he doesn't)." Kraft suggests that much of Jesus' worldview was shaped by the Hebraic background in which he lived in a small part of the wider Greco-Roman world, and as such, many of Jesus' perspectives would have been normative only for people of that setting (104). As a result, for Kraft, "a large number" of Jesus' Hebraic worldview perspectives with their related cultural practices would *not* also apply to us who are beyond that setting.

Kraft's suggestion may seem a little shocking. I am inclined to think that only a very few of Jesus' perspectives would *not* be applicable to us—for instance, utilitarian practices such as wearing long robes and reclining beside tables. I would be reluctant to dismiss too much of Jesus' values because we see how he challenges the Pharisees and teachers of the law on incorrect or incomplete understandings of Hebraic worldview perspectives, and all in the context of the law of love and what he is given to do and say by his Father. If we write off too much Israelite culture, which is based on law, we would also have to write off much of the Old Testament and the old covenant on which the new covenant is built. Jesus came to fulfill the law, show it from the perspective of completion, and build upon it. In the process, Jesus was unapologetically countercultural concerning relationship with outcasts and "sinners" and, crucially, explaining the means of coming into kingdom of God righteousness through being born of the Spirit rather than legalism.

Kraft's concerns about the limitations of Jesus' worldview perhaps, not surprisingly, show the Christian anthropologist's perspective from which Kraft deliberates. God works through culture and Kraft urges that, instead of looking to discover the particulars of an appropriate worldview,

Christians seek to discover and follow Jesus' *perspectives*, particularly in relation to the "kingdom perspectives" that are the central feature of Christ's teaching. For Kraft, living according to Jesus' perspectives marks out a Christian in any sociocultural setting (106). He suggests that the two key perspectives that challenge ungodly worldview beliefs involve power in relation to causality and love as the basis for interpersonal behavior, attitudes, and relationships (108). In summary, kingdom perspectives reveal our love of God, as shown through obedience, and love of our neighbor, as shown through servanthood.[12]

When we engage in interpretation of God's Word in relation to the different horizons, the subjective perspective that is stirred up from within us by the Holy Spirit will direct us concerning the significance and application of the truths discovered into specific cultural settings. When this direction is truly intuited by the Holy Spirit, it will violate neither the perspective of obedience due to love of God nor the principle of willing servanthood that shows love to others.

CONCLUSION

As we grow in intimacy with our Lord and Savior, so we will discover his Word challenging our assumptions and limited perceptions of how he can work in and through us. As we become more familiar with God's Word, we can also become deeper vessels from which to pour into the lives of our respondents. At the same time, as God works humility in our hearts and attitudes, we will be all the more able to hear and receive what God knows we need to learn from our respondents and intercultural friends.

QUESTIONS FOR REFLECTION
AND DISCUSSION

1. In the "As It Happened" scenario at the start of the chapter, how do you suspect the American missionary responded to the Thai student's interpretation of the text? What doctrinal issues were at stake, and how might the missionary have dealt with the Thai student's alternative interpretation of meaning?

---

12. See Kraft (1989, 108–14) for the complete list of the Kingdom Perspectives that Kraft derives from Jesus' teaching.

2. Which other aspects of the story of Jonah would you expect to have no compatibility with the rural China villagers' context and life setting? What else do you think I might have done to help the villagers have a richer understanding of Jonah's story from the perspective of their own context physically, emotionally, experientially, and spiritually?

3. Apply the code model and inference model to communicating the narrative of the wedding feast at Cana to Muslim teenagers for whom alcohol is forbidden. Be sure to identify the aspects of the narrative's context for which the respondents are likely to need explanation and bring out potential inferences related to needs in relation to the physical, emotional, and spiritual realms.

4. What would be an appropriate response if respondents come up with a bizarre and inappropriate interpretation of a Scripture text's meaning during a Bible discussion?

CHAPTER 11

Communication and Spiritual Growth: Teaching and Learning in Cultural Perspective

As It Happened: A teacher has invited a student from another culture to discuss together the student's progress.

> **Teacher:** How are you finding your studies here?
>
> **Student:** My parents wanted me to study here, teacher.
>
> **Teacher:** How are you finding the readings for the first assignment about followers of Christ and the temple tax? Are you also reading around the field as I suggested to the class?
>
> **Student:** Teacher, please, could you tell me which field you mean and how to find that field?
>
> **Teacher:** Well, that's just an expression; it's not a literal field. It means to take initiative and read wider than the actual title of the assignment. For instance, research the temple and what the temple tax was for, the development of its institution, by whom, how, and so on.
>
> **Student:** Ah, teacher, who are "Hoom How" and "So On"? Are they Chinese? Or Korean? Please tell me about these people.
>
> **Teacher:** I'm thinking perhaps you might be having problems with listening comprehension.
>
> **Student:** Teacher, I am listening, but please tell me, what is *comprehension?*

INTRODUCTION

We've probably all faced the frustration of not understanding a teacher figure's feedback whether face-to-face conversation or written. As we find ourselves looking to teach and inspire others, including our respondents, our communication needs to be shaped appropriately to bring about learning effectively.

In this chapter we examine different cultural ways of being and doing that we covered in earlier chapters but now in the context of teaching and learning. We might be looking to communicate in a way that facilitates spiritual discipleship or perhaps uses teaching as a platform to engage with respondents and potential respondents in another culture. Being aware of our preferences and the preferences of other cultures for both teaching and learning can help us contextualize teaching and learning so as to promote its effectiveness. Through enjoying intercultural relationships, respondents and/or students in formal settings can also be willing to risk acceptance of alternative ways of learning and engaging with ideas.

The chapter opens by discussing the potential difficulties associated with the timing of actually getting together. It then briefly examines the concept of learning and presents a variety of cultural orientations that can impinge on successful teaching and learning in both monocultural and multiple-culture situations. Having offered transferable principles to facilitate awareness, understanding, and overcoming of such barriers, the chapter concludes with devotional comments related to changing learned worldview beliefs.[1]

PERCEPTIONS RELATED TO TIME

In chapter 3 we examined the concepts of time orientation versus event orientation, and monochronism versus polychronism, and discussed how different cultures and individuals within cultures prefer one orientation over the other in varying degrees according to their cultural background. Whether we have planned to meet up with one person or many, being aware of their background culture's orientation can help us be realistic in our expectations of how the time agreed upon for the teaching and learning event might unfold. Regardless of whether the assigned time is for a formal class session or for informal interaction, we can expect that people will arrive in a manner coherent with their cultural norms. Some people will intentionally arrive at the appointed start time, others may arrive earlier, and others may arrive much later.

---

1. This chapter brings out and builds on principles from D-Davidson (2021) APTS Press and is used by permission. The basis for these principles is first seen in D-Davidson (2018).

As we saw in chapter 3, some cultures emphasize the careful expenditure of time, while others emphasize the quality of events, but as Lingenfelter and Mayers (2003, 49–50) urge, neither approach may be considered more godly. We need to acknowledge that God's approach to time is quite different from ours; no culture fully understands God's approach in terms of priorities or emphasis. While approaches that differ from our own preference might cause inconvenience or annoyance, keeping a healthy outlook in step with the Holy Spirit, particularly for informal and one-to-one events, helps enhance the quality of relationships and, consequently, the potential for enhanced teaching and learning. More formal settings require a little more care.

Example from a multiple-culture formal class setting: Filipino and Malaysian cultures are more event oriented than time oriented, and they differ in degree of orientation in relation to each other, with Filipinos being more laid back about time than Malaysians. Similarly, with Japanese culture being more time oriented than Hong Kong culture, Japanese students can be frustrated by their classmates from Hong Kong who show even mildly less attention to punctuality. A class professor coming from a relatively high level of time orientation can also be frustrated by non-time-oriented tardy students.

Important principle for multiple-culture formal theological teaching and learning settings: To resolve potential conflict and distress due to differing orientations, we can encourage new students (and visiting faculty) not only to be aware of their own cultural preferences but also to engage with school timetabling in a way that will best facilitate God's purposes through the school community culture in relation to classes, chapel ministry, and other school events.

When dealing with the difficulties resulting from differences in orientation preference, we can help non-time-oriented students meet time demands by offering them an appropriate means of motivation at a sufficient level. Whether we are instructing in Christian or secular settings, we can remind students of their desire to succeed in studies without "stealing" classmates' time; this will motivate them to follow time demands, such as refraining from being tardy for class and submitting course assignments on time. In Christian settings, it can be helpful to remind non-time-oriented students that God (or even their school community) could have other equally important events for them to be involved in that day as well as their current engagement. In contrast, for nonformal meetings, rather than allowing perceived limitations to cause frustration, it is best to be gracious concerning the balance of timing and event since the aim is to enjoy the time together and deepen relationships.

PERSPECTIVES ON LEARNING

As we look at different perspectives on learning, it is helpful to begin by asking, what do we mean by *learning*, and how does learning happen? The following sections examine some of the key theories related to the process of learning along with some cultural implications that can impact learning.

Prevailing Learning Theories

Writing in the context of differing cultural perspectives, Shade et al. (1997, 62) offer that "learning is a process that leads to some type of action." In this respect we might say that learning is more than merely communicating information or knowledge and hoping it will be received and correctly understood. Bloom's (1956) taxonomy of learning urged that learning happens on multiple levels, and increasing cognitive skills are required for more demanding learning and use of knowledge. His original taxonomy was updated by Anderson and Krathwohl (2001) to suggest that learning progresses from remembering facts, understanding information, applying knowledge in new ways, analyzing component parts in relation to each other, evaluating in order to make judgments, and ultimately creating new perspectives by synthesizing earlier perspectives and presenting something new.

Dewey (1938) saw experience as a crucial factor in learning, while Kolb (1984, 41) urged that "learning is the process whereby knowledge is created through the transformation of experience. Knowledge results from the combination of grasping experience and transforming it." Kolb presented learning in terms of a cyclical process that involves all of the four stages of concrete or hands-on experience through activity, followed by active reflection on the experience, then abstract reflection to bring out theoretical concepts, and lastly active experimentation that applies and tests out the evolving theoretical concepts. The cycle then starts again, with concrete activity related to the newly developed knowledge.

Kolb further suggested that individuals develop a preferred learning style in relation to one of the four stages (i.e., preference for presentation and reception of material in either abstract or concrete form, along with either active or reflective engagement in handling the material). As such, the learner likely prefers one of the four styles that sees learning come about through either a concrete-active approach, concrete-reflection, abstract-reflection, or abstract-active learning.

Howard Gardner proposed that intelligence is "the ability to solve a problem or create a product that is valued in society" (1983, 3) and his theory of multiple intelligences (1983; 2011) was the catalyst for recognizing learning styles related to the following:[2]

- linguistic—written and spoken words
- naturalist—learning outside or amidst manifestations of nature
- musical or rhythmic—thinking in relation to sounds and rhythm
- kinesthetic—tactile and physical movement
- visual or spatial—thinking that forms pictures and visual spatial mastery in relation to navigation, architecture, chess etc.
- logical/mathematical—thinking that follows a linear order
- interpersonal learning—learning with others in a collectivist manner
- intrapersonal learning—with independence and privacy

Later developments on learning styles include Fleming and Mills (1992) VARK[3] or *Visual, Aural, Read/write,* and *Kinesthetic* sensory modalities that are preferred in differing degrees by individuals and used for learning.

Whether or not one accepts the criticisms of "learning styles,"[4] adult learning theories have tended to build on Dewey and Kolb's theories.

---

2. Lest any area of human existence and engagement with life in the world should be considered a facet of intelligence, note that Gardner (2000, 27) does not attend to moral perspectives or issues of character and prefers that "those aspects of spirituality that have to do with phenomenological experience or with desired values or behaviors are best deemed external to the intellectual sphere."

3. This builds on the earlier VAK model of the 1920s.

4. Note Coffield et al.'s (2004) critique of instruments used to identify an individual's learning style. Coffield's team found that none of the most popular learning style theories [including VAK and VARK] had been adequately validated through independent research, leading to the conclusion that the idea of a learning cycle, the consistency of visual, auditory, and kinesthetic preferences and the value of matching teaching and learning styles were all "highly questionable." Despite Coffield et al.'s pronouncement of a learning cycle and learning style being highly questionable, plenty of anecdotal evidence, including my own, would suggest that Kolb's learning cycle has credibility.

While these theories are grounded in the context of Western academia, we can see that some of Gardner's multiple intelligences also overlap with non-Western cultural approaches to learning. Non-Western approaches include Gardner's collective learning and nonlinear learning, as well as learning in relation to other aspects of cognition and physicality additional to merely linear presentations of ideas and concepts.

Learning Theories in Practice

Kolb's richly enlightening learning theory assumes a preference for either active or reflective engagement with the material being taught, but it provides for no attention to learners whose teaching and learning environment expects activity by the teacher and passivity on the part of the students or learners. If experiential learning were to be forced upon them, students from cultures unaccustomed to it might be afraid to make mistakes and become the object of shame, or they may be uncomfortable with the potential for ambiguity and the uncertainty that comes from there appearing to be no control of the learning process. They may even resist fulfilling their full learning potential in case it would make them appear to be better than others and bring shame. Let us not forget that in all our relationship-building, teaching, and learning endeavors, maintaining the dignity of learners is of the utmost importance. Encouraging people into new and different ways of learning requires the same sensitivity to grace and graciousness as was initially needed for building the relationships.

> **Important principle:** Be aware that whether students have grown up accustomed to independence and learning on their own, or they find greater security through interdependence and working in groups, their experience will likely have been influenced by the degree to which they have grown up in either more individualist or more collectivist settings.[5]

Lingenfelter and Lingenfelter (2003, 57) affirm that in multiple-culture settings "teachers cannot possibly teach to all the potential differences [in a classroom setting] but they can become more culturally sensitive to the diversity of their students. One of the most important things they can do

---

5. Preference can also be influenced by the degree to which a student has either an extrovert or introvert personality.

is explain the context of what they are doing and make their teaching techniques explicit." As teachers, we can communicate to facilitate new ways of teaching and learning by including a mixture of receivable group activities and individual assignments.

In my experiences in multiple-culture theological classes, I have found that collectivist-background students accustomed to lectures tend to be unacquainted with experiential learning. This is especially true of those who grew up in environments that expected them to be passive in the classroom. When they are introduced to experiential learning, along with more individualist learning through small-group activity, they discover new empowering in learning (see D-Davidson 2011 on helping students move from passive to active learning). Learning is especially enhanced when they are made aware of how the personality facets of introversion and extraversion can affect group dynamics; in addition, the potential for shame in "giving wrong answers" is vastly reduced when group members look to mutually encourage each other and are willing to learn from each other. This takes humility and, in multiple-culture groups, a willingness by students to confront their own attitudes and prejudices toward people of other cultures within the group. As Gay (2018, 199) writes, "This confrontation forces them to come to terms with their own self-worth, self-image, and cultural pride, and encourage the transformation of their own personal worldview." Learning has then gone beyond acquisition of knowledge to heightened self-knowledge.

Similarly, students who have grown up with an individualistic learning mentality can discover for themselves through group activity the reality and wonder of more and differing perspectives. This gives them a greater pool of knowledge from which to solve problems. They gain the ability to recognize the truth of the body of students being more than the mere sum of its parts and gain a deeper appreciation of differences. For multiple-culture Christian groups, in addition to heightening self-knowledge, this also helps the individualistic-learning students value the mutuality and inclusivity of all members of the body of Christ.

Author's example: In my earlier years teaching and ministering in Asia, I put materials together, labored to translate them into Mandarin Chinese, and then taught them to the new believers each week with stories and visual aids. Dr. Co's major focus was dentistry and the pastoral care that interacting with distraught patients requires, while my focus outside working hours was on Bible and ministry teaching and training. Dr. Co had professed that she had little idea or experience in what to move on to after discipleship, so that is why the role fell to me, and I enjoyed it very much. Teaching passive learners to become active learners and, later on, teaching them to teach other passive learners was a big challenge and took even more creativity, and by God's grace, the earlier results were mostly positive. I did my best from my individualistic perspective, but a big difference came when I started asking Dr. Co what she thought of the material I was preparing. An even bigger and better difference came when we put our heads and hearts *together* in preparing materials. Together we have since taught mono- and multiple-culture classes across Asia and the Pacific Rim for many years, demonstrating the joy, empowering, and transforming communication that comes with intercultural coteaching.

COMMUNICATION AND APPROACHES TO TEACHING

After mastering graciousness in the timing of getting together and becoming familiar with different learning styles, we need to pay attention to contexting in our communication to prevent what we aim to communicate from being misunderstood. Appropriately presenting information with cultural expectations in mind can make the important difference between confusion and understanding. As we saw in chapter 2, low-context communicators will use specific words and phrases to capture the exact meaning of what they want the listener to hear and understand, while the intended meaning of high-context communicators relates more to the context of the communication and less to the words used. In formal teaching and learning settings, misunderstanding of contexting expectations can bring learning to a halt.

Examples from a formal classroom environment: In formal class settings, teachers coming from high-context communication cultures may give assignment instructions that seem vague and imprecise to students from lower-context communication settings. However, teachers from low-context communication backgrounds may be frustrated when high-context communication students do not appear to pay attention to the carefully listed details of course requirements. These students who are accustomed to high-context communication might be more focused on trying to work out meaning from what the teacher has *not* said or written.

Another factor to be aware of is the degree to which cultures and members within them are comfortable with ambiguity. Hofstede and Hofstede (2005, 163–205) describe the phenomena of uncertainty avoidance and its opposite, tolerance of ambiguity, in relation to preferences across cultures.[6] "Extreme ambiguity creates intolerable anxiety" (165) for which people develop coping skills common to their people-groups and national communities. Whilst "uncertainty is a subjective experience . . . [associated feelings] may also be partly shared with other members of one's society." Linking a desire for predictability with the desire to avoid uncertainty, Hofstede and Hofstede (167) write, "*Uncertainty avoidance* [is] *the extent to which the members of a culture feel threatened by ambiguous or unknown situations.*" Plueddemann (2018, 60) offers (albeit without providing sources or data to substantiate the suggestion), "There is often a correlation between a high tolerance for ambiguity and high-context cultures. High-context people tolerate ambiguity because events going on around them are more important than the disruption of a low-context clock. . . . How can one plan when the context is continually changing?"

Whilst the Hofstede study identified a wide range of preferences along the spectrum, with Greece ranking highest and Singapore lowest in relation to uncertainty avoidance, perhaps the most useful point is that cultures vary in how comfortable people are with ambiguity.[7] In relation to communication for teaching and learning, we can recognize that, at the extremes, some teachers prefer timetabling and lesson content scheduled down to the minutiae with no tolerance for change, whilst others are comfortable to

---

6. They build on the work of Geert Hofstede (1991) wherein he refers the term *uncertainty avoidance* back to Cyert and March (1963).

7. Note that the Hofstede studies were the result of research covering IBM manager-level employees worldwide in response to surveys. Whilst providing a rich source of cultural information in relation to business practice variables, limitations include the sample consisting largely of commercial business-minded, educated males. The Hofstede studies results are tabled with an uncertainty avoidance value for seventy-four countries (2005, 168–69) but with little means of predicting whether countries within a hemisphere or continent would score high or low and with the data potentially predisposed to bias by the business-minded orientation of the survey respondents.

throw out some ideas to the class and see what opens up as a result. Equally, some students prefer and feel most helped by the former, whilst others find that approach oppressive and prefer the seemingly unplanned creativity that can come from spontaneity and ambiguity. Apart from the degree of scheduling or ambiguity in teaching methodology to which our respondents or students were accustomed as they progressed through schooling, we can also see hints of preference in relation to personality, regardless of culture.[8]

> **Important principle:** Communication related to teaching and learning can be enhanced when we are aware of our respondents' or students' expectations for teaching and learning, since teaching and learning preferences for the presentation of material differs from culture to culture and personality to personality. Being aware of expectations can help us communicate in a way that is conducive to understanding even if expectations are not fully met. Incorporating feedback into the teaching and learning process is, as for any communication, also vital.

Linear learners prefer a logical approach in the progression of what is presented, whereas nonlinear learning may bring out a single theme by approaching it and illustrating it from multiple different perspectives. Nonlinear learning is often seen as unproductive and repetitive to linear learners, while their counterparts find it enthralling. Similarly, in some cultures, learners are accustomed to being given principles followed by the application of the principles. Other cultures focus on application before dealing with underlying principles. Storytelling cultures, for instance, first tell a story containing principles to be taught and then bring out important principles from the story.[9] This contrasts with teaching styles that present principles followed by illustrations or means of applying the principles.

> **Example from Kenya:** "Oral communication through stories always catches the ears of Kenyans in Africa. We love to hear stories. So use the story to teach, or the incidents of daily life to teach."

8. For some other easy-reading perspectives on learning style and personality, see LeFever (2011).
9. See for instance Steffen (1993, 59).

Example from Japan: "A Christian American was sharing the gospel to my friend, and my friend could not understand who *Kristo* [i.e., Christ] is. Our background is Shintoism, so people believe in many gods. It is always best to show pictures and diagrams that we can relate to and make it simple because it doesn't need to be complicated—the gospel isn't a lot of complicated theory!"

Giving the story or application first follows an inductive approach to learning, while beginning with principles takes more of a deductive approach. Learners can be best helped to reach understanding when teachers are aware of inculcated worldview beliefs about learning and which approach is more likely to appeal to the learners.[10] With a multiple-culture group or class, it will be all the more important for the teacher to recognize that different students might be more accustomed to one approach than the other. In this case, we do well to vary the delivery of material using assorted approaches, from highly ordered teaching session content versus ambiguity, linear versus nonlinear learning, and working through different stages of Kolb's learning cycle with respect to hands-on activity, reflection, theorizing, and practical experimentation.

Important adult-learning principles for online or in-person learning: Adult learners of any culture can only concentrate for a certain amount of time, after which they need a break.[11] Online teaching has seen advantages in reducing the length of time a teacher is lecturing and allowing students to prepare materials ahead of time so that they are ready to actively participate in the sessions. Breaking into smaller groups also allows for

---

10. Cf. Shade, Kelly, and Oberg (1997, 10): "Particular ways of perceiving, thinking and acting to meet the demands of the environment are shaped by a person's worldview" and so also have an impact on effectiveness of the teaching styles to which they are subjected.

11. Note that multitasking, or concurrently concentrating on multiple different tasks, is now being debunked as cognitively nonachievable. Instead, supposed multitaskers are actually task switching (i.e. switching between tasks) but, as a result, not actually achieving maximum productivity in any of the tasks! See, for instance, Hyman et al. (2009) who show that "cell phone usage may cause inattentional blindness even during a simple activity that should require few cognitive resources." This implies that students making calls during class, whether online or not, are more than likely unable to concurrently focus on the class session!

the adult learners to interact. The disadvantages of online learning include that it takes additional planning to help students get to know each other, and it often takes more time to prepare for class sessions. We are not looking to merely entertain through teaching. However, using visual aids and introducing a degree of unpredictability from session to session can help make lengthy sessions, when scheduled by necessity, more enjoyable for both linear and nonlinear learners. Both kinds of learners find it easier to reengage in concentration when sessions are broken up with short discussion, small group exercises, video clips, or in Christian settings, brief times of ministry when appropriate.

APPROACHES TO TEACHING AND STUDENTS' COGNITIVE PREFERENCES

Personality, adult maturity, and spiritual maturity, as well as culture, can all influence a student's preferred orientation and degree of orientation in relation to cognition and learning. In chapter 2 we saw the importance of being aware of dichotomistic thinking in contrast to comprehensive thinking. We saw the need to communicate in such a way as to encourage dichotomist respondents that there is often more than one way of engaging with issues and resolving problems and, importantly, to beware of judging others who have different opinions. Equally, we may need to encourage comprehensive thinkers to look beyond an array of possibilities and commit to one of the options.

In terms of cognitive starting points, we do well to ensure that we are teaching in such a way that we engage with whichever of relational priorities, postulated concepts, or intuitional perception is most helpful for the learners. Especially where we have representatives of more than one cognitive starting point, we can aim to teach in ways that make what we are presenting receivable from the different perspectives. For concrete thinkers, we should provide a concrete basis before moving on to theoretical concepts. For relational thinkers, we need to include an element that appeals to the emotions and relational perspectives. Conceptual thinkers find a logical progression of ideas to be most helpful, whilst intuitional thinkers appreciate an approach that provides for the thinker to analyze and evaluate ideas in relation to their inner leadings.

Example of communicating gospel truths from John 14:6: Jesus proclaimed, "I am the way and the truth and the life. No one comes to the Father except through me." For conceptual thinkers, we can communicate the logical progression from who Jesus is as the way, truth, and life to the means he *is* for people to come into relationship with God the Father and salvation because of who and what he is. For the relational thinker, we can focus communication on the relationship implications: Jesus indicates that his relationship with the Father is a crucial aspect of both salvation to be gained as well as the means to it. For the intuitional thinker, truth and life are validated by inner leading. Jesus' "I am" proclamation comes from the inner being of who he is, but it also impacts the outer environment in which he lives and moves. The life Jesus lives and presents, as well as the resulting change in the lives of others, is undeniable to those open to an unfathomably powerful perspective on life and its purpose. As we pray and they seek, intuitional thinkers can come into the affective reality of relationship that has the Spirit of Christ within them.

Teachers, consciously or subconsciously, reflect their orientation preference through the way they present information and new ideas in class. Younger students infrequently receive what is taught without questioning the content. Adult students, with more information, experience, and broader perceptions of life and possibilities, might also be accustomed to questioning what is presented. These adult students may desire to question what is presented in terms of black-and-white issues so as to investigate alternative gray-area possibilities, or vice versa. This can be reflected in their cultural perceptions of what makes for appropriate power distance.

TEACHING AND LEARNING IN RELATION TO POWER DISTANCE

As we saw in chapter 4, high power distance cultures expect members of society to respect the hierarchical structure of society by showing the expected level of respect for those with higher levels of authority. Titles make clear where authority lies and what kind of behavior is expected toward such title holders. In high power distance settings, the teaching and learning model leads to a preference for lectures since personal interaction between teachers and students is neither expected nor encouraged (Moreau et al. 2014, 166). In multiple-culture classes, students from high power distance, face-saving cultures are less likely to volunteer questions or answer questions in class to avoid potential embarrassment, but this silence can be misunderstood as lack of interest (Xiao and Petraki 2007).[12]

Not surprisingly, the most extreme high power distance cultures include those with a background that acknowledges the strict hierarchy of Confucianism, such as China, Korea, and Japan. Marginson (2011, 587) adds to these Taiwan, Singapore, and Vietnam and proposes that these "Confucian" education nations show a certain measure of effectiveness in supplying research from "world-class universities," albeit with "downsides for social equity in participation, and in the potential for state interference in executive autonomy and academic creativity." Confucian ideals recognize both the value of education and its role in bringing betterment for the student's entire family and wider community, but high power distance in teaching and learning is not limited to Marginson's "Confucian" education nations[13]—it affects the teaching and learning environment in other cultures too.

> **High power distance example from Myanmar:** "In my country people show great respect to those in authority, and power distance is a higher level than in the Philippines where I'm studying now. In my country, a student must go to the teachers, but the teachers never come to a student. In class we can't ask the teachers questions, and education in Myanmar is more about memorizing concepts than discussing or applying them."
>
> **High power distance example from Bhutan:** "In Bhutan, students cannot just pack their bags and get up and go once the class is finished. They may not leave the classroom until the professor has left. This is to show respect to the professor."

---

12. See too Dolzhikova et al. (2021) for teaching and learning cultural difficulties identified in a study of Chinese and Arab (Syrian and Egyptian) students in a multiple-culture university in Russia.

13. See also Hsiao and Yang (2014) on the differing effects of introducing "Confucius classrooms" into Cambodia and Myanmar with the Cambodian initiative being "enthusiastically championed by government and political leaders" (11), in contrast to Myanmar.

High power distance example from Thailand: "Generally, in Thai schools the learning is very passive. We are shy to ask the teachers questions if we are not clear, and actually, teachers are also offended if students ask them questions—they feel threatened because they believe that their authority is being challenged."

In contrast, low or small power distance cultures, typically Global North cultures, reflect values that prefer equality and mutual respect regardless of a person's title and position in society. Teaching and learning models in these cultures welcome interaction and discussion in classes (Moreau et al. 2014, 167). Students may publicly challenge or disagree with the teacher figure, but this should always be done with a respectful attitude in line with the associated and inculcated worldview beliefs. The teacher may be holding ultimate authority and power, but this may not be so obvious to the observer.[14]

Low power distance example from a female Mongolian: "Teachers can be friends and have a closeness with students, much like the relationship with a brother."

Difficulties can occur in multiple-culture class settings when students or teachers are unaware of the different cultural expectations related to power distance. Students or respondents from high power distance cultures are likely to be uncomfortable in settings where students from low power distance cultures challenge or appear to disagree with the teacher

---

14. The academic requirements of graduate level study call for the development of critical thinking skills and the ability to interact with multiple diverse and even competing ideas. Students from large power distance cultures can find it difficult to interact with and publicly disagree with the views of those perceived to be in authority. See D-Davidson (2013) for suggestions on how to help such students and others develop critical thinking skills including, for all students, encourage an outlook which sees the acquisition and use of critical thinking skills as more than an exercise in the academic setting and as a skill for lifelong learning; Christian students can be particularly encouraged to seek deeper intimacy in their relationship with God since that also has the potential to enhance the creative possibilities of the Holy Spirit in and through the critical thinking skills employed in their studies. See too Kuhn (2019), who sees critical thinking as a dialogic process. Prayerful internal dialoguing with self about others can aid heightening of effective dialoguing with those same others.

figure. Similarly, students or respondents from a lower power distance culture may find a higher power distance class environment both restrictive and frustrating. As we might expect, power distance differences have similar implications for dynamics within discipleship groups and Bible study sessions.

Projecting one's cultural power distance preference into the classroom setting may be helpful for students with a similar preference. However, it may act as "noise" to others and drastically reduce effectiveness in teaching. Amidst varying expectations of power distance, we can encourage a mutual respect of difference in secular settings, while in Christian settings we can encourage our respondents or students to be aware of different cultural outlooks and seek deeper intimacy with God so that graciousness prevails.

The Effects of Power Distance and Social Interaction on Class Interaction

Power distance affects expectations concerning social interaction with people of different levels of power and authority in communities. This can have major implications for interaction between our respondents or class members from high power distance cultural backgrounds who are from different levels of society (e.g., if one has the high-status level of a pastor but another is a church member devoid of status or role). Interacting together in class discussions or at fellowship events has the potential for difficulty because low-level class members would expect only higher-level members to voice opinions. Our role as teachers and learning facilitators in any setting is best served by seeking to heighten dignity amongst ourselves and those gathered and to model that we cherish the dignity of others. Without completely abandoning cultural expectations, we can recognize, affirm, and model that we are all equal in status and role before God as his beloved children. As we pray and the Holy Spirit moves in hearts and lives, God transforms cultural ways.

Author's example from rural China: When Dr. Co and I were ministering in the village in rural China, we began our mission work by helping new believers into a growing relationship with God through discipleship and with the goal of eventually establishing a church. As they shared their faith, we gave them different levels of responsibility for discipling and encouraging newer believers too. Eventually these emerging leaders were discipling and teaching several small groups of believers, and initially, anyone who desired to learn more about God's Word would join our ministry training sessions. Each small group had a leadership team of two or three believers who would take turns ministering from the Word, and Dr. Co and I would listen to what they had each prepared a week ahead. Apart from giving us an opportunity to make suggestions about the content, appropriate illustrations, and so on, it was also a time for mentoring and encouraging these dear friends. Most but not all were the fruit of our earliest evangelistic efforts, and some were the fruit of the first few emerging leaders, but they happily all came together to learn more about God. We did not use terms such as *church* or *leader* until our time to depart the area grew nearer. They were acting as leaders without the title, and with the understanding that the groups were all part of the worldwide body of Christ, which happened to be in their villages and communities. These men and women's academic backgrounds varied widely, and some had roles with distinctly higher levels of power and influence, but they showed love, humility, and mutual respect as they ministered together. After leaving the area we made occasional trips back to encourage the leaders and were also delighted to get phone calls asking how we were too. A few years later we were thrilled to hear that they had begun a fellowship for elderly members of the community who had become Christians. Parents and grandparents had seen the gospel lived out and heard how to also come into life in Christ. Counterculturally, the elderly folks' congregation was led by members of the younger generation of adults who were also teaching their elders from the Bible. Transformation occurred in God's timing and as the different generation members delighted in following his leading in their lives.

PATRON-CLIENT IMPLICATIONS FOR TEACHING AND LEARNING

As we saw in chapter 4, all cultures employ some kind of patron-client relationship mechanism with differing degrees of subtlety. Teachers and students will be aware of the patron-client obligations and expectations of their background culture, at least subconsciously. Difficulties and conflicts come when one or the other party assumes their own understanding is also the rule outside of the setting of their background culture.

Some students come from a culture in which the teacher, as patron, is expected to be a parental figure. There can be frustration when these students do not see their teachers' culturally cued actions and behaviors accompanying a parentlike care. Equally, for teachers facing different cultural expectations without awareness of their students' expectations, there can be frustration due to what might appear to be a naive lack of adult maturity on the part of the students.

Example from a Western English teacher in China: "I had come from a relatively high power distance teaching and learning setting in the USA, and in order to maintain consistent class discipline never changed my classroom approach since beginning teaching in China in the mid-1990s. I maintained the formalities of classroom interaction with, and by, students, and enjoyed consistently acceptable academic results. The cross-cultural teaching and learning aspect that had most surprised me on arriving in China was discovering that, as a teacher, I was also expected to provide a caring parentlike role for each student, and this while concurrently maintaining the boundaries of the high power distance relationship."

Expectations of teacher, learner, and teacher as learner can be crippled when misunderstanding exists concerning differing cultural patron-client obligations. In settings where the student's achievement (or lack thereof) has wider social implications in relation to maintaining the honor of both the student and the student's family, if the teacher is unaware of the cultural expectation clues, this has the potential to alienate on a long-term basis. Frustrations related to honor and shame can also arise.

Lingenfelter and Lingenfelter (2003, 73) advise that in honor-honoring societies, "the student's quest for learning and achievement is directly linked to the honor and expectations of the family. Students from Western cultures do not share this collective burden." While this might be seen as a rather simplistic perspective on students from Western cultures, as teachers we need to recognize and value the differing degrees of beliefs related to honor, guilt, and shame held by respondents and students from different cultures.

For our respondents who experience unfulfilled patron-client expectations in anticipated (but not achieved) academic success, we can communicate in a way that directs their attention to God's desires of faithfulness in study and use of individual giftings and abilities. Even with family honor at stake, regardless of supposedly accrued obligation in terms of a student's hoped for academic success, a teacher cannot put into the student or "make up for" what God has left out. As teachers we are also ongoing learners in God's eternal purposes and can be his vehicles for compassionate empathy. Whilst we aim to seek the highest and best of God's purposes for our respondents, urging them into accredited theology-related study is not advised if the groundwork has not been laid that gives them a desire and hunger for more of God. Seeking academic badges of honor can in no way substitute for seeking more of God through personal study of the Bible for the pure purpose of growing more in love with him and deepening our life in Christ.

CHANGING WORLDVIEWS AS AN IMPORTANT PART OF LEARNING

We saw in chapter 9 that turning to Christ does not mean turning away from every aspect of culture and inculcated worldview belief. We are communicating to bring appropriate change to worldview beliefs in relation to Christian perspectives as found in the Bible, and in a way that does not displace our respondents from the relationship networks within their community and society. As we saw in the example earlier in this chapter pertaining to establishment of the village church in rural China, the relationship networks that naturally exist within communities and societies are the means for communities and societies to be transformed "from the inside out." Flemming (2005, 150) writes that believers "will both reflect their culture and disrupt it." Kraft (1979, 145) argues that transformation aims "to increase the suitability of the culture to serve as a vehicle for divine-human interaction." He also suggests (1989, 200) that beliefs related to causality and power, particularly supernatural power, are the ones most likely to need change. In contrast, atheists and secularists need an opposite form of enlightenment that reveals the reality of supernatural power through the presence and touch of the Holy Spirit. How can we, in our role as learning facilitators, help ourselves and our respondents into the crucial aspects of worldview change, through transformation of previously learned worldview beliefs, which might then be a catalyst for transformation of the wider community? The devotional comments that follow offer some guidance.

Principles for Changing Worldview Beliefs
from a Devotional Perspective

1. Kraft (1989, 56–58) advises that culture does not possess any power in itself; rather, "it is habit that empowers cultural patterns." As we saw in chapter 3, we learn cultural patterns from childhood before we necessarily learn the worldview beliefs associated with them, and we then develop into adulthood with an established set of habits. We can encourage not only our respondents but also ourselves to periodically examine our lifestyle habits in relation to Christian perspectives of love, righteousness, and truth, and ask the Holy Spirit to show us and convict us of where our learned habits are due for change.

2. Be aware that resistance to change can arise if we or our respondents do not have the cognitive categories to validate or make sense of the change proposed (68). Moving into realms where belief is by faith and not by sight or understanding will be a continual life-long requirement for replacing old habits and outlooks with new ones as we cooperate with the Holy Spirit.

3. Recognize that it is the *will* to change a perspective that becomes crucial. As we progress through the stages of childhood into adolescence and from young adulthood into mature adulthood, we face many situations and times of instability that challenge us to rethink what others taught us to believe (69). Healthy change is about being willing to rise to the challenge, examining those beliefs and modifying them as appropriate—but this must be done willingly and without coercion. Are we willing to trust God for wisdom, revelation, and understanding as he deems we need it and provides it, or will we just give up and walk away? It's not easy to change a learned aspect of worldview or ingrained behavior, but if we are willing, and it is in line with something God would will, then it is certainly possible. God never forces anyone; by his grace, he acts on willingness.

4. Worldview change involves laying aside beliefs that previously fueled our sense of security but that either distracted us from or did not deepen our dependency on God. As we throw off those beliefs and hunger and thirst after more of God, we become vessels into which "new wine" can be poured and matured. The experience, whether by the senses or by faith, of God-given revelation or vision intuited to our inner being can be the forerunner to taking on a new untried spiritual perspective that is centered in the person and power of Jesus.

Example from Malaysia: "Many Muslims have shared testimonies about how they encountered God personally through visions or dreams from God by themselves, and then Christians help them into understanding how God is calling them into relationship with him through Jesus."

5. Kraft (1989, 94–95) suggests that "one of the biggest hindrances to change is lack of knowledge" concerning alternative perspectives and that intellectual, observational, and experiential knowledge are all important for willingness to change, to the extent that "there is absolutely no substitute for experience to bring one into a new perspective" (96). To this I add that we need to understand for ourselves and for our respondents that willingness is more than either an emotional conviction or mental assent provoked by new knowledge. Steps toward long-lasting change begin when the heart, mind, and will are all in agreement. When there seems to be no evidence or insufficient evidence from observation or experience to fuel that agreement, God can and does gift faith to us as we seek him. That is when faith displaces doubt and we discover with delight that he knows we are ready to trust him for what is important and timely from his perspective.

Devotional comment: Like many ministers, I have taught on 2 Corinthians 12:9–10 and Paul's declaration that God's "power is made perfect in weakness." Delighting in weaknesses, insults, hardships, persecutions, and difficulties was, for Paul, opportunity to own "For when I am weak, then I am strong." The reality of a response that delights as Paul did can long elude believers, as can seeing our weaknesses become vessels for God's glory. One of my mentors wondered why, when he preached about Christian lifestyle, some people were convicted but others felt condemned. My mentor decided that rather than preaching, "This is how the Bible says we *should* be," he would preach, "This is what the Bible says we *are*," because *oughts* and *shoulds* can easily bring people into condemnation.[15] In a bid to further reduce the potential for condemnation

---

15. From Rev. Dr. Hugh Osgood in 1987. He has become a cherished and influential mentor.

and doubt in relation to the reality of individuals' lifestyles (including my own), I have since encouraged Christian communicators and emerging leaders to avoid preaching, "This is how the Bible says we *should* be," but instead, with a careful eye to the Scripture content, preach "This is what the Bible says we *are* and/or what we *can become* in Christ." As we seek more of Christ and the Holy Spirit's direction for making choices and changes conducive to living out love, we submit ourselves to him so his presence within us *can* bring the changes, and Christ within us can live that love out through us for his glory.

CONCLUSION

While we are becoming familiar with our respondents and aware of their teaching and learning backgrounds, we must take responsibility for clear and appropriate communication. Meyer (2002, 258) urges that "a classroom environment be established to meet the individual needs of students in each class." A one-size-fits-all approach may end up being a poor fit for all and so undermine the potential for effective communication. Lingenfelter and Lingenfelter (2003, 52) note that "the teacher, who has the authority to define the classroom experience, must take responsibility for creating a context that bridges cultural differences . . . [and] create a learning context that is familiar to students yet stretches them beyond their previous experiences." As we engage with our respondents, who are hopefully now precious friends, we can expect that it will not just be these friends who are stretched but that *we* also will be stretched for God's glory and purposes as we sensitively seek appropriate ways to promote ongoing learning toward greater Christlikeness.

QUESTIONS FOR REFLECTION AND DISCUSSION

1. In the "As It Happened" scenario at the start of the chapter, where can you see examples of misunderstanding between the teacher and student? What aspects of miscommunication can you detect in relation to the teacher's and student's cultural backgrounds and preferred approaches to teaching and learning? What clues are there to suggest the teacher might be task oriented? How might the teacher have spoken to display some empathy?

2. Consider the following statements in response to someone's communication:
   - "I *hear* what you are saying."
   - "I *see* what you mean."
   - "I *think* I understand the point being made."
   - "I *feel* like I understand, but I might still be missing something."

3. Regularly referring to hearing, for instance, may indicate a cognitive learning style that prefers aural learning, while regularly referring to seeing may indicate a learning style that aligns with visual reception. Similarly, for verbal communication that regularly refers to either thinking or feeling, can you see the potential link with personality? Which of the responses can you personally relate to? Being aware of our own response styles can help us as ongoing learners. Importantly, listening to how our respondents communicate can help us teach and communicate according to their preferred approaches to learning and bring enhanced understanding.

4. Engage with the following scenario: An international, intercultural church congregation also has multiple-culture groups for children's ministry. The group for seven- to nine-year-olds is run by a female Korean teacher. Several non-Western children have told their parents they don't like the group and don't want to attend because the Western children in the group are rude and interrupt the teacher. You have been asked to help resolve the issue. Analyze the scenario. What is the underlying problem? Suggest different solutions that might help resolve the problem. Evaluate each option and decide which will bring the greatest benefit. What communication is required, and thinking creatively, how might you be able to bring even greater benefit in resolving the issue?

5. Which aspects of your worldview beliefs had to change when you became a Christian? Reflect on how the change came about. What other aspects of your current lifestyle and habits are you aware of that still need changing? In a time of quiet, ask God to show you his desires for your life in Christ, and what steps and choices you need to take to cooperate with him so that the necessary changes can come about.

CHAPTER 12

Communication and Spiritual Growth: Communicating for Spiritual Maturity and Multiplication

As It Happened: A man and his wife were preparing to cross a busy road. The husband was slightly ahead and managed to cross through several lines of traffic, but the wife was left behind carrying the shopping. There seemed to be no letup in the traffic, so the husband called out that he'd go on home and would pray for God to make a break in the traffic. The traffic flowed solidly by for another fifteen minutes and then, suddenly, for no obvious reason, it all came to a halt. After crossing the road between the lines of vehicles and returning home, the wife expressed her surprise to her husband at how the traffic had suddenly come to a complete halt. The husband jubilantly started praising God and thanking him for his kindness in answering prayer so specifically. The wife's response was quite different. Instead, she said, "Thank God? What's God got to do with it? It was just a lucky coincidence!" Their young son overheard his parents' words and, on Sunday, having pondered over the issue during the week, asked his church's youth group teacher, "So which of my parents was right? Was it God or just luck?"

INTRODUCTION

Have you noticed how children can ask questions about God with a charming simplicity and, of course, expect an instant answer? Imagine if you were the son's youth group teacher and were faced with that question. Could you have given an instant answer and your reasons why, or would you have needed to stop and think about how to answer? The question could have been a challenge to the teacher regardless of whether the son's youth group was monocultural or multiple-cultural. As we will see in this chapter, some cultural factors have the potential to confuse understanding about God.

We have seen that intercultural relationships are marked by mutual enrichment. In the quest for spiritual growth, our intercultural relationships provide the platform for mutual encouragement and the joy that comes from teachability and learning from each other. Just as engaging in the Bible together has the means for enriching both parties, so does growing into Christian maturity. This final chapter looks at communicating about Christian spiritual maturity, offers an assessment of facets of spiritual maturity, and discusses cultural tendencies that have the potential to limit spiritual formation. As the chapter unfolds, we examine transferable principles for engaging with and overcoming these worldview-belief-based limitations.[1]

CHRISTIAN SPIRITUAL MATURITY

Spiritual formation has been defined in classical terms by Mulholland (1993, 15) as "a process of being conformed to the image of Christ for the sake of others." It is universally recognized that growth of any kind of organism occurs via a process. In Christian terms, we have referred in earlier chapters to the concept of discipleship training, which when done appropriately (i.e., according to cultural contexts) can be a catalyst for the spiritual growth process. Discipleship as a training mechanism is a *means* to growing in Christlikeness, whereas discipleship as a lifestyle marks the state and status of our relationship to the Master, Jesus, and is a lifelong process. How do disciples look in our cultural contexts? Kraft (1989, 80) points out that they may appear differently in cultures other than our own and, as Moreau et al. (2014, 218) suggest, vary depending on a culture's national values. It is thus necessary to take an intercultural approach to communicating about spiritual growth.

The following New Testament Scriptures offer clear examples of the expectation that Christians should grow spiritually:[2]

---

1. This chapter brings out material from D-Davidson (2018, 168–72) and D-Davidson (2019), which first appeared in *Asia Pacific Theological Association (APTA) Symposium: Pentecostalism in Context; Challenges and Opportunities* (121–29), and which was recrafted with permission for *European Pentecostal Theological Association Symposium* (online), July 6–7, 2021. Used with permission of APTA.

2. The thoughts concerning the issue of expectation of spiritual growth according to the New Testament Scriptures cited, as well as the timescale for spiritual growth, were given to me many years ago by my cherished mentor Rev. John H. Price.

- **Hebrews 5:12–14:** "By this time you ought to be teachers . . . [but] you need milk, not solid food. . . . Anyone who lives on milk, being still an infant, is not acquainted with the teaching about righteousness. But solid food is for the mature, who by constant use have trained themselves to distinguish good from evil." This passage should encourage us to communicate to the new believer the benefit of getting familiar with the truths in the Bible and learning to distinguish good from evil from God's perspective.
- **1 Corinthians 3:1–3:** "Brothers and sisters, I could not address you as people who live by the Spirit but as people who are still worldly— mere infants in Christ. I gave you milk, not solid food, for you were not yet ready for it. Indeed, you are still not ready. You are still worldly. For since there is jealously and quarrelling among you, are you not worldly?" This passage should encourage us to communicate to new and growing believers that a sign of spiritual growth is marked by worldliness decreasing in the believer's life. We can urge new believers to consider and articulate what are mere worldly ways of being and doing from the perspective of their cultural background.

TIMESCALE FOR GROWTH

Following conversion, it is usually most helpful to communicate to new believers the biblical principles underlying basic topics that will help them understand what it means to be a disciple of Christ. This gives them the foundations of biblical perspectives appropriate for the new lifestyle, an understanding of the requirement of simple obedience to Christ, and the fruit of this commitment. It is also a means of breaking away from inappropriate behavior patterns. Rather than following preprepared materials or programs from other settings, it is most helpful for us to consider which aspects of the new life in Christ are most appropriate to begin with in relation to our respondent or respondents' cultural and situational specifics. At the same time, we can communicate that this new life and love is to be shared and given away to others because that is what Jesus commanded, and the Holy Spirit equips us to do this.

Example from Cambodia: "We are used to foreigners coming and sharing the gospel through social care projects, but the discipleship materials they used would be American publications that were written for individualists and were quite dichotomistic in format—not at all appropriate for our setting. Simple illustrations about being in Christ, talking with Almighty God, and sharing the gospel life to the whole family would be a better start than great long teachings about the origins of sin and everything that needs to change."

After three years, a new believer in a caring community of Christians should have shown signs of spiritual growth and should be at least starting to take some responsibility in using their gifts as a part of the body of Christ. Lack of growth by three years may well be a sign of either a spiritually unhealthy believer or an insensitive surrounding sector of the worldwide body of Christ.

Other markers of spiritual growth[3] vary in timing, order, and degree from person to person and may manifest differently from culture to culture. These markers include:

- Increasing intimacy in relationship with God (this will usually accompany increasing love for God's Word, praise, prayer, fellowship, and outreach)
- Increasing integrity and conviction to graciously challenge nonbiblical cultural values
- Emergence of fruit of the Spirit (Galatians 5:22–23)
- Stewardship of lifestyle in relation to time-bound opportunities: talking with and listening to God, intentionally helping others, diligently working, resting in a nonslothful way, and engaging in godly recreation
- Stewardship of spiritual gifts and natural abilities: used with individuals and among the church body so that all grow

---

3. Some rich spiritual formation material with universal application (once contextualized where necessary) include Nouwen (2011), which presents a beautifully fresh attempt at explaining and engaging with some of the paradoxes of change and growth; MacDonald (2004) on building resilience; Willard (1998) on lessons from the Sermon on the Mount; and Mulholland (1993), who unfolds the Catholic approach to the spiritual journey. Earlier classics include Foster (1980), which gives a Protestant interpretation of the traditional Catholic spiritual disciplines; Maxwell (1945) on our identification with Christ in his death and resurrection; and Oswald Chambers (1927; 1972) *My Utmost for His Highest* devotional teachings originally presented in Egypt at the YMCA (Young Men's Christian Association).

- Stewardship of resources including finances (with appropriate motives)
- Envisioning as to their part (and that of others) in God's kingdom work

ASSESSING SPIRITUAL GROWTH

How can we assess spiritual growth when only God knows the depths and motives of a person's heart and their degree of intimacy with him? Any assessment tool can only provide a degree of measurement according to the results shown by the tool, and the results may or may not actually match reality. Christians assessing their own spiritual growth invariably decide they are further along than they actually are.[4] Communicating during intercultural discipling or counseling requires careful listening to the respondent/counselee in their cultural context and sensitivity to the voice of the Holy Spirit, without jumping to conclusions about a believer's spiritual state.

Several of the examples throughout the book have referred to the missions work in a rural village that Dr. Co and I were privileged to carry out together as an intercultural team. Our missions platform provided dental treatment for the village and wider communities of villages, and dental training so that the work would be sustainable. We received a lasting welcome by the villagers, many of whom became Christians. They shared the gospel with family members and friends as well as with friends and relatives in other villages so that we were graced to set up a network of several small groups of Christians with each group led by teams of local believers. As part of the more advanced training, our mentoring included providing the emerging Christian leaders with guidelines to use as a tool to assess and set goals concerning their own spiritual growth as well as to assess the progress of the believers in their fellowship/church groups. The guidelines follow a "progression of stages" approach to a Christian's perceptions and practices of prayer, obedience to God, and degree of belief in God's sovereignty.[5]

---

4. This might be due, for instance, to unrealistic wishful thinking, cultural expectations in relation to honor, or worldly untamed pride.

5. These stages related to progression from immature perception to greater maturity are my combination and simplification of material drawn from Fowler's (1981) classic stages of faith approach and Oser and Gmünder's (1991) religious development. They have been reconstructed, modified, and adapted to reflect evangelical spirituality. I originally piloted and contextualized the material presented below with scenarios to respond to for the Chinese Christian villagers, but it has

A key factor in deciding how well any of us are growing in areas such as prayer and obedience depends on our underlying rationale for praying to and obeying God. In other words, we need to examine what we believe about prayer and obedience and why we pray and obey. Similarly, for the issue of God's sovereignty, we need to ask: What do we believe concerning God as sovereign, and to what extent, and how, do those beliefs work out in practice in everyday life?

When we are looking to communicate about these vital issues and expectations and possibilities for growth in spiritual maturity, we are likely to find greater ease when our relationships have developed from being merely cross-cultural to being intercultural because these relationships are marked by mutual respect, openness, and trust. This was beautifully the case with the Chinese villagers for whom I originally put together the assessment guidelines in this chapter. As with studying the Bible, there is the potential for mutual enrichment and growth as we learn from each other's cultural perspectives about how life in Christ can be fruitfully lived out.

Spiritual Growth in Relation to Prayer

Like any activity that is important to us, actually doing the activity rather than merely talking about doing it makes the difference between shallowness and depth of growing accomplishment. From that perspective we will examine the stages that Christians might go through for prayer to become an increasingly fruitful activity based on a growing relationship with God.

Stage 1: I Pray Because I Know I Should

This stage is marked by mental assent only. For Christians at this early stage, prayer is understood as talking to God because their parents or someone significant told them so. Although they mentally agree with the notion, praying is just an "as quick as possible," emotionless activity to get it over with.

> **Example from Malaysian Indian:** "I'd go to the temple with my family as a child and didn't even think about what was happening or why. After I became a Christian I had to really think about what prayer is."

since been welcomed as relevant by Christian leaders and laypeople from multiple Global North and Global South settings with appropriately recontextualized scenarios and examples.

Stage 2: I Pray to Avoid Losing the New Blessings

This early stage of prayer can be marked by an excited and even fearful urgency in ritualistic prayer, but it attends purely to prayer activity and shows little attention to God as the recipient of the activity.

Stage 3: I Pray to Get More Blessings

This early stage keeps the focus on the one praying; the people pray with something of a manipulative motive as they perceive prayer merely in terms of gaining additional benefit for the one praying.

Example from China: "People would think that becoming a Christian is just another way for getting richer, and that's why Christians pray."

Prayers at stages 1–3 show immaturity; they are fear-based or manipulative, reflecting little or no true relationship with God. We need to communicate to new believers that prayer is not a practice for selfishly getting what we want from God. Christians who see God in patron-client terms may be trying to manipulate him through prayer in the same way that their cultural patron-client relationships recognize manipulation and reciprocal obligations as part of the fabric of the relationship.

Important culturally influenced principles: We best help believers by discouraging them from drawing close to Christ in the same cultural way a client seeks to draw close to a patron. We must carefully communicate that our relationship with God has a unique spiritually engendered basis and cannot be equated to that of human patrons and clients. God cannot be manipulated (in the derogatory sense of the term) by our prayers. He has no material obligations toward us that we can call upon, and his responses to prayer and relationship with him are purely grace-initiated and of his nature of unconditional love. The many promises in God's Word are ours to claim but not in a petulant or demanding manner. God fulfils his promises to us not as obligations but as grace-wrapped gifts of love so that a spiritually healthy response is praise and thanksgiving.

Many religions (e.g., Islam and Buddhism) include prayer practices, so the measure for spiritual growth is not the manner in which or how much one prays but relates to the underlying rationale behind the practices. The first three prayer stages do not show a spiritually healthy rationale.

Important principles: We can help new and immature believers progress from stage 3 to stage 4 by modelling God-centered, Holy Spirit–inspired prayer and by communicating so as to ignite aspiration in these believers to discover, through prayerful relationship with God, which ways of being and doing bring the fulfillment in Christ the believers were created for. We can help them into the glorious adventure of God's plans and calling as we pray zealously with them and for them.

Stage 4: I Begin to Realize That God Has a Plan for My Life and I Pray So That I Can Understand and Walk in That Plan Cooperatively (Philippians 2:12–13)

Now we are seeing prayer that is both the fruit of relationship with God and the catalyst for deepening a relationship that walks according to God's leading. Prayer is no longer talking *at* God but *to* him and *with* him. Prayer is no longer fueled by selfishness. The rationale behind prayer is now engagement in a cooperative venture that communicates with God for God's purposes to come about in and through the praying Christian. Prayer clamors for the one praying to be a vessel for God's purposes.

Important principles: Believers might become discouraged if they see contentment as only based on seeing fruit come about. We must remind respondents that, in God's economy, some plough, some sow, some water, some reap, and all we are called to is to be faithful to God's leading. We may have hopes and dreams about specifics of fruitfulness, but fruitfulness is always on God's terms and from God's perspective.

In Luke 10:17–20, "The seventy-two returned with joy and said, 'Lord, even the demons submit to us in your name.' He replied, 'I saw Satan fall like lightning from heaven. I have given you authority to trample on snakes and scorpions and to overcome all the power of the enemy; nothing will harm you. However, do not rejoice that the spirits submit to you, but rejoice that your names are written in heaven.'" Commenting on this passage, Oswald Chambers (1927; 1972, 171) notes, "Jesus Christ says, in effect, Don't rejoice in successful service, but rejoice because you are rightly related to Me." It can be helpful to communicate to discouraged believers that rather than letting their self-esteem be based on achievements, let our self-esteem come from being a beloved child of God.

Author's example from rural China: Dr. Co and I knew that missionary ventures in the wider geographical area of the minority group villagers were documented as having seen no fruit at all in earlier decades. It was as though we were placed by God's grace in a timely way and manner to reap the fruit of not only our own prayers but also years of earlier prayers.

Important principles: As we grow in intimacy with God, we will not see spending time in prayer as something we ought to do but something we love to do. Times of silence and solitude prepare our hearts to not just pray as the Holy Spirit leads us to pray but also to spend time listening to the sometimes quiet murmurings and sometimes clear exhortations intuited to us by the Spirit of Christ in our inner being. As we wait on the Lord, he renews us from within with fresh strength and hope for the purposes we face, so that our prayers might bring God's will in the heavenly places to fulfillment on earth.

Example from Japan: "I used to have a regular quiet time as a sort of ritual, but after discovering in spiritual growth course sessions how to hear God[6] and that he really does speak to me when I spend time with him, I just want to even more be in times of quiet and solitude with him."

---

6. A helpful text that I use in both monocultural and multiple-culture spirituality and spiritual growth courses, including for those inexperienced or uncertain about hearing God, is Dallas Willard's (2012; 1st ed., 1983) *Hearing God: Developing a Conversational Relationship with God.*

Stage 5: I Pray So That I Can Continue to Grow in Intimacy in My Love Relationship with God; I Have Increased Willingness Toward the Sacrificial Prayer of Luke 22:42. In Prayer Times with God, I Speak Less and Listen More.

Whereas stage 4 shows the beginnings of maturity, stage 5 shows increasing maturity. In the garden of Gethsemane, Jesus asked his Father to take away the cup of suffering if he was willing. It seems, like us at times, Jesus would have preferred another option than the one he was headed toward. Despite this, Jesus further prayed, "Yet not my will, but yours be done" (Luke 22:42). Jesus modeled for us sacrificial prayer that is motivated by love. He prayed earnestly and continued on toward the Calvary-road death marked out for him, which would be the means for our attaining to new life and fruitfulness in him. As we grow in understanding and experience communing with God through prayer, so too will our prayer life be marked by willingly sacrificial prayer that is borne of our welcoming the paradox that great gain can come from seeming loss.

Stage 6: I Become Like Christ in Communication:
One with God, Mature, Complete, Perfect

As long as there remain vestiges of our selfish former self, we are unlikely to reach this stage this side of seeing our Lord and Savior face-to-face, but let us at least know what we are aiming for in developing a spiritually mature prayer life so that we can not only be aware for ourselves but also communicate about this matter coherently to our Christian brothers and sisters.

Spiritual Growth in Relation to Obeying God

Why is obedience important for spiritual growth? In our relationship with God through Jesus there are certain obligations. We are called to obey all of Jesus' commands and teach others to do so too (Matthew 28:20). The underlying rationale for this obedience is love, and this is what distinguishes the obedience of Christians from the obedience required of followers of religions such as Islam and Buddhism. As we grow in love with our Lord Jesus, so will our love-based obedience, but the increase is the fruit of a process through stages just as for spiritual growth in and through prayer.

Stage 1: I Obey God Because I Know I Should.
My Parents or Someone Told Me This

This stage is marked by mental assent only. As with prayer at this stage, obedience is taken as a requirement because some significant figure has informed the person that this is so.

Stage 2: I Obey to Avoid Losing the New Blessings

As with prayer activity at this stage, the act of obedience is undertaken to maintain what has been gained with a focus on self and benefit to self rather than as part of relationship with God.

Stage 3: I Obey to Keep the Blessing Coming, Get a Reward from God, and/or Avoid God's Punishment

At this stage, believers see obedience either consciously or subconsciously as the means to manipulate God to continue providing blessing, whether material, physical, emotional, or as otherwise desired. Believers might also perceive obedience as the means of avoiding God bringing punishment for sins committed or sins of omission.

At stages 1–3, acts of obedience, as well as understandings related to obedience, show immaturity. They may be fear based or intentionally manipulative; they show little or no true relationship with God. As for the prayer stages, evidence of obedience and degree of obedience may give a misleading suggestion of spiritual growth. The key to true growth requires a spiritually healthy underlying love-based rationale for obedience to God.

Important principles: We do well to communicate to new or less mature Christians that blessing from God's perspective might include trials that are presented to refine our faith and serve to draw us closer to him. It is helpful to communicate through study of his Word that God disciplines his children for their good like a father rearing children (Hebrews 12:7–11). However, whilst punishment has to do with getting what one deserves for wrongdoing and paying a price for that wrongdoing, only Jesus can pay the price for our sins and wrongdoings. We cannot. Jesus bore the punishment and paid the price for all our sins—past, present, and future—at Calvary.

Important culturally influenced principles: As for the prayer stages, we do well to communicate to new or less mature believers that any cultural obligations in relation to patron-client relationships have nothing in common with the obligation of obedience that God expects from his children. We do not obey God for what we can get from him but for what we can be and become in Christ so as to fulfil his desires for his children's lives.

Stage 4: I Become More Aware That God Has a Plan for My Life That Involves Abiding in Christ and Bearing Fruit (John 15:16) and I Want to Lovingly Obey So That I Can Walk in That Plan and Bear Fruit

In this stage, believers start learning to live out Jesus' teaching that whoever wants to follow him "must deny themselves and take up their cross daily. . . . For whoever wants to save their life will lose it, but whoever loses their life for me will save it" (Luke 9:23–24), but they do so still more on their own terms than on God's. They realize that God doesn't maliciously punish wayward children but rather disciplines them as a loving father disciplines a son. Although discipline is painful, believers at this stage have sufficiently grown in their love of God to realize its value.

Important principles: We can help less mature believers progress from stage 3 to stage 4 through not only modelling the joy that an appropriate rationale for obedience brings but also by encouraging them to seek God in prayer so as to discover which areas of their lives they have not submitted to him. We must communicate too that God is the "source of our transformation" and that he, not us, does the conforming (Mulholland 1993, 30). Where we are lacking in Christlikeness is where obedience for spiritual growth will be asked of us (37). It can be helpful to communicate too that sins are invariably distortions of the heart-longings that only life in Christ can fully satisfy, such as having a sense of security, love, self-worth, and purpose.

Communicating through prayer and Bible study times, as well as about communing with God during times of daily life both individually and together, moves God's children to discover what obedience they need to exhibit in various aspects of their lives so that their heart-longings can be satisfied and to bring about the fulfillment in life for which they were created. We are called to live every moment of our lives in Christ's love and so that his love overflows out to others. Brother Lawrence[7] gives a marvelous example of this lifestyle. He spent his day in the monastery kitchen preparing the meals for monks. Many would consider his life of service which involved peeling vegetables and cooking meals as a mundane uninviting lifestyle,

---

7. Brother Lawrence was a 17th century lay Carmelite monk. His writing, *The Practice of the Presence of God*, originally published in French in 1692, is widely available translated into English.

but he described the joy and wonder of "practicing the presence of God," by which he meant experiencing God's love in every moment of the day whether in simple or more demanding activities of service. He wrote (1982, 37–38),

> I have given up all but my intercessory prayers to focus my attention on remaining in God's presence. I keep my attention on God in a simple, loving way. This is my soul's secret experience of the actual unceasing presence of God. It gives me such contentment and joy. . . . My day-to-day life consists of giving God my simple, loving attention. If I'm distracted, He calls me back in tones that are supernaturally beautiful . . . in this state of enjoying God I desire nothing but His presence. . . . All I want is to be completely His.

We can communicate how obedience can be a catalyst for the release of both joy, wonder, and creativity. Communication will be heightened as we give examples of how that has happened for us. Deepening in relationship with God and discovering one's part in the body of Christ also opens believers up to the importance of both individual and corporate obedience as mutual love-based service.

Important culturally based principles: It will be helpful to be aware of the extent to which aspects of believers' background culture lend themselves (or not) to engaging with God and obeying God while recognizing God's infinite nature and purposes as present in both planned and seemingly unplanned temporalities. D-Davidson (2019, 122) advises:

> The monochronists' fixation with not "wasting" time, and preference for linear plans with a fixed order as the culturally-shaped default, might suggest that engaging with God and obeying him is merely a result of "getting the approach right" along with rolling out obedience-oriented, time-framed plans that promote a reluctance to potentially "waste" time by yielding to alternative possibilities. An over-emphasis on highly-planned structure and insistence on adhering to the minutiae of content details can be the mark of legalism in obedience rather than vibrancy in relationship with God. Spiritual growth might be limited by the resulting reluctance to flex with the planned structure so as to be open to the Holy Spirit and allow God

to work in *his* way and in *his* willed timing of bringing the eternal into the temporal.

In contrast, polychronists' freedom from pressure to follow a fixed order of time-coveting events also gives them the freedom to engage with God at multiple levels in the spontaneity of the moment and the seeming spontaneity of unplanned availability of people. Life in the now is delightfully less shaped or restricted by "ought to" and "should do" calls of the future. However, spiritual growth might be unhelpfully held back by a view that fails to see the benefit of achieving in a timely manner successful completion of shorter-term projects. Obedience in completing a progressive series of intentionally planned and carried out shorter-term projects can then be the means to achieve longer-term goals in God's purposes.

Example from Thailand: "Before the tsunami in 2004, the [foreigner-led] church hadn't always really been growing well or been particularly fruitful in outreach. The building is near the coast but on high ground. Once the tsunami happened, the church building became a central gathering place for medical treatment, finding displaced people, and establishing how to help the destroyed coastal communities. The result was that the gospel was shared in really practical ways, and cooperation with government officials brought increased credibility. Churches were planted in small communities through a combination of foreigner-led planning and Holy Spirit–inspired spontaneity in rising to meet multiple different needs that became the basis for longer-term projects." It was a new season of fruitfulness that required obedience through flexibility and different kinds of service.

Stage 5: I Increasingly Obey Because My Desire Is to Grow in Increasing Intimacy in Relationship with God

At this stage there is increased willingness toward greater depths of sacrificial obedience through self-denial and taking up of one's cross (Luke 9:23–24) on God's terms. Believers at this stage delight in the hidden service that pleases God and make intentional acts of self-denial sweet love offerings to him.

See how stage 4 shows the beginnings of maturity as the rationale underlying obedience is now being in a loving relationship with God, whereas stage 5 shows increasing maturity because the rationale underlying obedience is now unquestionably based on pursuing what delights and pleases God. The believer has learned to bring sufferings and difficulties to the cross rather than projecting the pain outward onto others. There is a lived out understanding that obeying Christ's foundational teachings of loving God and loving each other has no place for selfish ambition or roots of bitterness (Hebrews 12:14–15). Deepening life in Christ is a sweet discovery of the potential to grow in holiness as one willingly pursues the path of obedience that brings a Spirit-empowered desire to know Christ more deeply and embrace the power of his resurrection while desiring, like Paul, to somehow share in his sufferings (Philippians 3:10).

Stage 6: *I Become like Christ: Perfect in Obedience, Mature, Complete, Perfect*

As with the progression through the prayer stages, we are unlikely to reach this stage while our obedience works out through our earthly body. As also with the prayer stages, it is good to have some idea of what we are aiming for in terms of spiritually healthy rationale underlying obedience to God. We need to be aware not only for ourselves but also so that we can communicate about obedience to those we are ministering amongst.

Spiritual Growth in Relation to Degree of Belief in God's Sovereignty

We have seen how obedience is one of the Christian's obligations before God. Another obligation is to live by faith because "without faith it is impossible to please God" (Hebrews 11:6), and out of our growing love of God, we want our newborn lives to be pleasing to him. By faith we trust that God's ways are always for our good and that his plans come about in perfect timing, and this reflects our trust in his sovereignty. Like prayer and obedience, growing in trust of his sovereignty is a lifelong process marked by different stages.

Stage 1: *I "Know" God Is Sovereign Because My Parents or Someone Told Me He Is*

This stage is marked by mental assent only. At this stage, the believer has mentally taken on board this component of Christian belief, but neither their heart nor will has been engaged in a way that would make the concept of sovereignty either appealing or worth further understanding.

Stage 2: *I Begin to Test God's Sovereignty by Trying to*
"Manipulate" Him Through Prayer or the Obedience
That Seems to Have Also Been Imposed upon Me

We see this stage particularly with young children and new adult believers, although for adults possibly subconsciously, as they grapple with what it means practically to experience God as sovereign.

Stage 3: *Unanswered Prayers or Obedience That Does Not Produce the*
Results Hoped for Lead Me to Believe That God Is Not Sovereign in
Every Area of Life; Instead, I Believe That Luck, Chance, Animist Spirits,
Unknowable Forces, or Ancestral Spirits Are Unseen Causes of Events

Since their prayers or acts of obedience do not appear to have provoked God to supply the result hoped for, the child or adult draws a mental box compartmentalizing the areas of life in which their experience shows that God appears to be at work, and so these are aspects of life in which they are willing to trust God. For adults this may be subconsciously done, but the box excludes those aspects for which God has not been seen to produce results. Consequently, people at this stage believe that other forces have influenced those areas instead. Those people of background cultures who previously worshipped other deities or ancestral spirits may live in a syncretistic fashion to account for areas that appear to lack evidence of God's influence. For others, including children, luck or chance are believed to make up for where God is not perceived to be active.

Stages 1–3 show immaturity. If believers at this stage have a relationship with God, it is shallow, and as with prayer and obedience at these stages, the underlying rationale for trying out belief in God's sovereignty may merely be toward selfish or manipulative ends.

Important principles: Cultural expectations in relation to power distance can have important implications for a Christian's perception of God and relationship with God in his sovereignty. D-Davidson (2019, 127) notes:

> A spiritually-healthy balance is needed by all believers concerning recognition and acknowledgement of both God's glorious transcendence, and the gracious love and mercy-bound reality of His immanence. When cultural expectations of high power distance are misattributed to characteristics of one's relationship with God,

Christians (and especially new believers) in these large power distance cultures, and particularly those at lower social levels, might consciously or subconsciously prefer to emphasize the transcendence of God over His immanence. I.e. since God is the ultimate authority in His Divinity, mere humanity should engage with the obeisance of those at the lowest level of existence. But a God who is purely worshipped as Almighty, Omniscient and Omnipotent might also, by self-imposed limitation due to large power distance understandings, be considered to be a God who is distant and unreachable, and so not involved in the events of people's daily lives. Spiritual maturity has the potential to be limited if worldview beliefs that own relationship with an authority-figure as inappropriate, result in perceiving God as distant and unapproachable. There can then be a reluctance to engage in a personal relationship with God that deepens in intimacy as well as difficulty in acknowledging sovereignty that lovingly impacts every area of one's personal existence. This can also result from religious backgrounds in which God's transcendence has somehow been over-emphasized.

Example from a white British academic: "With my Catholic background, I find it difficult to relate to the idea of the personal relationship with God that many evangelicals write about. For me God is high and lifted up, and I revere him from afar and through the Catholic ordinances."

D-Davidson (2019, 127–28) further advises, in terms of prayer and obedience:

A large power distance, cold, non-personal approach to God can easily result in a legalistic, works-based relationship, or even a relationship based on manipulative practices of superstition and magic, rather than the vibrancy of life in deeply personal relationship with the One who is love beyond measure. God is certainly an authoritative figure but one of the paradoxes of the Christian faith rejoices in and welcomes the timeless truth of the concomitance of the transcendence and immanence of His presence and being.

At the other extreme, for Christians from small power distance cultures, spiritual maturity might be limited if an overemphasis of God's immanence breeds overfamiliarity and lack of reverence in relationship with God. In such a case, a right fear of God and horror of sin in light of God's holiness might easily be dismissed so that "the consciousness of . . . sin in the presence of moral purity" (Rowley 1956: 66)[8] becomes limited or underdeveloped.

This can not only have negative implications for obedience but also for resisting submitting to God in those difficult life situations that God, in his sovereignty, has seen fit to allow us to face. Where there are areas of our lives in which our faith excludes God's sovereignty, these areas can also be subtle catalysts that quietly destroy what faith there is.

Important principles: In chapter 9 we saw the importance of helping new Christians into at least a mental assent of God's sovereignty as early as possible. To help new believers progress from stage 3 to 4, in their cultural setting we can ask the Holy Spirit to lead us in communicating in such a way that they will become aware that other forces such as luck, ancestral spirits, or other superstition-based practices do not provide an assured basis for security in difficult times. As we live out and communicate our love of God and trust in his sovereignty, we can help usher the new believers into their own experience of faith that enjoys the reality of God's sovereign presence in events and moments and is marked by trust in his merciful sovereignty working in and through their lives. This can then bring about the needed heart agreement too as they discover and live in the truth that only God can provide true peace amidst turmoil and unmet desires as we turn to him in faith and prayer trusting in his sovereignty (Philippians 4:6–7).

Example from Myanmar: "Initially it was hard to believe that God is involved in events that happen in our lives. In my country high authority figures just don't get involved with you personally. I studied the Bible and

---

8. Cited in Motyer (1993, 71n3).

prayed and eventually came to realize that it must be God working things out in my life because there just wasn't any other explanation."

Example from Guatemala: "My mother became a Christian first and led me to the Lord as a child. I heard about the peace of God that you can have when you are in difficulty and you pray, but actually experiencing it was really amazing and grew my faith in what it means that God is in control."

Stage 4: As My Faith Grows so Does My Trust in God's Sovereignty so That I Acknowledge That God Has a Sovereign Plan for My Life and I Start Submitting to That Plan

Believers at this stage know there are aspects of their lives that they hold back from God and that there are also aspects they hold back that they are not yet mature enough to be aware of. They begin to recognize that they need to trust God and let God be in control of their relationship with him, and if they're being honest, they are not truly willing to do so. They are now less likely to feel the need to deny the paradoxes of Christian faith, but if they're honest, they still give them some private concern.

This can be a stage of long duration, but the foundations laid through reading God's Word and in prayer start bearing the fruit of true personal experience of his presence and the reality of his sovereignty working out in seemingly unconnected details of one's life. Submitting to God's hand can bring us into situations we would previously have preferred to avoid, but letting God be in control brings us into the freedom of trusting that "the One who brought us to it will also bring us through it."[9] As we walk in increasing trust, we discover God's hand in the details of myriad life situations past and present.

Example from China: "I think it's difficult for Chinese people to only walk by faith. We are pragmatic—we want to see the money, not just hope it will come. When I got married, I knew my father-in-law was well off so I wouldn't have to worry about providing for my wife. It was easy to believe she was

---

9. Thanks to Pastor Edmund Rowlands of New Life Family Church, Margate, UK, for this memorable encouragement. He and his wife spent many years as missionaries in the Congo.

the one God had chosen for me. Since then, I've seen God open doors that I couldn't open, but I have to admit, although I enjoy those experiences, at times I still tend to plan my own ways and hope they fit with God's plans."

Important principles: It can be helpful to communicate to growing believers that the reason we choose to follow our plan rather than God's plan is usually because we think we know what the end result will be. It seems easier to trust our projection of results than to walk into the unknown. But our plans can lead us astray and into holes that we then have to climb out of![10] By contrast, as we grow in experience of God's faithfulness and our trust in his sovereignty grows, we also grow in the ability to choose options where the results are unseen or less predictable. We have a deep-seated conviction of the promise that he will never leave us or forsake us and that, from his glorious perspective, he has only the best lined up for us, in both the details and bigger picture, as we depend on him. As our trust in God increases, the self-sacrifice that requires self-denial starts to become an obvious and freeing choice. We increasingly find delight in the Holy Spirit–empowered ability to resolve issues related to anger,[11] disappointment, and fear. We will also have less difficulty in discarding previous rationale that had fueled our compromising on both faith and belief in Christ's sovereignty.

Stage 5: I Continue to Grow in Intimacy of Relationship with God and in My Understanding of His Sovereignty. I Increase in My Willingness to Suffer so That His Plan and Purposes in and through Me Can Become a Reality in My Life, along with the Declarations of Philippians 3:10–11.

Believers at this stage are increasingly comfortable with the paradoxes of Christian faith. They hold back fewer and fewer areas of their lives and

---

10. Or return to trusting God and ask him to help us out of the hole by his grace!

11. Anger may seem to feel or be rationalized as justifiable. It may be due to any of: fear; blocked goals; sense of self-worth or personal values and priorities being undermined. As Dallas Willard (1998, 167) points out, anger wants to hurt the offender. "Anger indulged, instead of waived off, always has in it an element of self-righteousness and vanity. Find a person who has embraced anger and you find a person with a wounded ego!" Willard links anger with the sin of pride and further implores that "there is nothing that can be [achieved through] anger that cannot be done better without it" (169).

give God increasing control of their relationships with him because they have absolutely no doubts that he is in control of both the events he brings about for his purposes and those he allows to influence their lives that are the consequence of their poor choices or the poor choices of others. In this respect they are confident that God's sovereignty limits the power and effects of evil.

As with the prayer and obedience stages, stage 4 shows the beginnings of maturity, and stage 5 shows increasing maturity. At stage 5, confidence in God's sovereignty pervades far more areas of one's life than those that are still knowingly held back. The heart and life reality of Paul's declaration become an increasing desire that also becomes increasingly lived out: "I have been crucified with Christ and I no longer live, but Christ lives in me. The life I now live in the body, I live by faith in the Son of God, who loved me and gave himself for me" (Galatians 2:20). Life is increasingly marked by the ability to "rejoice always, pray continually, give thanks in all circumstances" with a delight in knowing that "this is God's will for you in Christ Jesus" (1 Thessalonians 5:16–18). As situations unfold that God is allowing us to face, we may find that others disagree with our perspective of his sovereign involvement, but even as we bring resolution by "agreeing to disagree," the other parties may find themselves challenged to examine their relationships with God.

Important principle for moving beyond stage 4: As we learn the simplicity of trusting God with childlike faith, we cannot avoid the reality of the changing seasons of life in which growing in faith requires us to trust God either in far deeper measure in familiar situations, in circumstances we have never encountered, or in matters that we have never had to trust him for before.

Stage 6: *I Become like Christ, Perfectly Submitting and Yielding to the Will of the Father—"Not My Will, but Always Yours Be Done"*

This stage points to a belief in God's sovereignty marked by a life that lives as Christ does, in relationship with his Father, that is mature, complete, and perfect. That day won't come until our lives on earth are finished or he returns, but let us rejoice at all that God is bringing us toward as we increasingly trust in his sovereignty and submit to him in all he allows to come our way. In the meantime, we can rejoice that "what we will be has not yet been made known. But we know that when Christ appears, we shall be like him for we shall see him as he is" (1 John 3:2).

Important point: Although we have looked at growth in relation to stages, growth toward maturity invariably does not unfold neatly from stage to stage. The degree to which we are living according to appropriate rationale for prayer, obedience, or trust in God's sovereignty is not likely to follow a consistent linear progression. We may have occasions or seasons when we return to earlier stages without even realizing. Being in fellowship with other Christians on the journey, to whom we can be accountable, can be crucial for helping us become revived, recover vibrancy in Christ, and continue onward again.

Devotional comment: As we live vibrantly in Christ, so we can also be vessels for him to overflow that life and love into the lives of others. May our hearts be hungering and thirsting for more of Jesus in our lives. When times of dryness come, those desert experiences can be opportunities to quiet our hearts in Christ. As we wait on him to show us the roots of the dryness, he may perhaps open our spiritual eyes to inner discontent, unresolved relationship frustrations, or even that it is a season to rest in him with no preconceived expectations. Only he can spring up again the inner streams of living water that the dry areas of our hearts and lives are crying out for. We can become again like the weaned child in Psalm 131:1–2 who enjoys contentment: "My heart is not proud, Lord, my eyes are not haughty; I do not concern myself with great matters or things too wonderful for me. But I have calmed and quieted myself, I am like a weaned child with its mother; like a weaned child I am content." An unweaned child makes endless and insistent demands for milk. Like the weaned child, let's not make demands but be content to receive whatever God chooses to give us as we quiet ourselves with him; let's find our contentment purely in our deepening relationship with him and not because of anything we are trying to acquire or achieve.

As we submit ourselves gladly to God's will, which is marked by love, righteousness, and truth, we can discover more of the unspeakable, glory-filled joy that motivated our Savior's earthly love-fueled choices and

that served to realize God's eternal purposes. As we make our home con-
tentedly in Christ and Christ makes his home in us, the Great Commission
adventure becomes an increasing and fruitful delight.

CONCLUSION

As we have seen throughout this book, communicating Christ to those
of other cultures requires far more than merely accumulating knowledge
about features of respondents' background cultures. Effective communication comes via the interculturality that develops relationships from being
merely cross-cultural to being marked by expressions of love-based empathy, increasing mutual respect, and welcoming of difference and diversity
that also become a means of creativity. In this chapter we have seen how
communication about spiritual maturity is more than a presentation of
facts. Effective communication requires sensitivity to both the communicator's and respondents' cultural ways and worldview beliefs, just as at any
stage of the process of communicating Christ and Bible principles, in order
to help bring forth lifestyles that display delight in following him.

Poor awareness of the implications of one's worldview beliefs and
resulting cultural practices can limit growth toward spiritual maturity
both individually and corporately. Self-awareness on the part of both the
communicator and respondents can make a crucial difference in reducing
the limits of spiritual growth due to cultural factors. This can be true particularly in conjunction with a desire to grow in intimacy of relationship
with God through Jesus and increase in sensitivity to the voice of the Holy
Spirit, regardless of how countercultural one's approach to life in Christ
might appear.

As we seek to communicate Christ by building relationships that move
from being cross-cultural to intercultural, we can prayerfully anticipate
becoming fruitful vessels for transforming communication. Fruitfulness
is always according to God's perspective, and as Christian communicators
enjoy the mutual respect of intercultural relationships with our respondents, who have now become dear friends, the creativity from diversity
can bring us into the mutual enrichment and deeper joy of learning from
each other. Our intercultural relationships then become the means for
greater multiplication of fruitfulness through life in Christ, our uniting
Lord and Savior.

QUESTIONS FOR REFLECTION
AND DISCUSSION

1. In the "As It Happened" scenario at the start of the chapter, if the young boy had asked you the question he asked his church youth group teacher, how would you have replied before studying this chapter? How would you reply now?

2. Here are two pairs of Scriptures from which you might teach that there is equality regardless of any cultural values concerning power distance when it comes to praising and worshipping God: Luke 2:8–20 with Matthew 2:1–12; and Galatians 3:26–4:7 with Revelation 7:9–17. For people from which kind of backgrounds might each set be initially more helpful? Why?

3. For developing our intercultural relationships, what can we learn from Jesus about obedience that is not merely based on earthly, culturally bound expectations, such as the expectations that result from patron-client relationships? How might you present Jesus' perspectives on obedience for those who began as something of a patron in relationship with you? Would your presentation need to differ with those who began as clients in relationship with you? Why or why not?

4. Why might the question of how God's sovereignty appears to work out cause disagreements? In which areas of your life are you currently or might you soon need to be trusting him in new ways? How can you prayerfully resist any unresolved issues or uncertainties from impacting your potential for living increasingly fruitfully and keeping your heart at home in Christ?

Personality Analysis Tool

Tick the adjectives that really do describe you. Total your scores for each column. The highest score will likely reflect your major personality type. The next highest, which may be a combination of types, will likely reflect your minor personality type. Be aware of both your strengths and weaknesses, especially when involved in conflict.

1. CHOLERIC: Extrovert and task-oriented	2. MELANCHOLIC: Introvert and task-oriented
Strengths:	*Strengths:*
Natural leader	Conscientious
Visionary	Very intelligent
Hardworking	Loyal
Practical	Serious
Optimistic	Attention to detail
Courageous	Quietly sensitive
Very active	Self-sacrificing
Decisive	Very orderly
Self-confident	Hardworking
Efficient	Creative
Determined	Thinks a lot
Independent	Self-disciplined

Weaknesses:	Weaknesses:
Demanding	Critical
Insensitive	Moody
Inconsiderate	Pessimistic
Unsympathetic	Inflexible
Severe	Legalistic
Hostile	Unrealistically perfectionistic
Sarcastic	Vengeful
Tough	Unsociable
Unforgiving	Judgmental
Domineering	Negative
Opinionated	Isolationist
Prejudiced	Picky
Cruel	Persecution prone
Strong-willed	Moralistic/preachy
3. PHLEGMATIC: **Introvert and people-oriented**	**4. SANGUINE:** **Extrovert and people-oriented**
Strengths:	**Strengths:**
Good listener	Lively
Encourages harmony	Avoids detail
Sympathetic	Enthusiastic
Supportive	Stimulating
Easygoing	Talkative
Respectful	Carefree
Caring	Generous
Loyal follower	Very, very friendly
Agreeable	Spontaneous
Comfy to be with	Enjoys variety
Conforms to rules	Compassionate
Patient	Optimistic

Weaknesses:	Weaknesses:
Reluctant leader	Exaggerates
Stingy (mean)	Disorganized
Lazy	Manipulative
Selfish	Unproductive
Dislikes change	Over-excitable
Stubborn	Undependable
Indecisive	Egotistical
Avoids conflict	Easily distracted
Spectator	Talks endlessly/Shows off
Easily embarrassed	Spiteful
Dependency-prone	Negligent
Self-protecting	Restless
Lacks self-confidence	Loud
Fearful of being disliked	Distracts people

Note: It can be more helpful to just total the strengths scores as we are often less willing to acknowledge weaknesses and/or may not be aware of them!

If you are uncertain in discerning your major personality type from the scores, then ask: Am I more introvert or more extrovert? Or more task oriented or more people oriented? Asking someone who knows you well to look over how you have assessed yourself can also be helpful to get a more accurate picture.

Owned Characteristics of Multiple Different Cultures

The following material was acquired through cross-cultural and intercultural interviews as referred to in chapter 8.

BHUTAN

The majority of Bhutan are Buddhist. It will be great if Christian communicators can learn the local language, Dzongkha. If missionaries can converse in Dzongkha, Bhutanese will be impressed, and they will be interested to talk to you, and you can easily develop the friendship. But you have to build a strong relationship and a deep trust before you share the gospel because it is illegal to share the gospel. In Bhutan, we have everything we need, like English lessons and medical care, and they're free, so Christian communicators have a hard time coming to my country. If they come using their profession, they end up not being able to share the gospel because they're scared of becoming blacklisted. When they try to build relationships, they're not able to focus on their work properly. Bhutanese Christians who share the gospel can get stripped of their citizenship.

Bhutanese are event oriented—most of the church services start on time, but overall people will not come on time. We love to spend time with people even if we haven't finished scheduled work.

Generally, people are holistic thinkers as they tend to be more flexible in the way they handle things or in organizing events, but we have a more dichotomistic church culture concerning rules to follow.

High respect is shown to authority figures. When it comes to exposing vulnerability, we are perhaps more likely to do so with foreigners that we've made friends with than with our own local people.

CHINA (MAINLAND)

There are many different tribal groups, and there can be tension between Han Chinese and minority groups. Family and relationship with people are the most important things for the Chinese people; as of Confucianism, parents should be respected and obeyed. When the children get married, they will move to another house but always close to their parents. When parents grow old it is the responsibility of the children to take care of and pay for their parents' expenses.

In the cities, time is very important, but in the countryside, village people will meet on the street and will talk for an hour.

When there is a wedding in a village, everybody will participate and cooperate somehow. In the city, people will be more task oriented, but if I ignore the needs of people, I might lose my friends. Chinese are holistic thinking people because of China's social structure. The economic development is changing the society; in my opinion, development is polluting Chinese society.

Many of the people in my city will prepare their house before the rain comes. Also they will save their money in the bank for future needs, and this provides some peace of mind and security for the family. We would always prefer to conceal our vulnerability. Chinese value appearance; even if they don't have money, they will pretend that they have money. It is very hard for people to admit failure. Chinese culture values personal achievement, and there is a lot of competition between young people. We seek the opinions of family members and the people around us before making decisions. It's a high power distance culture, and communism demands that all its citizens listen and obey. This mentality has crept into the church authorities. Communication is high-context: people prefer indirect interactions and avoid criticizing others in public, even if they want to confront someone. We have to use a very nice way of saying no.

CZECH REPUBLIC

The Czech Republic is one of the most homogeneous countries in Europe. There are few foreigners living in the Czech Republic (around 600,000, less than 5 percent). Czech people are friendly, but they keep their private lives to themselves until they get to know you better. To communicate effectively, you must learn the language. To get closer to individuals, you have to accept cultural differences, customs, and traditions.

Czech Republic is geographically divided into Bohemia and M
Members of the Moravian church, the oldest known Protestant den
nation in the world, had to flee to exile because of persecution in the eig
teenth century. Moravian brothers were united in Herrnhut (Germany)
and sent hundreds of missionaries to different parts of the world. Yet today,
Czech Republic is one of the most unreligious nations in the world.

Czech people are a mixture of personalities, but generally speaking,
they are more time oriented than event oriented. They are more people
oriented then task oriented, and they are crisis preventative. Czechs are
not willing to expose vulnerability. It is considered a weakness. There is a
saying, "Real men don't cry." Dichotomistic thinking is more prevalent than
holistic thinking.

Czech culture has low power distance, so students do not have a
problem interacting with their teacher during class sessions. But in terms
of interaction with superiors in the workplace, they are more restrained.
They are individualistic in their decision-making process.

In general, Czech people have low context communication. They
always speak their minds and they are not intentionally wanting to offend.

DOMINICAN REPUBLIC

Generally, like the Filipinos, our people are not on time because we were all
colonized by Spaniards. We take our time. We prefer to focus on the event
that is happening and consider the hospitality and the comfort of our guests.
We are people oriented. We like to engage, relate to each other, and talk.

We respect our elders' decisions. The oldest man holds authority,
makes public decisions, and is responsible for the welfare of the family.
The oldest married woman commands her household, delivers the more
private decisions, and nurtures the family. Married sons and their wives
and children are part of the extended family and have a strong allegiance to
their fathers. Married daughters become part of their husbands' families.
Dominican Republic is very collectivistic in the sense that individuals go
to their community or family to ask for help if needed and they will not
make important decisions on their own; they will always take into consideration the opinion of close friends and family around them. Outlook is
more holistic. People are open to debate, and they tend to see things with
an open perspective. They like to hear others' opinions to make decisions.
Society has low power distance because everyone can approach and talk to
each other regardless of their social or financial status. Society is marked

munication because our people are very open to say no. ...uble speaking the truth, and they communicate what ...vithout having any real issue in this. They are straight- ... their minds and their feelings even if they offend ...is a strength, and the opposite is seen as a weakness or

Our people who have an education are more crisis preventative; they have foresight before a problem occurs. However, in the village people are more non-crisis preventative, and those who are not very well educated tend to be non-crisis oriented. Self-image is important, but when vulnerabilities are exposed, people don't try to hide them; they will share their problems with the community and seek help among other families. They are very open also to help others; this is a characteristic of most of the Latin-American cultures. Moreover, they are not afraid to share their personal situations; this is a strength for them.

INDIA

India is a big country. It's divided in two main parts, north and south, and has twenty-eight states, each of which has its own culture and traditions, so the rules are different from place to place. Eighty percent of the country is Hindu. India follows the caste system, but it's changing. For example, I have friends in every caste, and in my state, which is Christian, we don't see castes discrimination. In churches we have people from every caste. I think Indian people are more people oriented, but maybe it's changing because of Western influence. Often people will trust white missionaries more than local pastors, but they can't hold authority; you have to work under the pastor. Timewise, services or other events will start whenever people show up. The tendency is toward collectivism because it's a very family oriented and extended family society.

Society is very much characterized by high-context communication because people don't say directly what they want or mean. Confrontation is indirect and even carefully sarcastic. We are not very open to discuss our problems and vulnerabilities because of the potential for shame.

JAPAN

Japan is mostly Buddhist, but there are many traditional customs like Shintoism too. Maintaining harmony is very important. People are very shy; most people do not want to communicate with people of another country. They are not very open to showing feelings, and they try to always be kind and have a smile on their faces even though they might be going through difficult situations. Showing emotions and vulnerability is considered a weakness.

Japanese are very time oriented. Since we value manners and etiquette very much, punctuality is very important; people will even arrive ten minutes ahead of an appointment. Although community and relationship are important, Japanese can be very task oriented and also value personal space. People like to focus on their goals, on the things they need to accomplish, and they will work and focus on their appointments until they finish all their work. Japanese people don't want to fail because that brings shame and a bad reputation within the community.

Japan is high power distance with clear hierarchy, and respecting those in authority is very important. To greet a person that is in a higher position than you, you must bow instead of shaking hands—the angle of the bow depends on the level of authority: the higher the ranking, the deeper the bow.

Communication is high-context and non-direct. The phrase "I'm sorry" means a variety of things, including "thank you" or "excuse me," so it looks like Japanese are always apologizing or afraid to offend another person. Japanese are dichotomistic thinkers which is seen in the importance of following rules and being highly organized, and they always think ahead and try to handle the crisis long before it happens. They will sacrifice time, enjoyment, or rest in order to have everything under control or to avoid future crisis.

In general, Japan exhibits a collectivist culture, but sometimes the senseis and others in authority make their own decisions based only on what they think. Japanese culture includes the public bathtub. For instance, all ladies will be naked in one bathtub and enjoy talking together while they bathe.

MONGOLIA

Mongolians have a nomadic culture, and we have a direct character. This direct character means that we can be quite direct in speaking. Like Westerners, the people of Mongolia are also quite dichotomistic in thinking. Some might misunderstand and think that we are very proud and unfriendly, but actually we just want to say what we feel and what we want directly. We do not just keep quiet and obey other people. In addition, the people of Mongolia want freedom and independence. Church starts on time, but people come whenever they want.

We are crisis preventive in some aspects but flexible in others. We have a very cold climate in our country, so it is already a common practice to prepare everything ahead because we can see that problems might happen in the future. We more prefer to conceal vulnerability, but it depends on your trust level in relationships. We're low power distance, so Global North Christians get on well with us, but Koreans have a hard time.

MYANMAR (FORMERLY BURMA)

In my county we have eight major tribes that speak different languages, plus 135 other official languages, but the main language, Burmese, is what children learn in school. Burmese worship deities and evil spirits, and life is based on rituals including animal sacrifice. Only 7 or 8 percent of Burmese are Christians.

We are more people oriented than time oriented, and we will wait for our friend even if he is two hours late because he is more important than the waiting time. Burmese don't bother about future crises; they will start preparations when the rain starts and not before. We tend not to think about the future. In our mindset, everyone wants money but only just enough to live by. Friends are like gold, and people will ask not how much money you have but how many friends you have.

We tend to be dichotomist, perhaps because we like to follow rules. We have something called "habhab" in the church: if someone does something wrong, the pastor will just tell the wrongdoer to get out of the church without offering explanation. There are special ways of showing respect in interacting with different age groups, especially to honor the elderly.

Usually people will hide problems and not want to show weakness; if you are not part of the family, you may never know what is really happening in their lives. Because of this, strong relationships should be built with the people, and this takes time.

Burmese society is characterized by high power distance and great respect for authority figures. Religion and military control are not separated. Worldview beliefs include the need to respect or else something bad will happen. We usually consult the opinions of others and make decisions collectively. Communication is high-context, especially to avoid offending anyone; people will always make up excuses before saying "no."

NAIROBI

We don't do "on time"; we love events and love connecting with people. It is not about finishing the services, even in church, but more about fellowshipping, not thinking of the time. We're more non-crisis. We avoid taking action and rely on the head of the village to make decisions when crisis arrives, and we're very much people oriented. We prefer to conceal vulnerability. Many Kenyans believe that the spiritual realm affects the natural realm supernaturally. There is a saying, "I am because you are!" Things are not done individually. Group effort is important. "Ubuntu" means group work in a village.

NEPAL

The majority of the people in Nepal are Hindus, and there is a caste system that's more obvious in villages. There are many tribal groups in the countryside, with millions of people who remain unreached by the gospel.

Nepalis are people oriented and basically very friendly; we like to have visitors and will treat the visitors very warmly, especially in the villages.

We love gathering together and live an event oriented, collectivist community lifestyle. Church does not usually start on time, and the way we organize events is pretty flexible. We tend to take things very easy. People don't arrive on time. These days, Nepali people tend to save money and be prepared for the future: the most important thing for us is to have a concrete house.

Some people still practice animism; for example, some building contractors will secretly perform human blood sacrifice and practice rituals as they believe the project will move on smoothly. Jesus is perceived as one of the lower caste "gods."

I suppose we are dichotomist thinkers because we tend to think in one way or another without considering much the aspects around us. Some think this way because they have not been trained to critically consider the circumstances for themselves before making a decision, so they just follow the others.

Our culture is male dominated, and we tend to conceal vulnerability, especially women. People don't freely talk about problems other than with people that they deeply trust. We generally won't take up projects that we might fail in.

NIGERIA

Nigerians in general tend to be event oriented. It's normal not to keep time. We have what we call "African time," which can mean two hours later than the agreed set time. Events like weddings won't start on time, usually because the bride comes late.

Generally, we tend to be more dichotomistic than holistic. Older traditional Nigerians especially see things as black and white. For example, things like homosexuality are considered evil, and that's it—no reasoning or explanations necessary. Businesses have rules and principles that must be followed, and they come with various consequences. Most people are not open to alternative views and ideas; instead, they stick to what they already know.

Nigerians don't prepare ahead for crises. For example, there are no warning systems for natural disasters; we just deal with what comes. There are not enough quality healthcare facilities. Immigration failed to detect Ebola coming in because they were not trained to detect the symptoms of the virus. For financial planning, most people have no knowledge about insurance or investments. Cars are the only item insured, as it is required for getting a car permit.

Nigerians are generally people oriented and value relationships because these are more valuable than completing tasks. The public sector work culture is generally laid-back, with people having entitlement mentality and not exerting themselves on the job. A typical Nigerian is always more interested in rewards than assigned responsibilities. In this case, relationship can be abused. In workplaces, employees generally prefer a leader who is warm and supportive of subordinates over a leader who is highly authoritative.

Nigerians generally do not like exposing their weaknesses and failures as they want to create the impression that everything is fine in their lives. In church, people are willing to share spiritual aspects of life but using other people's life examples rather than their own. Depending on the closeness of relationships, they don't usually easily share their problems with each other because they want to protect their self-image.

Nigeria is high power distance. Everybody has a place in the hierarchy which needs no further justification. Students highly esteem their teachers and usually do not raise questions. The male elders in the family usually make decisions for the clan and do not necessarily ask the approval of their members. Emphasis is placed on full obedience without explanation.

Nigerians are typically collectivist in culture. They make decisions as a unit, like as a family, for example. Loyalty knits together each member of the family, extended family, or extended relationships. Life is communal with a collective effort that allows communal ownership of resources and effort. Trust and loyalty are very important.

Communication is very high-context: There is more beyond what is said. The listener must be discerning of what the real meaning is. For instance, if someone invites you to a meal, they are not always *really* inviting you to a meal, often it's just polite talk. Mothers speak to children often and continually through the day as a means for communicating expectations and teaching correct behavior. Usually, Nigerian parent-child interactions and speech more closely resemble teacher-pupil talk.

PAKISTAN

Islam is the state religion, and around 95 percent of Pakistanis are Muslims. You need to know the history of Pakistan. Pakistan was part of India and also has castes. Christianity is a religion of the low caste people; that's why now, most of the churches are among poor people.

Pakistanis do not keep to time. Most people come one hour behind schedule. They do not place an emphasis on time; they are event-oriented people, even in churches. In offices there is a huge lack of commitment; for example, the officers will feel proud if they deliberately arrive late because that gives them the sense of power. But a recent president is changing society toward more time consciousness, even in churches.

In the workplace, whether government servants or private companies, there are always two kinds of people: one is very committed and one is just very lazy. Pakistanis can be pretty disorganized. Overall they follow holistic thinking, are more relaxed, and take life very easy. They give priority to friends rather than their unfinished tasks. Family, relatives, and friends are important to them. Every year, there is flooding in Pakistan, yet people never take any advanced preventative action; they do not anticipate and prepare for future events because people believe they cannot control their fate. Pakistanis are very flexible, and they can find a solution for every problem.

People in lower social positions don't make eye contact with the people in higher positions. The higher-level person expects that the lower-level person will greet them first. Communication is high-context: nonverbal communication and the tone of the voice influence meaning.

PAPUA NEW GUINEA

It is important that you speak Pidgin, which is our national language. Knowing how to speak Pidgin would bring acceptance, especially in the villages. If you plan to reach the university students then there is no need to study the Pidgin language. We are more people oriented and very event oriented. If you organize an event in a community, the people will attend anytime they want, and if the meeting extends that is okay, no big deal, the people will stay until the whole event is finished. Church services usually start on time, but the majority of the people can arrive late to the service and it's acceptable. We don't like being controlled, but we're collectivist: one cannot make any decision about events that will affect people unless he discusses with the whole group that he belongs to; in the villages there are committees to help with the resolution of village problems. When there's a problem, they confront it and deal with it immediately. We're not crisis preventative. We don't plan much or think ahead; we wait for things to happen before taking action, and the community helps together. People talk quite directly and express their real situations and feelings freely. There's a big gap between the few rich people and the poor, but every individual is respected equally regardless of their social status.

SAUDI ARABIA

Islam and Allah are the center of everything: society-influences, law, cultural behavior, and both collective and personal dealings. The people are people oriented and event oriented, collectivist and dichotomistic. Social norms prevent interaction between sexes, especially unmarried men and women. The people of Saudi Arabia are unwilling to expose vulnerability. High power distance is seen through great respect for authority. Communication by authority figures is low context—what they say is exactly what they mean. Wealth brings both privilege and community responsibility.

THAILAND

Ninety-five per cent of the population is Theravada Buddhists. Buddhism is embedded in Thai identity and culture with a lot of idols too. The majority of Thai do not speak English, so missionaries have to learn the local language to communicate effectively. Thai people are people oriented and friendly, and they love to have gatherings and a community lifestyle. To be honest, they are not very open to outsiders; they also tend to group among themselves.

Thai are event oriented: churches don't start on time, and a meeting scheduled from 5 pm to 7 pm can last until 11 pm. They won't take on any project where they lack confidence that they can do it successfully. They are holistic, not dichotomistic; for instance, they're not so strict and organized in lifestyle. They are flexible and always just "go with the flow." Thai people are largely non-crisis preventative, and when they do not agree on something, they will not voice it out, even in a formal meeting, but they will complain after the meeting because this allows them to avoid confrontation. Communication is high-context: many times what we say we do not actually mean.

Thai culture is based on the shame-honor principle, so we are afraid to lose face in public. As in Buddhism, we see that everything revolves around karma: life goes on in a circle, so there are no extremes. Decisions are made collectively with the family and authorities. This has made Thailand a nationalistic country. This factor has also impacted our religious decisions. It is understood that to be Thai is to be Buddhist.

TURKEY

Turkish people highly value hospitality, respect, and morality. It is largely a Muslim country. Turkish people tend to be more event oriented. For example, at the small church we attended in Istanbul, rather than starting at the "agreed upon" starting time, we would wait to start until everyone was there.

Authority figures and elders are highly respected. Most parents prefer an authoritarian, disciplined classroom (which is a contrast from the common parenting style, which tends to be very permissive). Students do interact with teachers but must show respect—coming late to class is very disrespectful. Religious authority is respected as well. Most imams do not appreciate being questioned about doctrinal issues—it probably puts their authority and expertise into question.

Turkey is more of a collectivist culture. Maintaining the status quo and going along with the family/community consensus is valued. Communication is high-context: People will rarely give a direct "no." Life is "Inshallah," "if God wills it," which provides an ambiguous non-committal response to any question or issue. People tend to be honor/shame oriented. Telling "white lies" to "soften" the truth is justified as better or more loving than to be accurate or honest. Deception is only a problem when it is exposed, thus "shaming."

UNITED ARAB EMIRATES

The culture is more people and event oriented, though they also have a slave mentality. People tend to be non-crisis oriented: they react rather than prevent. It is a shame/honor society. Only those very close to you will expose a vulnerability. However, they may share their problems with a deeply-trusted foreigner more than with a relative or someone from their own culture. They tend to be dichotomistic: there's a black/white tendency although the culture is not logically based—they compartmentalize and seem to have truth boxes that can contradict each other. They also quickly believe conspiracies; something is generally believed to be true until proven false.

Generally there is high power distance; however, a local student has a higher level than a foreign teacher. Nationals, whatever their position, are higher than any foreigner. In the workplace if a foreign boss wants to dismiss a local for failing in his job, it is not the local who will most likely end up being dismissed!

In general they are collective decision-makers rather than individualistic, though that may be changing due to social media amongst the young. They tend to say what will please you. However, if they ask you to do something then you are expected to carry out that request regardless of whether you think it is a good idea or not. Rulers like to be obeyed and not to have thinkers around them. The people worship money. How much one earns is more important than of what faith one comes. The richer one is, the more status one has.

In the past, missionaries have made the mistake of seeing people as objects rather than as people and trying to use methods that appeared to have worked in one area in another. Just because the environment looks modern and Western, the culture is not, and that trips up foreigners.

Foreigners can quickly become influenced by materialism and get drawn in by its deception. They may feel like they are being treated like a paid slave in the workplace and get frustrated.

UNITED STATES OF AMERICA

People often think Americans are just white and rich, but that is not so. For instance, there are also African American, Chinese American, and Latin

American communities. White Americans are generally time-oriented people. Being on time shows politeness and respect and means being a good steward of time for the right purposes. Church services, professional meetings, and business meetings start on time. Except for occasions like parties, where time can be flexible, Americans regard time as precious. Even casual meetings amongst friends happen at the agreed upon time.

Typically, Americans tend to be more dichotomistic in outlook. They would debate the two sides of an issue but still, after discussion, can be very divided in their opinions. To consider many people's opinions about an issue would be very troublesome.

In general, Americans are crisis-preventative. They like saving things for different seasons to prepare for the future. Most people at least have savings for anything that may suddenly come. In school, they have fire drills, lockdown practices, and earthquake drills to prepare children for if calamities come.

The working culture of Americans is very task oriented. Companies and businesses focus on numbers, money, and achievement. However, outside the workplace, Americans value relationships and are delighted in spending time with their families and friends.

Most Americans do not want to show their weakness or failure as it is embarrassing. However, they can share lesser problems. For instance, they will openly share that they are having difficulty maintaining a Bible-reading plan, but not perhaps that they are having marriage problems. When they are having troubles, they tend to withdraw from social groups. Americans can pretty much share their feelings without difficulty.

American culture is a low power distance culture, and there is not much of a hierarchy in society. Students can express their opinions and ask questions in the classroom. They are not being rude as they do so because they are taught to ask questions in a polite manner. People call each other by first names as well. They regard everyone equally, with respect. Parents allow their children to choose what they want to do in the future. At eighteen years, the children can be independent, have their own jobs, and take care of themselves. This way, they learn to live on their own and become mature enough to deal with life.

Typically, Americans tend to be individualistic. They make decisions for themselves on their own. They value other people's opinions as well, but it does not mean they agree with them. Sometimes they voice their own opinions, but they cannot tolerate other people's opinions toward them.

Communication is usually very low context. What they say is what they mean. Americans are very explicit and direct except for some areas in the Midwest, where people are a bit more laid back and less direct.

VIETNAM

Vietnam is a communist country. We are not time conscious at all. If you are invited to a party at 7 pm then you can arrive at 9 pm, and we'll wait for everyone to come before the party starts because we are more event oriented and are very much people oriented. Even if the task is not done, as long as you can fellowship with people, that's fine. Vietnamese are more dichotomistic in thinking than holistic. An example is that during the war, they would view people as either friends or enemies. Even in this generation where preaching the gospel is not totally free, one should be careful in their behavior so as not to be labeled as an enemy. We conceal vulnerability and cover up the mistakes of others because it is a shame-based culture. If a family member does wrong, the family will cover up for the other, especially if there is a foreigner involved.

Bibliography

Allen, Roland. 1912; 1962. *Missionary Methods: St Paul's or Ours?* Reprint of 1912 1st ed. London: World Dominion; Grand Rapids: Eerdmans.

Anderson, Lorin W., and David R. Krathwohl, eds. 2001. *A Taxonomy for Learning, Teaching, and Assessing: A Revision of Bloom's Taxonomy of Educational Objectives.* New York: Longman.

Anderson, Perry. 1998. *The Origins of Postmodernity.* New York: Verso.

Argyle, M. 2013. *Bodily Communication.* London: Routledge.

Balconi, Michela, Davide Crivelli, and Maria Elide Vanutelli. 2017. "Why to Cooperate Is Better Than to Compete: Brain and Personality Components." *BMC Neuroscience* 18, no. 1: 68. https://bmcneurosci.biomedcentral.com/articles/10.1186/s12868-017-0386-8.

Balconi, Michela, and Maria Elide Vanutelli. 2017. "Empathy in Negative and Positive Interpersonal Interactions. What Is the Relationship Between Central (EEG, fNIRS) and Peripheral (Autonomic) Neurophysiological Responses?" *Advances in Cognitive Psychology* 13, no. 1: 105–20. DOI: 10.5709/acp-0211-0.

Baltes, Boris B., Marcus W. Dickson, Michael P. Sherman, Cara C. Bauer, and Jacqueline LaGanke. 2002. "Computer-Mediated Communication and Group Decision Making: A Meta-Analysis." *Organizational Behavior and Human Decision Processes* 87, no. 1: 156–79. https://doi.org/10.1006/obhd.2001.2961.

Bariso, Justin. 2018. *EQ Applied: The Real-World Guide to Emotional Intelligence.* Germany: Borough Hall.

Barnland, D. C. 1968. *Interpersonal Communication: Survey and Studies.* Boston: Houghton Mifflin.

Benedict, Ruth. 1946. *The Chrysanthemum and the Sword: Patterns of Japanese Culture.* Boston: Houghton Mifflin.

Bennett, Milton J. 1979. "Overcoming the Golden Rule: Sympathy and Empathy." In *Communication Yearbook 3.* International Communication Association, 406–22. New Brunswick, NJ: Transaction.

———. 1986. "A Developmental Approach to Training for Intercultural Sensitivity." *International Journal of Intercultural Relations* 10, no. 2: 179–96.

———. 1993. "Towards Ethnorelativism: A Developmental Model of Intercultural Sensitivity." In *Education for the Intercultural Experience*, edited by R. M. Paige, 2nd ed., 21–71. Yarmouth, ME: Intercultural.

———. 1998. "Intercultural Communication: A Current Perspective." In *Basic Concepts of Intercultural Communication: Selected Readings*, edited by M. J. Bennett, 1–34. Yarmouth, ME: Intercultural.

———. 2004. "Becoming Interculturally Competent." *Towards Multiculturalism: A Reader in Multicultural Education*, edited by J. Wurzel, 2nd ed., 62–77. Newton, MA: Intercultural Resource Corporation.

———. 2013. *Basic Concepts of Intercultural Communication: Paradigms, Principles, and Practices*. 2nd ed. Boston: Intercultural.

Bennett, M. J., and I. Castiglioni. 2004. "Embedded Ethnocentrism and the Feeling of Culture: A Key to Training for Intercultural Competence." *Handbook of Intercultural Training*, edited by D. Landis, J. Bennett, and M. Bennett, 3rd ed., 249–65. Thousand Oaks, CA: Sage.

Berger, P., and T. Luckmann. 1967. *The Social Construction of Reality: A Treatise in the Sociology of Knowledge*. Garden City, NJ: Anchor.

Berlo, David. 1960. *The Process of Communication*. New York: Holt, Rinehart & Winston.

Bhaskar, Roy. 1975. *A Realist Theory of Science*. London: Verso.

———. 1979. *The Possibility of Naturalism: A Philosophical Critique of the Contemporary Human Sciences*. Hemel Hempstead, UK: Harvester.

Birdwhistell, Ray L. 1952. *Introduction to Kinesics: An Annotation System for Analysis of Body Motion and Gesture*. Washington, DC: Department of State Foreign Service Institute. https://books.google.co.th/books?id=Ad99AAAAMAAJ&printsec =frontcover&dq=Birdwhistell+Ray,+L.+Kinesics&hl=en&sa=X&ved=0ahUKE wjbgeC8mIvqAhWD7XMBHQINBe8Q6AEIPzAD#v=onepage&q=Bird whistell%20Ray%2C%20L.%20Kinesics&f=false.

Bloom, Benjamin Samuel, ed. 1956. *Taxonomy of Educational Objectives: The Classification of Educational Goals. Handbook 1, Cognitive Domain*. New York: Longman, Green.

Boa, Kenneth. n.d. "12. Christ and Cultures: Multiculturalism and the Gospel of Christ." *Mission for the Third Millennium* (blog), March 27, 2006. https://bible.org /seriespage/12-christ-and-cultures-multiculturalism-and-gospel-christ.

Bosch, D. 1991. *Transforming Mission: Paradigm Shifts in Theology of Mission*. Maryknoll, NY: Orbis.

Brandner, Tobias. 2009. "Mission, Millennium, and Politics: A Continuation of the History of Salvation from the East." *Missiology*, 37: 317–32.

Brinkman, Rick, and Rick Kirschner. 1994. *Dealing with People You Can't Stand: How to Bring Out the Best in People at Their Worst*. New York: McGraw Hill.

———. 2002. *Dealing with People You Can't Stand: How to Bring Out the Best in People at Their Worst*. Revised and updated ed. New York: McGraw Hill.

Broome, John. 2013. *Rationality through Reasoning*. Oxford, UK: Wiley-Blackwell.

Brother Lawrence. 1982. *The Practice of the Presence of God*. Springdale, PA: Whitaker House.

Burnett, David. 1992. *Clash of Worlds*. Nashville: Oliver-Nelson.

Capps, John. 2019. "The Pragmatic Theory of Truth." *Stanford Encyclopedia of Philosophy*. March 21, 2019. https://plato.stanford.edu/entries/truth-pragmatic/.

Carter, Craig A. 2006. *Rethinking Christ and Culture: A Post-Christendom Perspective*. Grand Rapids: Brazos.

Chakwera, Lazarus McCarthy. 2000. "The Development of the Eleventh Hour Institute to Be Utilized as a Means of Mobilizing, Training, and Sending Missions Workers from Malawi and Nearby Countries to Unreached Peoples." Diss., DMin, Trinity International University.

Chambers, Oswald. 1927; 1972. *My Utmost for His Highest*. London: Marshall, Morgan & Scott.

Chan, Sam. 2018. *Evangelism in a Skeptical World: How to Make the Unbelievable News about Jesus More Believable*. Grand Rapids: Zondervan.

Chao, M. M., R. Takeuchi, and J. L. Fahr. 2017. "Enhancing Cultural Intelligence: The Roles of Implicit Culture Beliefs and Adjustment." *Journal of Personnel Psychology* 70: 257–92.

Chapman, Gary. 1995. *The Five Love Languages: How to Express Heartfelt Commitment to Your Mate*. Chicago: Northfield.

Clark, David K. 2003. *To Know and Love God: Method for Theology*. Wheaton, IL: Crossway.

Concise Oxford English Dictionary. 2004. 11th ed. CD-ROM ©. Oxford: Oxford University Press.

Chu, Michael K. 2019. *Intercultural Competence: Cultural Intelligence, Pastoral Leadership, and the Chinese Church*. Macquarie Park, NSW: Morling.

Cloud, Henry, and John Townsend. 2017. *Boundaries: When to Say Yes, How to Say No to Take Control of Your Life*. Updated and expanded ed. Grand Rapids: Zondervan.

Coffield, F., D. V. Moseley, Elaine Hall, and K. Ecclestone. 2004. *Should We Be Using Learning Styles? What Research Has to Say to Practice*. London: Learning and Skills Research Centre. http://hdl.voced.edu.au/10707/64981.

Cyert, R. M., and J. G. March. 1963. *A Behavioral Theory of the Firm*. Englewood Cliffs, NJ: Prentice-Hall.

Dance, Frank. 1967. *Human Communication Theory*. New York: Holt, Rinehart & Winston.

Davis, John R. 1998. *Poles Apart: Contextualizing the Gospel in Asia*. Bangalore, India: Theological Book Trust.

D-Davidson, Vee J. 2011. "From Passive to Active Learning: A Worked Example of Theological Education in Rural China." *Journal of Adult Theological Education* 8, no. 2: 186–95.

———. 2012. "Mission and Education in Rural China: Birthing a Community-Oriented Mission-Minded Body of Christian Believers." *Evangelical Missions Quarterly* 48, no. 2: 226–31.

———. 2013. "Pentecostalism's Potential for Helping Theological Students Develop the Essential Critical Thinking Skills Related to MA and MDIV Level Studies in Preparation for the Theory and Practice of Pentecostal Ministry." Presentation at Pentecostal World Conference, World Alliance for Pentecostal Theological Education (WAPTE) Consultation on Pentecostal Ministry Formation, Kuala Lumpar, Malaysia, August 26–28, 2013.

———. 2018. *Empowering Transformation: Transferable Principles for Intercultural Planting of Spiritually-Healthy Churches.* Oxford, UK: Regnum International.

———. 2019. "Engaging with Cultural Factors That Have the Potential to Limit Spiritual Formation in Cross-Cultural Pentecostal Ministry." Paper presented at Asia Pacific Theological Association (APTA) Symposium, Hong Kong, September 2–4, 2019.

———. 2021. "Non-Western Students in Majority World Asian Settings: Understanding and Overcoming Barriers Inherent in Cross-Cultural Teaching and Learning." *Asian Journal of Pentecostal Studies* 24, no. 1: 7–20.

De Dreu, Carston K. W., and Laurie R. Weingart. 2003. "Task Versus Relationship Conflict, Team Performance, and Team Member Satisfaction: A Meta-Analysis." *Journal of Applied Psychology* 88, no. 4: 741–49.

De Oliveira, Stephanie, and R. E. Nisbett. 2017. "Culture Changes How We Think About Thinking: From 'Human Inference' to 'Geography of Thought.'" *Perspectives on Psychological Science* 12, no. 5: 782–90.

Dewey, John. 1938. *Experience and Education.* New York: Collier.

———. 1941. "Propositions, Warranted Assertibility, and Truth." *The Journal of Philosophy* 38, no. 7: 169–86. https://doi.org/10.2307/2017978.

Dietz, Gunther. 2018. "Interculturality." In *The International Encyclopedia of Anthropology*, edited by Hilary Callan, 1–19. London: Wiley-Blackwell. DOI: 10.1002/9781118924396.wbiea1629.

Dodd, C. H. 1987. *Dynamics of Intercultural Communication.* 2nd ed. Dubuque, IA: Brown.

Dolzhikova, Anzhela, Victoria Kurilenko, Yulia Biryukova, Elena Baryshnikova, Olga Shcherbakova, and Okksana Glazova. 2021. "Why Did They Keep Silent? Some Peculiarities of Intercultural Academic Communication." *Intercultural Education* 32, no. 1: 83–89. https://doi.org/10.1080/14675986.2020.1845043.

Duvall, J. Scott, and J. Daniel Hays. 2005. *Grasping God's Word: A Hands-On Approach to Reading, Interpreting, and Applying the Bible.* 2nd ed. Grand Rapids: Zondervan.

Dwyer, Judith. 2013. *Communication for Business and the Professions: Strategies and Skills.* 5th ed. Frenchs Forest, NSW: Pearson Australia.

Earley, P. C., and S. Ang. 2003. *Cultural Intelligence: Individual Interactions across Cultures.* Stanford University Press.

Ekman, Paul. 1999. "Basic Emotions." In *Handbook of Cognition and Emotion*, edited by T. Dalgleish and M. Power, 45–60. New York: Wiley.

———. 2009. *Telling Lies: Clues to Deceit in the Marketplace, Politics, and Marriage.* 4th ed. New York: Norton.

Elliott, John H. 1993. *What Is Social-Scientific Criticism?* Minneapolis: Fortress.

Elmer, Duane. 1993. *Cross-Cultural Conflict: Building Relationships for Effective Ministry.* Downers Grove, IL: InterVarsity Press.

———. 2002. *Cross-Cultural Connections: Stepping Out and Fitting In around the World.* Downers Grove, IL: InterVarsity Press.

Erickson, Millard J. 1998. *Postmodernizing the Faith: Evangelical Responses to the Challenge of Postmodernism.* Grand Rapids: Baker.

Fee, Gordon D., and Douglas Stuart. 1983. *How to Read the Bible for All Its Worth: A Guide to Understanding the Bible.* 2nd ed. Grand Rapids: Zondervan.

———. 2003. *How to Read the Bible for All Its Worth: A Guide to Understanding the Bible.* 3rd ed. Grand Rapids: Zondervan.

Fee, Gordon D., Mark L. Strauss, and Douglas Stuart. 2018. *How to Read the Bible for All Its Worth Video Lectures: An Introduction for the Beginner.* Grand Rapids: Zondervan.

Ferraro, Gary, P. and Elizabeth K. Briody. 2017. *The Cultural Dimension of Global Business.* 8th ed. New York: Routledge.

Fleming, Neil D., and C. Mills. 1992. *Helping Students Understand How They Learn.* The Teaching Professor. 7, no. 4. Madison, WI: Magma.

Flemming, Dean. 2005. *Contextualization in the New Testament: Patterns for Theology and Mission.* Downers Grove, IL: InterVarsity Press.

Foster, George M. 1973. *Traditional Societies and Technological Change.* 2nd ed. New York: Harper and Row.

Foster, Richard. 1980. *Celebration of Discipline.* London: Hodder & Stoughton.

Fowler, J. W. 1981. *Stages of Faith: The Psychology of Human Development and the Quest for Meaning.* San Francisco: Harper Collins.

———. 2000. *Becoming Adult, Becoming Christian: Adult Development and Christian Faith.* San Francisco: Jossey-Bass.

Fujino, G. 2009. "Towards a Cross-Cultural Identity of Forgiveness." *Evangelical Missions Quarterly* 45, no. 1: 22–28.

Fukuyama, Francis. 2000. "Social Capital." In *Culture Matters: How Values Shape Human Progress,* edited by Lawrence E. Harrison and Samuel P. Huntington, 98–111. New York: Perseus.

Gadamer, H. G. 1975. *Truth and Method.* Translated by G. Barden and J. Cummings. New York: Seabury.

———. 1976. *Philosophical Hermeneutics.* Translated by David E. Linge. Berkeley: University of California Press.

Gardner, Howard E. 1983. *The Theory of Multiple Intelligences.* New York: Perseus.

———. 2000. "A Case Against Spiritual Intelligence." *The International Journal for the Psychology of Religion* 10, no. 1: 27–34. DOI: 10.1207/S15327582IJPR1001_3.

———. 2011. *Frames of Mind: The Theory of Multiple Intelligences.* New York: Basic.

Gay, Geneva. 2018. *Culturally Responsive Teaching: Theory, Research, and Practice.* 3rd ed. New York: Teachers College Press, Columbia University.

Georges, Jayson, and Mark D. Baker. 2016. *Ministering in Honor-Shame Cultures: Biblical Foundations.* Downers Grove, IL: InterVarsity Press.

Gilliland, Dean S., ed. 1989. *The Word among Us*. Dallas: Word.

Goleman, Daniel. 1995. *Emotional Intelligence: Why It Can Matter More than IQ*. New York: Bantam.

———. 2006. *Social Intelligence: The New Science of Human Relationships*. New York: Bantam Dell.

Grant, Harold, Magdala Thompson, and Thomas E. Clarke. 1983. *From Image to Likeness: A Jungian Path in the Gospel Journey*. Ramsey, NJ: Paulist.

Gulick, Sidney Lewis. 1914. *The American-Japanese Problem: A Study of the Racial Relations of East and West*. New York: Scribner's.

———. 1962. *The East and the West: A Study of Their Psychic and Cultural Characteristics*. Rutland, VT: Tuttle.

Gutt, Ernst-August. 1991. *Translation and Relevance: Cognition and Context*. Oxford: Blackwell.

Hagner, Donald A. 1993. *Matthew*. Word Biblical Commentary. CD version. Waco: Word.

Hall, Edward T. 1959. *The Silent Language*. New York: Doubleday.

———. 1963. "A System for the Notation of Proxemic Behavior." *American Anthropologist*, New Series, 65, no. 5: 1003–26.

———. 1966. *The Hidden Dimension*. Garden City, N.Y., Doubleday.

———. 1973. *The Silent Language*. New York: Anchor.

———. 1976. *Beyond Culture*. New York: Anchor.

Handford, M., J. Van Maele, P. Matous, and Y. Maemura. 2009. "Which 'Culture'? A Critical Analysis of Intercultural Communication in Engineering Education." *J Eng Educ*. 108: 161–77.

Hanifan, Lyda Judson. 1916. "The Rural School Community Center." *Annals of the American Academy of Political and Social Science* 67: 130–38.

Harris, Ruth. 2016. "Schweitzer and Africa." *The Historical Journal* 59, no. 4: 1107–32.

Hastings, A. 2003. "The Clash of Nationalism and Universalism within Twentieth-Century Missionary Christianity." In *Missions, Nationalism, and the End of Empire*, edited by Brian Stanley and Alaine M Lowe, 15–33. Grand Rapids: Eerdmans.

Heslop, A. 1992. "Qualities of the Effective Counselor." *The Child Care Worker* 10, no. 6: 10–11.

Hesselgrave, David J. 1991. *Communicating Christ Cross-Culturally: An Introduction to Missionary Communications*. 2nd ed. Grand Rapids: Zondervan.

Hiebert, Paul G. 1985. *Anthropological Insights for Missionaries*. Grand Rapids: Baker.

———. 1994. *Anthropological Reflections on Missiological Issues*. Grand Rapids: Baker.

———. 1999. "Cultural Differences and Communication of the Gospel." *Perspectives on the World Christian Movement: A Reader*, edited by R. Winter and S. Hawthorne, 3rd ed., 373–83. Pasadena: William Carey.

———. 2008. *Transforming Worldviews: An Anthropological Understanding of How People Change*. Grand Rapids: Baker.

Higgins, Kevin. 2010. "Diverse Voices: Hearing Scripture Speak in a Multicultural Movement." *International Journal of Frontier Missions* 27, no. 4: 189–96.

Hofstede, Geert. 1991. *Cultures and Organizations: Software of the Mind*. New York: McGraw Hill.

Hofstede, Geert H., and Gert Jan Hofstede. 2005. *Cultures and Organizations: Software of the Mind*. New York: McGraw Hill.

Hogbin, H. Ian. 1958: *Social Change*. London: Watts.

Holliday, A. 1999. "Small Cultures." *Applied Linguistics* 20, no. 2: 237–64.

———. 2013. *Understanding Intercultural Communication: Negotiating a Grammar of Culture*. London, England: Routledge.

Holliday, A., J. Kullman, and M. Hyde. 2017. *Intercultural Communication: An Advanced Resource Book for Students*. 3rd ed. London: Routledge.

Holmes, Arthur F. 1979. *All Truth Is God's Truth*. Downers Grove, IL: InterVarsity Press.

Hsiao, Hsin-Huang Michael, and Alan Hao Yang. 2014. "Differentiating the Politics of Dependency: Confucius Institutes in Cambodia and Myanmar." *Issues & Studies* 50, no. 4: 11–44.

Hughes, Earnest Richard, ed. 1937. *The Individual in East and West*. London: Oxford University Press.

———. 1938. "The Village and Its Scholar." In *China, Body & Soul*, edited by E. R. Hughes, 44–62. London: Secker and Warburg.

———. 1967. "Epistemological Methods in Chinese Philosophy." In *The Chinese Mind: Essentials of Chinese Philosophy and Culture*, edited by Charles A. Moore with Aldyth V. Morris, 77–103. Honolulu: East-West Centre Press.

Hyman, Ira E., Jr., S. Matthew Boss, Breanne M. Wise, Kira E. McKenzie, and Jenna M. Caggiano. 2009. "Did You See the Unicycling Clown? Inattentional Blindness While Walking and Talking on a Cell Phone." *Applied Cognitive Psychology* (December). https://doi.org/10.1002/acp.1638.

Iyadurai, Joshua. 2015. *Transformative Religious Experience: A Phenomenological Understanding of Religious Conversion*. Eugene, OR: Pickwick.

James, William. 1907; 1975. *Pragmatism: A New Name for Some Old Ways of Thinking*. New York: Longmans, Green. Reprint, Cambridge, MA: Harvard University Press.

Jenkins, P. 2002. *The Next Christendom: The Coming of Global Christianity*. Oxford: Oxford University Press.

———. 2006. *The New Faces of Christianity: Believing the Bible in the Global South*. Oxford: Oxford University Press.

Johnson, Alan R. 2015. "Context-Sensitive Evangelism in the Thai Setting: Building Capacity to Share Good News." *Becoming the People of God*, edited by Paul DeNeui, 63–92. Pasadena: William Carey.

Katz, David. 1937. *Animals and Men*. New York: Longmans, Green.

Kirby, Alan. 2009. *Digimodernism: How New Technologies Dismantle the Postmodern and Reconfigure Our Culture*. New York: Continuum International.

Kirk, Andrew J. 2000. *What Is Mission? Theological Explorations*. Minneapolis: Fortress.

Klein, William W., Craig L. Blomberg, and Robert L. Hubbard Jr. 1993. *Introduction to Biblical Interpretation*. Dallas: Word.

Klopf, D. W. 2001. *Intercultural Encounters: The Fundamentals of Intercultural Communication.* 5th ed. Englewood, CO: Morton.

Knapp, Mark L., Judith. A. Hall, and Terrance G. Horgan. 2013. *Nonverbal Communication in Human Interaction.* 8th ed. Boston: Cengage Learning.

Kolb, D. A. 1984. *Experiential Learning: Experience as the Source of Learning and Development.* Englewood Cliffs, NJ: Prentice-Hall.

Kostić, Alexandra, Derek Chadee, and Jasmina Nedeljković. 2020. "Reading Faces: Ability to Recognise True and False Emotion." In *Social Intelligence and Nonverbal Communication,* edited by Robert J. Sternberg and Aleksandra Kostić, 255–82. Camden, UK: Palgrave Macmillan.

Kraft, Charles H. 1979. *Christianity in Culture: A Study in Dynamic Biblical Theologizing in Cross-Cultural Perspective.* Maryknoll, NY: Orbis.

———. 1983: *Communication Theory for Christian Witness.* Nashville: Abingdon.

———. 1989. *Christianity with Power: Your Worldview and Your Experience of the Supernatural.* Manila: OMF.

Kitayama, S., S. Duffy, T. Kawamura, and J. T. Larsen. 2003. "Perceiving an Object and Its Context in Different Cultures: A Cultural Look at New Look." *Psychological Science* 14, no. 3: 201–6.

Kubota, Mayumi. 2019. "What Is 'Communication'? Beyond the Shannon and Weaver's Model." *International Journal for Educational Media and Technology* 13, no. 1: 54–65.

Kuethe, J. L. 1962. "Social Schemas." *Journal of Abnormal and Social Psychology* 64, no. 1: 34–38.

Kuhn, D. 2019. "Critical Thinking as Discourse." *Human Development* 62: 146–64. https://doi.org/10.1159/000500171.

Küster, Dennis. 2020. "Hidden Tears and Scrambled Joy: On the Adaptive Costs of Unguarded Nonverbal Social Signals." In *Social Intelligence and Nonverbal Communication,* edited by Robert J. Sternberg and Aleksandra Kostić, 283–304. Camden, UK: Palgrave Macmillan.

Kwarst, L. E. 2009. "Understanding Culture." In *Perspectives on the World Christian Movement,* edited by R. Winter and S. Hawthorne, 4th ed., 397–99. Pasadena: William Carey.

Labarre, Weston. 1947. "The Cultural Basis of Emotions and Gestures." *Journal of Personality* 16: 49–68.

LaHaye, T. 1993. *The Spirit-Controlled Temperament.* Revised ed. Wheaton, IL: Tyndale.

Landes, D. 2000. "Culture Makes Almost all the Difference." *Culture Matters: How Values Shape Human Progress,* edited by Lawrence E. Harrison and Samuel P. Huntington, 2–13. New York: Perseus.

Lasswell, Harold. 1964. "The Structure and Function of Communication in Society." In *The Communication of Ideas,* edited by L. Bryson, 37–52. New York: Jewish Theological Seminary of America.

LeFever, Marlene. 2011. *Learning Styles.* Colorado Springs: David C. Cook.

Levinson, D. J. 1978. *The Seasons of a Man's Life.* New York: Knopf.

Lingenfelter, Judith E., and Sherwood G. Lingenfelter. 2003. *Teaching Cross-Culturally: An Incarnational Model for Learning and Teaching*. Grand Rapids: Baker Academic.

Lingenfelter, Sherwood G., and Marvin K. Mayers. 2003. *Ministering Cross-Culturally: An Incarnational Model for Personal Relationships*. 2nd ed. Grand Rapids: Baker Academic.

Little, Kenneth B. 1965. "Personal Space." *Journal of Experimental Social Psychology* 1, no. 3: 237–47.

Lustig, Myron W., and Jolene Koester. 2003. *Intercultural Competence: Interpersonal Communication Across Cultures*. 4th ed. Boston: Allyn and Bacon.

Lustig, Myron, W., Jolene Koester, and Rona Halualani. 2018. *Intercultural Competence: Interpersonal Communication Across Cultures*. 8th ed. New York: Pearson

Lynch, Michael P. 2009. *Truth as One and Many*. New York: Oxford University Press.

Ma Wonsuk. 2016. "A 'Fuller' Vision of God's Mission and Theological Education in the New Context of Global Christianity." *The State of Missiology Today: Global Innovations in Christian Witness*, edited by Charles E. Van Engen, 84–106. Downers Grove, IL: InterVarsity Press.

MacDonald, Gordon. 2004. *A Resilient Life: You Can Move Ahead No Matter What*. Nashville: Nelson.

Macek, J. 2005. "Defining Cyberculture." In *Média a Realita*, translated and edited by P. Binková and J. Volek, 35–65. Prague, Czech Republic: Masaryk University Press.

Marginson, Simon. 2011. "The Confucian Model of Higher Education in East Asia and Singapore." *Higher Education* 61, no. 5: 587–611.

Markus, H. R., and S. Kitayama. 1991. "Culture and the Self: Implications for Cognition, Emotion, and Motivation." *Psychological Review* 98, no. 2: 224–53.

Marston, William Moulton. 1928. *Emotions of Normal People*. New York: Harcourt, Brace.

Marx, Karl. 1970. *Critique of Hegel's "Philosophy of Right"*. Joseph O'Malley, trans. Annette Jolin and Joseph O'Malley. Cambridge: Cambridge University press.

Masuda, Takahiko, Richard Gonzalez, Letty Kwan, and Richard Nisbett. 2008. "Culture and Aesthetic Preference: Comparing the Attention to Context of East Asians and Americans." *Personality and Social Psychology Bulletin* 34, no. 9: 1260–75.

Maxwell, L. E. 1945. *Born Crucified*. Chicago, IL: Moody Press.

McCrae, Robert R., and Oliver P. John. 1992. "An Introduction to the Five-Factor Model and Its Applications." *Journal of Personality* 60, no. 2: 175–215.

McGavran, Donald Anderson. 1974. *The Clash Between Christianity and Cultures*. Washington, DC: Canon.

———. 1980. *Understanding Church Growth*. Revised ed. Grand Rapids: Eerdmans.

McLeod, Hugh, and Werner Ustorf. 2003. *The Decline of Christendom in Western Europe, 1750–2000*. Cambridge: Cambridge University Press.

McQuail, Denis. 1984. *Communication*. 2nd ed. Essex, UK: Longman.

McQuail, Denis, and Sven Windahl. 2015. *Communication Models for the Study of Mass Communications*. London: Routledge.

Meyer, Arlin G. 2002. "Teaching Literature as Mediation: A Christian Practice." *Teaching as an Act of Faith: Theory and Practice in Church-Related Higher Education,* edited be Arlin C. Migliazzo, 253–76. New York: Fordham University Press.

Meyer, Erin. 2014. *The Culture Map: Breaking Through the Invisible Boundaries of Global Business.* Philadelphia, PA: Perseus.

Misar, S. R. 2010. *Journey to Authenticity: Discovering Your Spiritual Identity through the Seasons of Life.* Cape Coral, FL: Master.

Molinsky, A. 2007. "Cross-Cultural Code-Switching: The Psychological Challenges of Adapting Behaviour in Foreign Cultural Interactions." *Academy of Management Review* 32, no. 2: 622–40.

Moreau, A. S., E. H. Campbell, and S. Greener. 2014. *Effective Intercultural Communication: A Christian Perspective.* Grand Rapids: Baker Academic.

Motyer, J. Alec. 1993. *The Prophecy of Isaiah: An Introduction and Commentary.* Downers Grove, IL: InterVarsity Press.

Movius, Hal. 2020. "How to Negotiate—Virtually." *Harvard Business Review,* June 10. https://hbr.org/2020/06/how-to-negotiate-virtually.

Mulholland, M. Robert, Jr. 1993. *Invitation to a Journey: A Road Map for Spiritual Formation.* Downers Grove, IL: InterVarsity Press.

Mutua, Eddah and Kikuko Omori. 2018. "A Cross-Cultural Approach to Environmental and Peace Work: Wangari Maathai's Use of Mottainai in Kenya." *The Journal of Social Encounters.* 2(1): 22–36. Available at: https://digitalcommons.csbsju.edu/social_encounters/vol2/iss1/3.

Myers, I. 1962. *Manual: The Myers-Briggs Type Indicator.* Palo Alto, California: Consulting Psychologists Press.

Navon, D. 1977. "Forest before Trees: The Precedence of Global Features in Visual Perception." *Cognitive Psychology,* 9(3): 353–83.

Newell, Marvin J. 2016. *Crossing Cultures in Scripture: Biblical Principles for Mission Practice.* Downers Grove, IL: InterVarsity Press.

Newberry, Warren B. 2005. "Contextualizing Indigenous Church Principles: An African Model." *Asian Journal of Pentecostal Studies* 8, no. 1: 95–115.

Newbigin, Lesslie. 1994. *A Word in Season.* Grand Rapids: Eerdmans.

Nguyễn, vănThanh. 2013. "Biblical Foundations for Interculturality." *Verbum SVD* 54, no. 1: 35–47.

Nida, Eugene Albert. 1952. *God's Word in Man's Language.* New York: Harper and Row.

———. 1960. *Message and Mission: The Communication of the Christian Faith.* New York: Harper and Row.

———. 1964. *Toward a Science of Translating: With Special Reference to Principles and Procedures Involved in Bible Translating.* Leiden: Brill.

Niebuhr, H. Richard. 1951. *Christ and Culture.* London: Faber and Faber.

Nisbett, R. E., K. Peng, I. Choi, and A. Norenzayan. 2001. "Culture and Systems of Thought: Holistic versus Analytic Cognition." *Psychological Review* 108, no. 2: 291–310.

Northrop, F. C. S. 1953. *The Meeting of East and West: An Inquiry Concerning World Understanding.* New York: Macmillan.

Nouwen, Henri. 2011. *Spiritual Formation: Following the Movements of the Spirit.* London: SPCK.

Oetzel, John, and Stella Ting-Toomey. 2003. "Face Concerns in Interpersonal Conflict: A Cross-Cultural Empirical Test of the Face Negotiation Theory." *Communication Research* 30, no. 6: 599–624.

Oetzel, John, Stella Ting-Toomey, Tomoko Masumoto, Yumiko Yokochi, Xiaohui Pan, Jiro Takai, and Richard Wilcox. 2001. "Face and Facework in Conflict: A Cross-Cultural Comparison of China, Germany, Japan, and the U.S." *Communication Monographs* 68: 235–58.

Omori, Kikuko. 2017. "Cross-Cultural Communication." *The SAGE Encyclopedia of Communication Research Methods,* edited by Mike Allen, 309–12. Thousand Oaks, CA: SAGE.

Osborne, Grant R. 1991. *The Hermeneutical Spiral: A Comprehensive Introduction to Biblical Interpretation.* Downers Grove, IL: InterVarsity Press.

Oser, F., and P. Gmünder. 1991. *Religious Judgment: A Developmental Approach.* Birmingham, AL: Religious Education.

Oxford Languages. "Word of the Year 2016." https://languages.oup.com/word-of-the -year/2016/#:~:text=After%20much%20discussion%2C%20debate%2C%20and,to %20emotion%20and%20personal%20belief'.

Payne, Geoff, and Judy Payne. 2004. "Positivism and Realism." In *Key Concepts in Social Research,* 171–74. London: Sage.

Peng, K., and R. E. Nisbett. 1999. "Culture, Dialectics, and Resonating about Contradiction." *American Psychologist* 54, no. 9: 741–54.

Perkins, Dwight H. 2000. "Law, Family Ties, and the East Asian Way of Business." *Culture Matters: How Values Shape Human Progress,* edited by Lawrence E. Harrison and Samuel P. Huntington, 232–43. New York: Perseus.

Perry, Edmund. 1958. *The Gospel in Dispute: The Relation of Christian Faith to Other Missionary Religions.* Garden City, NY: Doubleday.

Phillips, Bob. 1989. *The Delicate Art of Dancing with Porcupines: Learning to Appreciate the Finer Points of Others.* Ventura, CA: Regal. [Drawn from research of David W. Merrill and Roger H. Reid.]

Plueddemann, James E. 2018. *Teaching Across Cultures: Contextualizing Education for Global Mission.* Downers Grove, IL: InterVarsity Press.

Popenoe, David. 2000. *Sociology.* 11th ed. Upper Saddle River, NJ: Prentice Hall.

Porpora, Douglas. 2010. "Inside the American State: Reconciling Structural and Interpretive Analyses within a Critical Realist Perspective." *Scientific Realism and International Relations,* edited by Jonathan Joseph and Colin Wight, 88–100. London: Macmillan.

Porter, Michael E. 2000. "Attitudes, Values, Beliefs, and the Microeconomics of Prosperity." *Culture Matters: How Values Shape Human Progress,* edited by Lawrence E. Harrison and Samuel P. Huntington, 14–28. New York: Perseus.

Preston, Diana, and Michael Preston. 2010. *A Pirate of Exquisite Mind: The Life of William Dampier: Explorer, Naturalist, and Buccaneer.* New York: Random House.

Reddi, C. 2009. *Effective Public Relations and Media Strategy.* New Delhi: PHI Learning Private Limited.

Richards, E. Randolph, and J. Brandon O'Brien. 2012. *Misreading Scripture with Western Eyes: Removing Cultural Blinders to Better Understand the Bible.* Downers Grove, IL: InterVarsity Press.

Richards, E. Randolph, and Richard James. 2020. *Misreading Scripture with Individualist Eyes: Patronage, Honor, and Shame in the Biblical World.* Downers Grove, IL: InterVarsity Press.

Rowley, H. H. 1956. *The Faith of Israel.* London: SCM.

Rozell, Jack V. 1983. *Agape Therapy: A Christian Approach to Counseling.* Springfield: International Correspondence Institute.

———. 1997. *Christian Counseling: An Independent Study Text Book.* Springfield, MO: ICI University Press.

Sampson, P., V. Samuel, and C. Sugden. 1994. *Faith and Modernity.* Oxford: Regnum Books International.

Schramm, Wilbur Lang. 1954. "How Communication Works." *Process and Effects of Mass Communication,* edited by W. Schramm, 3–26. Illinois: University of Illinois Press.

Schweitzer, Albert. 2001. *The Quest of the Historical Jesus.* Edited by John Bowden. Translated by W. Montgomery, J. R. Coates, Susan Cupitt, and John Bowden. Minneapolis: Fortress. [Translated from the German *Geschichte der Leben-Jesu-Forschung.* Tübingen: Mohr, 1906, 1913, 1950. 1st English translation of the 1913 2nd ed.]

Sedlmeier, Peter, and Kunchapudi Srinivas. 2016. "How Do Theories of Cognition and Consciousness in Ancient Indian Thought Systems Relate to Current Western Theorizing and Research?" *Frontiers in Psychology* 7, art. 343. March 15, 2016. https://doi.org/10.3389/fpsyg.2016.00343.

Shade, Barbara J., Cynthia Kelly, and Mary Oberg. 1997. *Creating Culturally Responsive Classrooms.* Washington, DC: American Psychological Association.

Shannon, Claude, E., and Warren Weaver. 1949. *The Mathematical Theory of Communication.* Urbana: University of Illinois Press.

Shaw, Daniel R., and Charles E. Van Engen. 2003. *Communicating God's Word in a Complex World: God's Truth or Hocus Pocus?* New York: Rowman and Littlefield.

Smalley, W. A. 2009. "Cultural Implications of an Indigenous Church." *Perspectives on the World Christian Movement,* edited by R. Winter and S. Hawthorne, 4th ed., 497–502. Pasadena: William Carey.

Smalley, Gary, and John Trent. 1990. *Two Sides of Love.* Wheaton, IL: Tyndale House.

Sommer, Carl J. 2007. *We Look for a Kingdom: The Everyday Lives of the Early Christians.* San Francisco: Ignatius.

Sommer, R. 1959. "Studies in Personal Space." *Sociometry* 22: 247–60.

Sperber, Dan, and Deirdre Wilson. 1986. *Relevance: Communication and Cognition.* Cambridge, MA: Harvard University Press.

———. 1995. *Relevance: Communication and Cognition.* 2nd ed. Oxford: Blackwell.

Spinney, Laura. 2017. *Pale Rider: The Spanish Flu of 1918 and How It Changed the World.* London: Cape.

Steffen, Tom A. 1999. *Passing the Baton: Church Planting that Empowers.* 2nd ed. La Habra, CA: Center for Organizational and Ministry Development.

Sternberg, Robert J., and Aleksandra Kostić, eds. 2020. *Social Intelligence and Nonverbal Communication.* Camden, UK: Palgrave Macmillan.

Stetzer, Ed. 2003. *Planting New Churches in a Postmodern Age.* Nashville: B&H.

Swindells, C., E. Maksakov, K. E. MacLean, and V. Chung. 2006. "The Role of Prototyping Tools for Haptic Behavior Design." *Proceedings of 14th Symposium on Haptic Interfaces for Virtual Environments and Teleoperator Systems, IEEE-VR'06.* Alexandria, Virginia, March 2006. https://ieeexplore.ieee.org/abstract/document /1627084.

Thiselton, A. C. 1980. *The Two Horizons: New Testament Hermeneutics and Philosophical Description with Special Reference to Heidegger, Bultmann, Gadamer, and Wittgenstein.* Grand Rapids: Eerdmans.

Thomas, Kenneth W., and Ralph H. Kilmann. 1974. *Thomas-Kilmann Conflict Mode Instrument.* Tuxedo, NY: Xicom.

Ting-Toomey, Stella. 2017. "Facework and Face Negotiation Theory: Cross-Cultural Communication Theories, Issues, and Concepts." In *The International Encyclopedia of Intercultural Communication.* June 27, 2017. https://doi.org/10.1002 /9781118783665.ieicc0105.

Ting-Toomey, S., and L. C. Chung. 2012. *Understanding Intercultural Communication.* 2nd ed. New York: Oxford University Press.

Ting-Toomey, S., and A. Kurogi. 1998. "Facework Competence in Intercultural Conflict: An Updated Face-Negotiation Theory." *International Journal of Intercultural Relations* 22: 187–225.

Tino, James. 2008. "A Lesson from Jose: Understanding the Patron/Client Relationship." *Evangelical Missions Quarterly* 44, no. 3: 320–27.

Tippett, Alan R. 1975. "Christopaganism or Indigenous Christianity." In *Christopaganism or Indigenous Christianity,* edited by Charles Taber and Tetsunao Yamammori, 13–34. Pasadena: William Carey.

Travis, John J. 1998. "The C1 to C6 Spectrum: A Practical Tool for Defining Six Types of 'Christ-centered Communities' ('C') Found in the Muslim Context." *Evangelical Missions Quarterly* 34, no. 3: 407–8.

Turney, J. Russell. 2013. *Leave a Legacy: Increasing Missionary Longevity.* Baguio, Philippines: APTS Press.

Uyl, Anthony, ed. 2018. *The Practice of the Presence of God: The Best Rule for a Holy Life by Brother Lawrence.* Ontario: Devoted.

Wagner, C. Peter. 1976. "Full Circle: Third World Missions." In *Readings in Third World Missions: A Collection of Essential Documents*, edited by Marlin L. Nelson, 57–66. Pasadena: William Carey.

Währisch-Oblau, Claudia. 2009. *The Missionary Self-Perception of Pentecostal/Charismatic Church Leaders from the Global South in Europe: Bringing Back the Gospel*. Leiden: Brill.

Walsh, Catherine. 2006. "Interculturalidad y colonialidad del poder: Un pensamiento y posicionamiento otro desde la diferencia colonial" [Interculturality and Coloniality of Power: Thinking and Positioning Otherwise from Colonial Difference]. In *Interculturalidad, Descolonización Del Estado Y Del Conocimiento* [Interculturality, Decolonization of the State and of Knowledge], edited by Catherine Walsh, Álvaro García Linera, and Walter Mignolo, 21–70. Buenos Aires: Ediciones del Signo.

Weber, Max. 1947. *The Theory of Social and Economic Organization*. Translated by A. M. Henderson and Talcott Parsons. London: Free Press of Glencoe.

Westley, Bruce. H., and Malcolm. S. MacLean Jr. 1955. "A Conceptual Model for Communications Research." *Audio-Visual Communications Review* 3 (Winter): 3–12.

———. 1957. "A Conceptual Model for Communications Research." *Journalism Quarterly* 34, no. 1: 31–38.

Wiener, Norbert. 1948. *Cybernetics: Or Control and Communication in the Animal and the Machine*. New York: Wiley; Paris: Hermann et Cie.

Willard, Dallas. 1998. *The Divine Conspiracy: Rediscovering Our Hidden Life in God*. London: Fount.

———. 2012. *Hearing God: Developing a Conversational Relationship with God*. Downers Grove, IL: InterVarsity Press.

Williams, Mark S. 2007. "What Legacy Do We Leave to Believers in Contextualized Communities?" *Journal of Asian Mission* 9, no. 1–2: 59–70.

———. 2011. "Revisiting the C1-C6 Spectrum in Muslim Contextualization." *Missiology: An International Review* 39, no. 3: 335–51.

Wright, C. Thomas. 1998. "Contextual Evangelism Strategies." In *Missiology: An Introduction to the Foundations, History, and Strategies of World Missions*, edited by John Mark Terry, Ebbie Smith, and Justice Anderson, 450–66. Nashville: Broadman and Holman.

Xiao, Hong, and Eleni Petraki. 2007. "An Investigation of Chinese Students' Difficulties in Intercultural Communication and Its Role in ELT." *Journal of Intercultural Communication* 13, https://www.immi.se/intercultural/nr13/petraki.htm.

Yang, K., and M. H. Bond. 1990. "Exploring Implicit Personality Theories with Indigenous or Imported Constructs: The Chinese Case." *Journal of Personality and Social Psychology* 58: 1087–95.

Załuski, Wojciech. 2018. *Law and Evil: The Evolutionary Perspective*. Cheltenham, UK: Elgar.

Index